D1071648

POTS AND POTTERS

CURRENT APPROACHES IN CERAMIC ARCHAEOLOGY

EDITED BY PRUDENCE M. RICE

Monograph XXIV

Institute of Archaeology

University of California, Los Angeles

Book design: Dejon Dillon

The Institute of Archaeology Monographs include preliminary
and final excavation reports, symposia papers, and accounts
of research in progress in such subjects as archaeometry,
ethnoarchaeology, and paleodemography.

Editor: Ernestine S. Elster
Advisory Board: Giorgio Buccellati, Rainer Berger,
  Christopher Donnan, Timothy Earle, Clement W.
  Meighan, James R. Sackett, and David S. Whitley

Institute of Archaeology Director of Publications:
  Ernestine S. Elster

Preparation of this manuscript for publication

was funded by

the Department of Anthropology and

the Liberal Arts Research Office

of the College of the Liberal Arts,

The Pennsylvania State University

and

the College of Fine and Applied Arts,

Rochester Institute of Technology

Table of Contents

CHAPTER
Page

List of Contributors

RUTH AMIRAN
   The Israel Museum, P. O. Box 1299, Hakirya, Jerusalem 91000, Israel

DEAN E. ARNOLD
   Department of Sociology and Anthropology, Wheaton College, Wheaton, IL 60187

FRANK ASARO
   Lawrence Berkeley Laboratory, 70-103, University of California, Berkeley, CA 94720

GARMAN HARBOTTLE
   Department of Chemistry, Brookhaven National Laboratory, Upton, NY 11973

THOMAS W. JACOBSEN
   Program in Classical Archaeology, Indiana University, 422 North Indiana Avenue, Bloomington, IN 47401

ROBERT H. JOHNSTON
   College of Fine and Applied Arts, Rochester Institute of Technology, One Lomb Memorial Drive, Rochester, NY 14623

DIANA C. KAMILLI
   715 Coors Street, Golden, CO 80401

MAUREEN F. KAPLAN
   Analytical Sciences Corporation, One Jacob Way, Reading, MA 01867

W. DAVID KINGERY
Department of Materials Science and Engineering, Massachusetts Institute of Technology, Cambridge, MA 02139

CHARLES C. KOLB
Department of Anthropology, Pennsylvania State University, The Behrend Campus, Erie, PA 16563

EDITH PORADA
Department of Art History and Archaeology, Columbia University, Schermerhorn Hall, New York, NY 10027

PRUDENCE M. RICE
Department of Anthropology, 1350 GPA, University of Florida, Gainesville, FL 32611

EDWARD V. SAYRE
Department of Chemistry, Brookhaven National Laboratory, Upton, NY 11973

DODO SHENHAV
The Israel Museum, P. O. Box 1299, Hakirya, Jerusalem 91000, Israel

WILHELM G. SOLHEIM II
Department of Anthropology, University of Hawaii at Manoa, Porteus Hall 346, 2424 Maile Way, Honolulu, HA 96822

ARTHUR STEINBERG
Anthropology/Archaeology Program, Massachusetts Institute of Technology, Cambridge, MA 02139

FRED STROSS
Lawrence Berkeley Laboratory, 70-103, University of California, Berkeley, CA 94720

HOMER A. THOMPSON
School of Historical Studies, The Institute for Advanced Study, Princeton University, Princeton, NJ 08540

SANDER E. VAN DER LEEUW
Institute for Pre- and Protohistory, University of Amsterdam, Singel 453, 1012 WP, Amsterdam, Netherlands

KAREN D. VITELLI
Program in Classical Archaeology, Indiana University, 422 North Indiana Avenue, Bloomington, IN 47405

Preface

Given the universally acknowledged importance of pottery in archaeological studies, and the day to day significance of fired clay articles in many people's cooking or food storage activities, it is surprising that there are relatively few general or survey texts on ceramic studies. The literature on pottery is vast, but is generally area-, site-, or village-specific. For a long time, the major integrative or survey texts were only Anna O. Shepard's Ceramics for the Archaeologist (1971), a manual on technical analysis and Frederick R. Matson's Ceramics and Man (1965), a broad temporal and geographical survey of primarily sociocultural issues in pottery studies. Now the technical side has been updated with Owen Rye's (1980) Pottery Technology: Principles and Reconstruction, and a burgeoning crop of edited volumes has appeared, dealing with a broad range of techniques, regions, and individual ceramic wares.

Pots and Potters: Current Approaches in Ceramic Archaeology is intended as an outgrowth and updating of Ceramics and Man, with a primarily anthropological emphasis. As in Ceramics and Man, the objective here is to demonstrate how pottery from a variety of temporal and geographical contexts—when studied by a variety of methods and points of view—can be informative both as to the nature of the pottery itself as well as the people who made and used it.

The emphasis of this collection of papers was deliberately chosen to reflect the philosophy and teachings of the scholar in whose honor the volume was compiled, Frederick R. Matson. Frederick Matson pioneered in what has become a popular academic specialization in recent years, obtaining a Ph.D. in 1939 from the University of Michigan in "ceramic archaeology" with a combined program of ceramic engineering and archaeology. During the war years, he put his technical training to practice in industry, before receiving an academic appointment in the Department of Sociology and Anthropology at The Pennsylvania State University in 1949. While at Penn State, he served as Research Professor of Archaeology and as Dean of Research of the College of the Liberal Arts. Also during his long professional career, he helped found the Society for American Archaeology and served as president of the Archaeological Institute of America, receiving from the latter organization the 1981 Pomerance Award for Scientific Contributions in Archaeology.

Matson's research interests stretched from Afghanistan to Ohio, from the Neolithic at Jarmo to modern potters in Egypt, from ancient kilns in Greece to nuclear reactors and electron microscopes in the United States, from Egyptian plasters to Greek horses. He has aided hundreds, perhaps thousands, of scholars in their comprehension of ceramic materials, not only through his teaching at Penn State but in his many years of guest lecturing, visiting professorships, committee participation, consultancies, and simple generosity with his time, interest, and expertise. Thorough, meticulous, and a perfectionist, Professor Matson expected no less from students and colleagues.

The present collection of papers written by Fred's colleagues and students was compiled following his retirement in 1978 from The Pennsylvania State University. The tripartite organization of the book reflects the major ceramic research foci and contributions of Frederick R. Matson during his long career: "ceramic ecology," experimental archaeology, and ceramic technology.

REFERENCES

Matson, F.R. (ed.)
    1965   Ceramics and Man. Viking Fund Publication no. 41. Chicago: Aldine.

Rye, O.S.
    1980   Pottery Technology: Principles and Reconstruction. Manuals on Archaeology 4. Washington: Taraxacum.

Shepard, A.O.
    1971   Ceramics for the Archaeologist. Carnegie Institution of Washington, Publication 609. Washington.

Introduction

Unless ceramic studies lead to a better understanding of the cultural context in which the objects were made and used, they form a sterile record of limited worth.

— Frederick R. Matson, <u>Ceramics and Man</u>, p. 203.

One of my favorite anecdotes to emerge from my last few years as a professor concerns a student who came to me for academic advisement at the beginning of one year. He said he wanted to major in archaeology and was interested in what courses he should take. As I asked the appropriate questions about what sorts of things he was interested in and gave him the usual song and dance about university course distribution requirements, I noted a look of dismay gradually spreading over his face. Upon questioning, he revealed that he had decided to major in archaeology because then he "wouldn't have to take any courses in chemistry, physics, history, foreign language, and especially math . . . just (<u>sic</u>.) archaeology." So much for the popular view of archaeology.

I begin with this story because the interdisciplinary research orientation at the core of contemporary archaeology, of which this student was woefully unaware, is even more an integral part of current ceramic studies. Chemistry, physics, history, languages, and statistics are the diverse paths by which today's ceramic scientists realize the objective stated in the quotation above, that is, an understanding of the cultural context of ceramic products. And this multidisciplinary approach is also at the heart of the present volume.

Ceramic objects—articles formed in whole or in part of clay and subsequently fired (from the Greek keramos, meaning "burnt stuff")—have served humanity in many functions, ranging from the mundane to the arcane, for more than nine millennia. For today's scholars, archaeologists, anthropologists, and art historians among others, the cookpots and storage jars continue to be useful, this time as a record of people's activities in a host of realms, including economic, social, dietary, ceremonial, and technical. Although ceramic vases and bowls are fragile and ephemeral, once broken the fragments form a voluminous and virtually indestructible data set for scholars to measure, analyze, and classify toward a multitude of ends.

The study of pottery has been approached from a number of different starting points. As ancient objets d'art, ceramic vessels have had their decorative symbolism, costuming, life scenes, symmetry, and other aspects analyzed and described to achieve a greater understanding of the vessels' artistic execution and the cultural context in which their artisans operated. As a large corpus of ancient cultural debris (one might even say "garbage"), ceramic vessels and vessel fragments from archaeological excavations throughout the world have been sorted, classified, described, and intercompared in order to date sites and assess their social, political, and economic interrelationships. As craft products of contemporary, usually nonindustrialized peoples, both the pottery and the potters themselves have been studied from the point of view of social, environmental, economic, artistic, and technical behavior and productive interactions in resource procurement, manufacture, distribution, and "consumption" of ceramic goods. And finally, as the product of physicochemical reactions among common geological materials—clay, water, various rock or mineral fragments—ceramic resources and vessels, ancient and modern, have been subjected to sensitive physical, chemical, and mineralogical analyses, using equipment ranging in sophistication from a hand lens to a nuclear reactor.

The business of studying pottery, then, is as complex and multifaceted as its subject. Great strides have been made in accumulating information about pottery since the days when the unoxidized dark core between oxidized exteriors of a sherd was thought to indicate three layers of clay sandwiched together. One of the most significant efforts to compile such data, primarily on the sociocultural aspects of pottery, was the 1965 publication Ceramics and Man, edited by Frederick R. Matson. Having a wide-ranging geographical coverage, the volume provided a summary and integration of chronological, social, and technical information resulting from an eleven-day series of conferences held in 1961. The final chapter of his volume, entitled "Ceramic Queries," clearly pointed to the need for more work in a variety of areas, new questions arising as old ones decline in immediacy.

The present volume is a collection of papers, also broad in geographical coverage, that reflect this attention to new questions. Important new methodological directions have become prominent in ceramic studies, and contributions to this volume in these areas, primarily physicochemical analysis and "ethnoarchaeology," reflect this trend. The volume is organized into three sections, the first being the social and physical environment of pottery making, the second consisting of ethnoarchaeological studies, and the third covering technological analysis.

Part I, entitled "Potters in their Environment," treats the interactions of ancient pottery and the socioeconomic and physical milieu in which it is produced. Study of the physical resources for pottery manufacture as well as the social stimuli that operated in its decoration, distribution, and use is a significant means of increasing the breadth of our knowledge about the past art and artisans of pottery-making. The papers in Part I bear strong testimony that Matson's "ceramic ecology" emphasizes integration of social as well as physical contexts.

Papers in Part II, "Ethnoarchaeological Studies," exemplify the increasing popularity of this interface between ethnographic and archaeological studies that is so useful in analysis of material culture. Called variously "ethnoarchaeology," "experimental archaeology," and "action archaeology," this hybrid subdiscipline deals with the formation of the archaeological record by analogy with contemporary cultural processes and/or direct experiments with raw materials and nonindustrial techniques of manufacture. The ethnoarchaeological contributions in this volume include experiments with raw materials and tools of pottery-making, analysis of decorative patterns, and study of the variables in forming the archaeological record, all with assessments of their value and significance for archaeologists.

Part III, "Technological Analysis of Pottery," consists of papers in a growing area of ceramic research, physicochemical analysis. The papers include surveys of some of the applications and contributions of these sorts of analyses, as well as case studies that demonstrate the skillful integration of research problems and the analytical methodology brought to bear in their solution. Technological analysis, whether it involves macroscopic study of physical properties or extremely sensitive microscopic or trace chemical analyses, affords many advantages in objectivity and replicability. These studies establish a critical data base for formulating and testing hypotheses about many past and present socioeconomic activities, such as organization of ceramic production, distribution, and trade, as well as about ancient technologies in general.

PART I

Potters in their Environment

Part I

The environment—social and natural—of pottery-making has traditionally been and continues to be of interest to students of ceramics. Origins of pottery-making, the inspiration for and context of use of the beautifully decorated Greek, Chinese, or Maya vases that have survived for hundreds or thousands of years, and the patterns of manufacture and trade of vast quantities of both plain and fancy vessels and other objects of clay, fall within this general research area.

Unfortunately, efforts to reconstruct such contexts are often limited to sheer speculation. For example, evidence of early humans' recognition of clay as a useful resource is difficult to pinpoint, as are the earliest stages of any technology. Ceramic beginnings may be more problematical than the origins of other technologies, however, because it is entirely possible that the first objects made of clay were not fired, and therefore would not have survived the millennia to allow present-day archaeologists to discover and study them. Bison modeled in clay from a French Upper Paleolithic cave site and both fired and unfired figurines from Dolni Vestonici in Central Europe hint that clays may have already been skillfully formed into objects fifteen thousand or more years ago.

Knowledge of the role of fire in transforming clay objects into more durable goods similarly is a matter of conjecture. Clay-lined baskets or sun-dried clay containers (e.g., parching trays) accidentally encountering a fire may have resulted in the first fired vessels, it is frequently hypothesized. Or, the use of clay to line fire pits or in some other heating procedure (e.g., heat-treating flint) may have led to the discovery and/or intentional experimentation with the effects of fire on shaped clay objects.

Pottery is one of the hallmarks of the "Neolithic way of life," along with agriculture and sedentary village settlement. Although the underlying rationale for this categorization has traditionally been that pottery vessels were too heavy and fragile to be part of the material inventory of peoples leading a nonsedentary existence, the significance of pottery is that it represents a new set of technical, social, and economic relationships within human groups and between societies and their environment. For archaeologists, pottery represents a new kind of information about people and culture, highly sensitive to numerous sources of variation, and occurring in copious quantities. The ubiquity of pottery in archaeological sites makes it one of the most useful kinds of data on chronology, site-to-site relationships, ritual practices, costuming, dietary practices, economic relationships of production and exchange, and many other kinds of cultural behavior.

The pursuit of these kinds of interpretations of ceramic data has not always been consistent. The majority of archaeological ceramic studies, especially in the New World, have maintained a traditional focus on the creation of ceramic typologies, and the use of these classifications to build chronologies and reconstruct culture history. It is only comparatively recently, with the widespread adoption of radiocarbon dating and other chronometric techniques to ease the burden of chronology weighing heavily on ceramicists' shoulders, that archaeologists have begun intensively and systematically exploiting their ceramic data base in search of answers to a totally different set of questions. Among the most interesting of these questions are those involving the environment of pottery-making, particularly the availability of clay and other resources. Matson has focused attention on this perspective through what he termed "ceramic ecology." Ceramic ecology places emphasis on relating "the raw materials and technologies that the local potter has available to the functions in his culture of the products he fashions" (1965:203).

Several studies since Matson's 1965 publication have attempted, implicitly or explicitly, to put "ceramic ecology" to work. One of the best of these is Dean Arnold's (1975) study of the pottery of Ayacucho, Peru. Arnold studied the social and physical context of pottery-making in this highland region, and attempted to trace the development of a ceramic craft specialty back to pre-Columbian times. In discussing such a development, he identified "permissive factors," "limiting factors," and "forcing situations" in the interactions of human populations with their environment—interactions that may have led to abandonment of agriculture and adoption of a craft as a livelihood at some point in the past.

The five papers in Part I of this volume deal in one way or another with the concept or scope of ceramic ecology. The focus of this section is on illuminating the broader archaeological setting of the pottery, stressing the social and physical contexts of its manufacture and use which are the emphases of ceramic ecology. The papers deal with very different subject matter and very different approaches to ceramic data gathering, however, despite their common theme.

The first two papers are substantive contributions, providing examples of how ancient paintings and carvings can yield information on pottery-making and its social setting. Their approach is more "humanistic," an orientation that was much decried with the jargon of the "new archaeology," but is still very important to ceramic ecology. The first paper, treating the pictorial scenes on Athenian vases, examines the social environment and stimuli for the scenes depicted on the vessels in terms of the bustling market and ceremonial activities of the Agora where potters had their workshops. The second briefly treats a common "farm" scene on Mesopotamian and Iranian cylinder seals. These depictions may actually portray pottery-making activities and the use of a coiling rather than wheel-throwing technique for manufacture of some very large jars, and thus help illuminate the pottery-making technology of the period.

The third paper is in some ways akin to those in the second section of the book. Investigating a relatively little-explored topic in archaeology, pastoralism, Jacobsen employs ethnographic data on modern pastoralists in the northeast Peloponnese of Greece to suggest a model for the distribution of archaeological sites bearing a distinctive Middle Neolithic pottery type, "Urfirnis Ware" (see also Chapter 9, this volume). The paper is a good example of "ceramic ecology" in terms of using the environmental variables and particular economic adaptations in discussing the distribution of pottery at archaeological sites.

The fourth paper is "ceramic ecological" in its theoretical approach, treating the problem of craft specialization. Much of the pottery from complex societies that archaeologists work with was probably made by specialists of some sort, but archaeological definitions of craft specialization and an understanding of its evolution are still relatively unexplored. This paper suggests some methodological considerations for the study of ceramic craft specialization, emphasizing the resources locally available and study of patterns of variability in the vessels themselves.

The final paper shares a similar methodological objective, but with a different focus, that is, the trade or distribution of pottery. Identification of "trade wares" and paths of "contact" or "influence" between sites or regions has been an important goal of archaeologists' studies of ceramic collections, significantly aided by the kinds of precise analyses treated in Part III of this volume, and there seems to be a general sense of satisfaction in the skill in which this objective can be achieved. Van der Leeuw's paper, illustrated with archaeological and ethnographic examples, suggests caution in such interpretations, demonstrating the complexity of the variables involved in the various steps of pottery-making and in distinguishing the products of different manufacturing workshops. Our understanding of pottery-making and trade is intimately linked with our understanding of other aspects of the socioeconomic and physical environment, and all need more systematic investigation.

REFERENCES

Arnold, D.E.
    1981 Ceramic ecology in the Ayacucho Basin, Peru: implications for prehistory. Current Anthropology 16:185-203.

Matson, F.R. (ed.)
    1965 Ceramics and Man. Viking Fund Publication no. 41. Chicago: Aldine.

Chapter 1

The Athenian Vase-Painters and their Neighbors

Homer A. Thompson

Athenian vase-painting of the Classical Period (6th-4th century B.C.) is strikingly different from that of any other contemporary school. This emerges clearly from a stroll through a representative collection of Greek vases, or even from the perusal of a good picture book on Greek ceramics (Arias, Hirmer, and Shefton 1961). The special quality of the Athenian school lies chiefly in its predilection for depicting human activity. Often, to be sure, the human actors are thinly disguised as gods or heroes, but in very many instances we are presented with vignettes based directly on human life: scenes of war, worship, domestic life, sports, festive gatherings, occupational activities, the theater, occasionally even civic life (Webster 1972). Such scenes do occur occasionally in Corinthian vase-painting of the same period, but there they are usually little more than pale imitations of the Athenian, while the various South Italian schools with their lively scenes of human life are for the most part offshoots of the Athenian.

The strongly humanistic quality of Athenian vase-painting is paralleled, of course, in other branches of Athenian art and literature, but it may be worthwhile to consider whether the vase-painters may not have been influenced also by the setting in which they lived and worked (Figure 1), in addition to this humanistic tradition.

The Potters' Quarter (Kerameikos) of ancient Athens occupied a large area in the northwestern part of the city (Thompson and Wycherley 1972:186). From the literary and epigraphical evidence, the district is known to have embraced the Agora or city center (Figure 3), and to have extended outward to include the principal cemetery of the city, reaching even the famous old gymnasium, the Academy. The sheer extent of the district is enough to attest the importance of the industry in the life of the city.

At various points within this vast area, traces of potters' activity have been found in the course of the archaeological excavations of the past fifty years. The earliest known thus far is a mass of waste from a potter's shop of the Protogeometric Period (10th century B.C.) recovered from a well beneath the Odeion of Agrippa in the very middle of the classical Agora. Deposits of similar waste dating from the 7th century B.C. were encountered outside the southeast corner of the Agora, while a potter's kiln, also of the 7th century, came to light near the southwest corner of the square.

With the formalization of the Agora in the early 6th century, the potters were compelled to withdraw from that specific area, but they did not go far. An abandoned mining shaft on the northeast slope of Kolonos Agoraios, the hill that bordered the west side of the Agora, was used as a dumping place by neighboring potters from the middle of the 6th century until the Persian sack of 480/79 B.C. A well near the southeast corner of the Agora, which was also closed as a result of the Persian sack, yielded a great quantity of similar waste. The construction of the Stoa of Zeus on the west side of the Agora, begun ca. 420 B.C., involved the demolition of a potter's shop. Kilns of the 5/4th centuries have been found by German excavators outside the city wall to the west of the Dipylon Gate.

We are not here concerned with the evidence that attests the continuing activity of potters in this part of Athens into late antiquity, but the brief survey given above leaves no doubt that in the period with which we are concerned potters were plying their craft in immediate proximity to the Agora, to the great esplanade that led from the Agora to the Dipylon (the main gate of the city), and to the principal cemetery of Athens outside the city wall.

The potters' choice of location was presumably dictated by a conjunction of natural advantages: deep beds of clay in the valley of the Kephisos just to the west of the city; a convenient source of water in the Eridanos, a stream which flowed through the Kerameikos; proximity to the Agora as a sales place; and ready access by road to the harbor of Piraeus, through which especially fine potter's clay could have been brought in from Cape Kolias, and through which certainly passed all pottery intended for export.

Very little remains above ground of the buildings in which the potters lived and worked. On the analogy of the better preserved remains of the Classical Period in an industrial area of sculptors and metal workers west of the Areopagus, we may suppose, however, that their living and working quarters were often in the same building (Thompson and Wycherley 1972:185-191). The buildings that have come to light in the industrial quarter vary greatly in size and shape. They were simple in plan, comprising from two to ten rooms grouped on or around a courtyard in which was a well. Columnar porches and mosaic floors were rare. The floors were normally of clay, the walls plastered and painted in solid colors. There is nothing to suggest either poverty or affluence.

The vase-painters paid little attention to domestic architecture—on vases the presence of a house was normally suggested by a solitary column. The furniture shown in domestic scenes, though sparse by the standards of later periods, is tasteful and often elegant (Richter 1966). The chairs, couches, tables, and wash basins are such as one would expect to find in the homes of well-to-do people. The often elaborate dress, coiffure, and jewelry of the women are rendered with such easy mastery and delight as to indicate familiarity with a life of comfortable circumstances.

School scenes are among the favorite subjects drawn from everyday life. They were depicted especially by the early red-figure painters (Boardman 1975:217). The subjects taught are reading, writing, music, and gymnastics. Here again, where the artist shows such sure feeling not only for technicalities but also for the psychological relationship between teacher and pupil, we must believe that he is drawing on personal experience. That many of the vase-painters had indeed profited from schooling is evident from the frequent occurrence of inscriptions on the vases and, more significantly, from the painters' knowledge of mythology which was surely derived from epic poetry.

A comparatively high economic and cultural status is attested for the potters by their dedications on the Acropolis; these dedications were presumably made to the goddess Athena as the patron divinity of the arts and crafts (Webster 1972:4-8). Painted vases were the most numerous class of offering, and the hundreds of specimens found in the excavation of the 1880's, although sadly fragmentary, include some of the finest black-figure and red-figure ever produced in Athens. Not all these vases need have been dedicated by potters, but this is at least probable in the case of several that show potters at work. Of the inscribed bases for sculptural dedications in bronze or marble that have been found on the Acropolis, at least five were dedicated by potters with another half dozen probable dedications and three doubtful. This is certainly the largest representation from any craft or profession in Athens, and it is probably without parallel in any other city or sanctuary of Greece.

Among the major dedications made by potters on the Acropolis is the so-called "Potter's Relief" (Brouskari 1974:131f.). The dedicator sits proudly erect holding a pair of drinking cups (kylikes) in his hand. The date is ca. 510 B.C. The fragmentary inscriptions give us only the final letters of the dedicator's name, "-ios," and the initial letters of the maker's name which has been restored with probability as "Endoios," one of the leading sculptors of the day. The dedication is described in the inscription as a tithe, and since it was one of the most impressive monuments to be set up on the Acropolis by a private citizen of the period, we may infer that the dedicator was a man of very considerable means.

Athena shared the patronage of the arts and crafts with the god Hephaistos. Soon after the middle of the 5th century, when the Athenians felt able, for the first time after the Persian Wars, to erect a really fine marble temple, they chose to dedicate it to Athena and Hephaistos (Thompson and Wycherley 1972:140-149). They selected for its location the hilltop to the west of the Agora, on the slopes of which the excavators have found abundant traces of the casting of bronze statues and the making of fine pottery in the Classical Period. These decisions are not likely to have taken the sculptors and potters by surprise.

Like modern painters doing studio scenes, the Athenian vase-painters have left us a number of pictures showing potters and pot-painters at work. These scenes are of value not only as illustrations of technical procedure but equally as evidence of the professional pride of the potters. In this respect the most illuminating example is the scene on a red-figured water jar of ca. 460 B.C. (Figure 1), now in Milan, painted by the Leningrad Painter (Noble 1965:XIV, 54, 56). Four men and one woman are busily engaged in painting vases. It is prize-giving day, and wreaths are being presented. The proprietor, marked as such by his high-backed chair, receives his accolade from none other than the goddess Athena. The two junior male craftsmen are about to be wreathed by Victories (Nikai); the woman, alas, goes unrewarded. This is how the potters liked to picture themselves: busily engaged in the creation of beautiful things with the encouragement of the gods. One is reminded of Homer's repeated appeal to the goddess, the Muse, for help in the telling of his tales.

The vase-painters have also given us some revealing depictions of their fellow craftsmen with whom they shared this part of town. Alongside the remains of potters' establishments on the slopes of Kolonos Agoraios, excavators have come on pits sunk into the soft bedrock to hold the moulds for the casting of bronze statues (H.A. Thompson and Wycherley 1972:188-191). Five such casting pits have come to light, ranging in date from the middle of the 6th to the 2nd century B.C. The archaeological remains are meager: fragments of the clay moulds, bits of fused bricks from the furnaces, bronze drippings.

Fortunately, this evidence can be supplemented by several red-figure vase-paintings. The most familiar and informative was painted ca. 470 B.C. by the so-called Foundry Painter; it is a drinking cup (kylix) now in West Berlin (H.A. Thompson 1964). In a medallion on the floor of the cup, we see Hephaistos, god of the forge, putting the finishing touches on a helmet while Thetis, the mother of Achilles, stands by ready to carry this and the rest of a suit of armor to her warrior son, Achilles. On the outside of the cup are two scenes in human studios. One depicts a furnace from which has come the molten bronze for making a statue of Achilles in the guise of a runner, which is now being assembled from its component parts. In the other picture workmen polish a finished statue of Achilles as warrior in the presence of the proprietor of the shop and a distinguished looking visitor. Here again one admires both the skill of the draftsman in making the operation intelligible and his sensitivity in suggesting the atmosphere of human-divine collaboration in artistic creativity. The drawing in its circumstantial detail is evidently based on close first-hand observation, and it has been done with the utmost respect and sympathy on the part of the vase-painter for his fellow craftsmen.

The area in which the bronze-casters operated on the slopes of Kolonos appears also to have been the center of the making of arms and armor—a natural collocation. Extremely little Athenian armor of the Classical Period has survived, but some idea of its beauty and quality is conveyed by a number of ancient impressions taken in soft clay from the designs in high relief on helmets, cuirasses, and belt buckles (D.B. Thompson 1969:242-251). These date chiefly from the late 5th and 4th centuries B.C. We may suspect that the extraordinarily intimate knowledge of fine armor shown in the black-figure and red-figure vase-painting derives from direct observation by the vase-painters of the activities of their neighbors, the makers of armor.

Nor were the humbler crafts beneath the notice of the vase-painter. One of the more numerous and delightful series of genre scenes of this kind concerns the shoe-maker. Examples are to be found in both black-figure and red-figure pottery. Sometimes we are shown a solitary craftsman keeping close to his last. More often the scene represents a fitting in which figure the shoe-maker and his assistant, the person being fitted, some accompanying member of the family and occasionally a casual visitor. The atmosphere is caught no less successfully here than in the studio of the sculptor: the customer complains of the fit, the shoemaker expostulates, his assistant nervously awaits instructions, the visitor (who might well be the vase-painter) looks on calmly as the various personalities reveal themselves.

One might ask what evidence exists for the presence of shoe-makers' shops in the Potters' Quarter. The ruins of one such shop came to light in 1953 immediately outside the posted limits of the Agora at its southwest corner (D.B. Thompson 1960:234-240). It was, as one might expect, a modest establishment consisting of a room and a shed that faced on a courtyard in which opened a well. The identification is assured by the discovery of numerous iron hobnails of a kind used in ancient boots. Among the household pottery of the late 5th century was found the base of a drinking cup inscribed with the name of the owner, "Simon." There seems no reason to doubt that this is the shoemaker of that name on whom Socrates frequently called and who is reported to have written a number of Socratic dialogues. Philosopher and vase-painter alike found the shoe-maker's shop a good place in which to observe human behavior.

Such workshops as those just described were called ergasteria. The same term was used, somewhat metaphorically, for brothels. Numerous references in the ancient authors indicate that the environs of the Agora were the most notorious "red-light district" of the city. Thus a character in the 4th century comedy, Pyraunos, by Alexis, desiring experience of the hygros bios (=dolce vita) strolled for three days in the Kerameikos and found no less than thirty instructors in that way of life. It also appears from the literary testimonia that "call girls" were available in the Agora, especially in the vicinity of the small shrine called the Leokorion, which came to light in 1971 near the northwest corner of the Agora. It is little wonder that hetairai figure prominently in the vase paintings: the painters did not have far to go in search of models. Moreover, the assurance with which love-making is depicted on the vases could only derive from first-hand experience (Boardman and La Rocca 1978).

But there were other perfectly respectable ways in which the vase-painters might observe female activities. One way was to loiter by the public fountains to which the girls of neighboring households came to draw water from the everflowing spouts. Fountain-house scenes are among the most charming genre pictures in both black-figure and red-figure painting, commencing with the famous Francois Vase of ca. 570 B.C. This most common domestic chore is rendered in a great variety of ways as the girls fill their large water jars (hydriae) and swing them upon their heads for the homeward journey, chatting the whole time. The fountain houses in these graceful scenes are the most common and most realistic renderings of architecture in Athenian vase-painting. They show great variety of design, and the drawings were undoubtedly inspired by the actual fountain houses which became common when the Tyrants in the 6th century provided the city for the first time with a good supply of running water. The largest fountain house of the Archaic Period yet known in Athens stood at the southeast corner of the Agora where it was readily accessible to the potters; it dates from ca. 520 B.C. (Lang 1968:21-28).

In addition to such mundane happenings, many special events took place in the Agora in full view of the vase-painters (Trendall and Webster 1971). According to the literary tradition it was in the Agora, on the Dancing Floor (orchestra) that the earliest dramatic contests took place; this was before the construction of a permanent theater at the south foot of the Acropolis at the beginning of the 5th century. A good many pictures of comedy in its primitive phases and of choral singing in honour of Dionysos (dithyramb) are to be found in Athenian black-figure pottery of the late 6th century. One the other hand, there are surprisingly few representations directly inspired by the presentation of classical tragedy and comedy; for this one must await the red-figure pottery of South Italy, where such scenes are common. It is tempting to believe that their scarcity in Athenian vase-painting of the 5th and 4th centuries may have been due to the "interference" of the Acropolis which stood between the Kerameikos and the Theater of Dionysos.

But the Agora continued to be the scene throughout the Classical Period of many other festive events which took place in full view of the vase-painters and which undoubtedly provided the inspiration, direct or indirect, for many of their compositions. Such was the procession in which the national festival, the Panathenaia, culminated, and which is idealized in the marble of the Parthenon frieze (Brommer 1977:199-202). Also, each year at the time of the Eleusinian Mysteries the Sacred Objects of Demeter passed through the Agora escorted by the ephebes, first from Eleusis to the Eleusinion on the north slope of the Acropolis, then, a few days later, back from the Eleusinion to Eleusis. Less frequent but larger and more stately was the Pythais, the sacred mission sent by the Athenians to Delphi after lightning had been observed over Mount Harma. The band comprised the priest of Apollo, the highest civil magistrates, ephebes and riders, singers and musicians—a colorful array. The Agora was the setting for certain equestrian displays, notably the apobates race in which the passenger in a four-horse chariot was required to dismount and remount while the chariot was in full motion. Through the Kerameikos, we are told, passed all three of the principal Athenian torch races, those in honor of Prometheus, Hephaistos, and Athena; they are vividly described on a number of red-figure vases.

Nor must it be forgotten that until the construction of the Stadium outside the city walls in the second half of the 4th century, the track events of the Panathenaic Festival took place on a race course running from north to south through the Agora. The northern starting line has recently come to light near the Altar of the 12 Gods, an arrangement in keeping with Greek practice (Wycherley 1978:36). Here, then, the vase-painters had an excellent opportunity to observe the various athletic events that are represented with such sureness especially on the Panathenaic amphorae, the terracotta jars containing the olive oil that was given as prizes for the principal events.

An event of civic importance that had great attraction for the vase-painters was the annual inspection of the cavalry (dokimasia), both men and horses (Cahn 1973:3-22). The inspection was conducted by a committee of the Council of Five Hundred. It took place in all probability on the broad esplanade that extended from the Agora to the Dipylon Gate. The remains of the Cavalry Headquarters (Hipparcheion) may be recognized at the Agora end of the esplanade, and a quantity of the small lead tablets recording the official evaluations of the horses came to light in a nearby well in 1971 (Kroll 1977). The inspection is represented in a number of vase-paintings both black- and red-figure. The young men ride proudly past, each carrying a pair of javelins and wearing a cloak and broad-brimmed hat. In one case we see a secretary seated and making notes dictated by a member of the Council's Committee. In preparation for the inspection, the youths practice riding in this same area which came to be a very "horsey" part of town. The opportunity to observe such activities, involving the best horses in the country ridden by well-trained young men, will help account for the vase-painters' uncanny mastery of the anatomy, the movements, and the temperament of the horses.

Another consequence of the topographical location of the Potter's Quarter was to expose vase-painting to the influence of the major arts. Perhaps the most significant example of such influence is the impact on vase-painting made by the great murals painted just before the middle of the 5th century (Robertson 1975:240-270). These were the creations of the leading artists of the day: Polygnotos, Mikon, and Panainos the brother of Phidias. They were to be seen in the sanctuary of the Dioskouroi (the Anakeion) on the north slope of the Acropolis, in the sanctuary of Theseus (the Theseion) at the north foot of the Acropolis, and in the Painted Stoa (Stoa Poikile) on the north side of the Agora. The subjects were for the most part traditional and mythological, except for the Battles of Marathon and Oinoe in the Painted Stoa. Of the three buildings only the Painted Stoa has as yet been found: it came to light in 1981 on the north side of the Agora, but nothing remains of the paintings.

Neither in choice of subject nor in the treatment of iconography did the murals, insofar as we can judge from the brief literary references, differ significantly from earlier Athenian vase-painting. With the murals, for the first time in Athens such subject matter was dealt with on a monumental scale and was given full public exposure. Scholars are probably right in attributing to the influence of the major paintings certain developments which occur in vase-painting around the middle of the 5th century: greater interest and skill in the modelling of figures and in the suggestion of distance in landscape; a heightened ability to depict ethos, whether in individual figures or groups; and a preference for some of the themes employed later in the murals, especially the Centauromachy and the Amazonomachy.

We must not suppose that the vase-painters were influenced by the murals in any slavish or mechanical way. Athenian vase-painters of the period, the best of them, were still inventive and extremely able draftsmen. But through constant viewing of the glorious new murals that were being done in buildings within sight of their workshops they were undoubtedly influenced, perhaps for the most part unconsciously, in many important ways.

The murals appear also to have stimulated some technical developments in vase-paintings. Notable is the more common use of a white background, especially for oil flasks (lekythoi) intended for the grave, for it appears to have been the practice in Athens to do mural paintings on white-plastered wooden panels set against the wall.

Already within the Classical Period a number of free-standing sculptures had been set up in the Agora, and some of these appealed to the vase-painters. One of the earliest, and throughout antiquity the most famous, sculptural monument in the square was the pair of statues honoring Harmodios and Aristogeiton for their assassination of the Tyrant's son, Hipparchos, in 514 B.C. (Ridgway 1970:79-83). The original pair of statues was carried off by the Persians in 479 B.C. and replaced by new versions in 477/76 B.C.; the old group was sent back to Athens after Alexander's conquest of Persia. Thereafter the two groups stood near the northwestern corner of the square. Their prominent location combined with their historical association and striking style drew the attention of later artists in all media. A half dozen

The Athenian Vase-Painters and Their Neighbors

straightforward copies are known in vase-paintings, while the gestures and modelling of the great bronzes left their mark on the style of a whole generation of vase-painters (Brunnsåker 1971:99-120).

The next most prominent sculptures in the Agora in the 5th century were the schematic representations of the god Hermes, referred to conventionally as "Herms." A whole grove of these figures is known to have stood at the north-western corner of the Agora bordering the principal entrance—an appropriate location for the god of travel, of commerce, and of entrances. Remnants of a score or more of Herms have come to light in the excavation of the area. We may assume that it was these most readily accessible representations that chiefly inspired the vase-painters in their very frequent depiction of Herms in many different contexts (Zanker 1965).

Another category of sculptures with which the potters had constant and intimate contact was the grave sculpture in the Dipylon Cemetery. There are striking similarities in respect to style and composition between the earliest red-figured vases of the last quarter of the 6th century and the low reliefs on the marble bases of some of the great tomb statutes. Here there was undoubtedly both give and take between painter and sculptor. It seems probable, for instance, that the vase-painters were induced to shift from the black-figure to the red-figure technique by observing the practice of the sculptors who, as fine marble came into common use, left their figures in the white of the marble while painting the background dark (Boardman 1975:14).

The potters were influenced in other ways also by their close proximity to the principal cemetery of the city. In the 8th century B.C., long before grave monuments of sculptured stone or marble had come into vogue in Athens, a few well-to-do families marked their graves with colossal vases painted in the current Geometric style; the painting normally included a funeral scene (Kurtz and Boardman 1971:56-55). The largest of these wheel-turned vases are as tall as an adult, yet their walls seldom exceed the thickness of one's finger. The popularity of these huge vessels is likely to reflect in part their ease of transportation, because of the propinquity of pottery and graveyard. At the same time, however, the choice of such grave monuments on the part of leading families may be interpreted as a remarkable indication of the esteem in which the potter's art was held in early Athens.

In later periods vases of various types were made by the potters to be placed in the grave. The most characteristic and the most striking category is the white-ground lekythos which was in vogue chiefly in the second half of the 5th century (Kurtz and Boardman 1971:102-105). A large proportion of these lekythoi bear pictures of family groups mourning beside a grave. The circumstantial detail in these scenes, coupled with their very sensitive rendering of mood, remind us that the painters of the vases constantly witnessed such scenes as they went about their daily work.

Can we draw any conclusions from these random observations? Above all, can we decide whether the Athenian potters chose to remain in their traditional location as the city grew up around them because they were interested in human activity, or did they devote themselves to depicting the human scene because they found themselves surrounded in the Classical Period by the bustling life of the city? There may be truth in both views. One would be naive to regard sheer physical propinquity as the sole determinant in this matter. Athenian tragedy, after all, and Athenian sculpture of the Periclean period, are each distinguished by a local quality just as marked, as unmistakable, and as mysterious as that of Athenian vase-painting. Nevertheless the examples discussed show that the Athenian vase-painter was influenced by his setting in the choice of subject matter, that his rendering of the human scene is based on firsthand observation, and that he took advantage of his location to profit from contact with other forms of art. In any event we must count ourselves incredibly fortunate in having received from the vase-painters such a wealth of direct and vivid reportage on the people of Athens in the days of their greatness.

Figure 1. Red-figured Hydria by the Leningrad Painter in Milan, ca. 460 B.C. Vase-painters at work; the goddess Athena and Nikai distribute prizes in the form of wreaths. (From J.V. Noble, The Techniques of Painted Attic Pottery, Fig. 74., by permission).

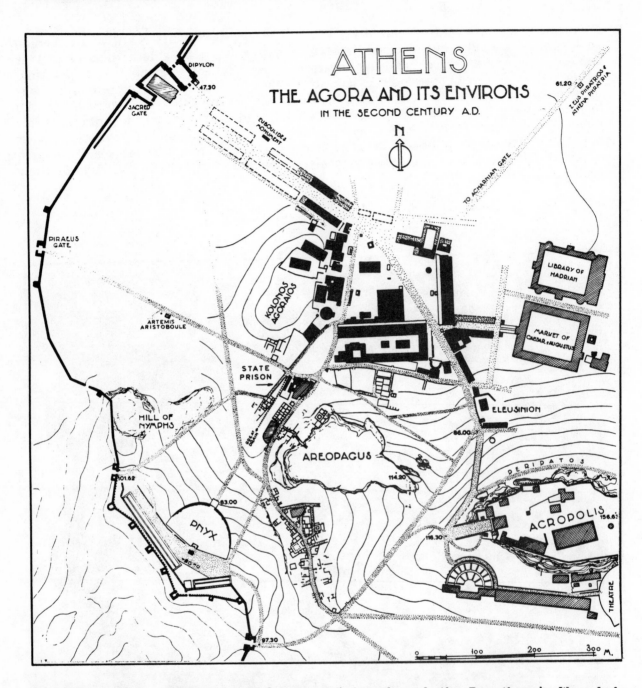

Figure 2. Athens: Northwestern Quarter. A broad road, the Panathenaic Way, led down from the Acropolis, passed diagonally through the Agora, issued through the city wall by the Dipylon Gate, passed the principal cemetery of Athens, and continued to the Academy, which lay ca. 1½ kms. beyond the Dipylon. The Potters' Quarter (Kerameikos) extended from the Agora to the Academy. (Drawing by John Travlos. Courtesy American School of Clasical Studies at Athens)

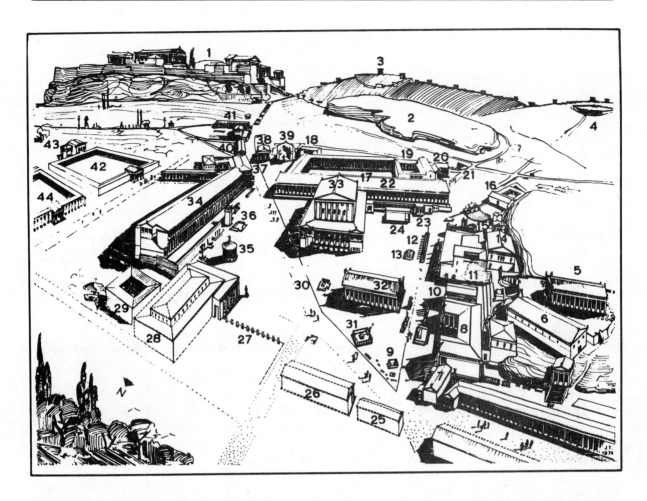

Figure 3. The Athenian Agora seen from the Northwest, ca. A.D. 150. 1. Acropolis; 2. Areopagus; 4. Pnyx; 5. Temple of Hephaistos and Athena; 6. Arsenal (?); 7. Royal Stoa; 8. Stoa of Zeus; 9. Leokorion; 18. Southeast Fountain House; 26. Painted Stoa; 30. Panathenaic Way; 31. Altar of the 12 Gods; 32. Temple of Area; 33. Odeion of Agrippa; 34. Stoa of Attalos; 41. Eleusinion; 42. Market of Caesar and Augustus. (Drawing by John Travlos. Courtesy of American School of Clasical Studies at Athens).

REFERENCES

Arias, P.E., M. Hirmer, and B. Shefton
   1961   Greek Vase Painting.   New York: Harry N. Abrams, Inc.

Boardman, J.
   1975   Athenian Red Figure Vases: the Archaic Period.   London: Thames and Hudson.

Boardman, J. and E. La Rocca
   1978   Eros in Greece.   London: John Murray.

Brommer, F.
   1977   Der Parthenonfries.   Mainz: Philipp von Zabern.

Brouskari, M.S.
   1974   The Acropolis Museum.   Athens: The Commercial Bank of Greece.

Brunnsåker, S.
   1971   The Tyrant-Slayers of Kritios and Nesiotes.   Stockholm: Svenska Institutet i Athen (Skrifter, Series Prima, 17).

Cahn, H.A.
   1973   Dokimasia.   Revue Archéologique.   1973 fasc. 1.

Kroll, J.H.
   1977   An archive of the Athenian cavalry.   Hesperia 46:83–140.

Kurtz, D.C. and J. Boardman
   1971   Greek Burial Customs.   Ithaca: Cornell University Press.

Lang, M.
   1968   Waterworks in the Athenian Agora.   In, Excavations of the Athenian Agora, Picture Book No. 11.   Princeton: American School of Classical Studies at Athens.

Noble, J.V.
   1965   The Techniques of Painted Attic Pottery.   New York: Watson–Guptill Publications and the Metropolitan Museum of Art.

Richter, G.M.A.
   1966   The Furniture of the Greeks, Etruscans and Romans.   London: Phaidon.

Ridgway, B.S.
   1970   The Severe Style in Greek Sculpture.   Princeton: Princeton University Press.

Robertson, M.
   1975   A History of Greek Art.   Cambridge: Cambridge University Press.

Thompson, D.B.
1960   The house of Simon the shoemaker. <u>Archaeology</u> 13:234-240.

1969   Mourning Odysseus. <u>Hesperia</u> 38:242-251.

Thompson, H.A.
1964   A note on the Berlin Foundry cup. In, <u>Essays in Memory of Karl Lehmann</u> (<u>Marsyas</u>, Suppl. 1). Locust Valley, N. Y.: J.J. Augustin.

Thompson, H.A. and R.E. Wycherley
1972   <u>The Agora of Athens</u> in <u>The Athenian Agora</u> Vol. XIV. Princeton: American School of Classical Studies at Athens.

Trendall, A.D. and T.B.L. Webster
1971   <u>Illustrations of Greek Drama</u>. London: Phaidon.

Webster, T.B.L.
1972   <u>Potter and Patron in Classical Athens</u>. London: Methuen.

Wycherley, R.E.
1978   <u>The Stones of Athens</u>. Princeton: Princeton University Press.

Zanker, P.
1965   <u>Wandel des Hermesgestalt in der attischen Vasenmalerei</u>. Bonn: Habelt.

Chapter 2

Pottery in Scenes of the Period of Agade?

Edith Porada

Among the rare representations of daily life in Mesopotamia are scenes in a farmstead, usually associated with the figure of a man riding on the back of an eagle in the sky, while shepherds and their dogs look upward at the extraordinary sight (Figures 1a and b). These have been dated to the Agade Period, ca. 2300 to 2160 B.C. (Boehmer 1965:190). The scenes have been interpreted as illustrating the dramatic moment in the story of Etana, who is listed among the rulers of the legendary dynasty of Kish, which followed upon the Flood. He is said to have been "Etana, a shepherd, the one who to heaven ascended" (Pritchard 1966:114).

Henri Frankfort commented on the delightful freedom with which these scenes are rendered and describes one of them, the impression of a cylinder seal found at Ur (Figure 1c), as follows: ". . . the herdsman, who has driven the flock out of the reed enclosure where they passed the night, halting at the door to turn and speak to a companion who remains behind for dairy work. He is cleaning a large vessel while others stand around, among which we recognize a churn for the preparation of buttermilk. Outside the enclosure some cheeses are shown put out on a mat to dry. The suggestive atmosphere of the early morning of a rural day is completed by the bird perched on the top of the enclosure" (Frankfort 1939:139, pl. XXIVg).

While every viewer will share Frankfort's pleasure over this detailed image of farm life, some of the items enumerated by him may be differently interpreted. A representation on a cylinder in the Iraq Museum (IM2203) shows a bird with spread wings in the sky beside a gate which may stand for an entire structure. Below bird and structure are a large vessel and symmetrical rows of rings, one above the other. The four elements—bird, structure, vessel, and rings—obviously belong together in some sort of context other than the early morning atmosphere around a farmstead.

The key to that context, however, remains to be discovered. For scholars encouraged for years by Fred Matson to pay special attention to ceramics in every phase of their manufacture, use, and distribution, these scenes present a special interest in the variety of vessels shown and the possibility that some of the items may be connected with making these vessels, or at least with adding significant parts to them.

The item which is of special concern here is the one referred to by Frankfort as "cheeses put out on a mat to dry." The ring-shaped objects, referred to by Frankfort as "cheeses," occur frequently, though not always within the confines of a rectangle, usually placed close to one or more large vessels. In one case (Figure 1a), a man in the posture of working (one knee up, the other bent and probably meant to be resting on the ground), seems to be about to form, from what looks like a coil of clay, a vessel using one of the rings. Three rows of the rings appear next to two vessels on a ledge. The feet or supports of these vessels are not visible: I therefore thought that the rings might have been clay intended to be shaped into feet for the vessels.

Such an interpretation would eliminate the idea of the rings representing cheeses. This had seemed most unlikely anyhow in view of the nature of Near Eastern cheeses, which are either kept in containers because of their semiliquid consistency, or are formed into lumps. Neither I nor any scholar familiar with present-day village life in Iraq (which may not have changed since antiquity in such traditional matters as preparing cheese) has seen a ring-shaped cheese in that country. Thorkild Jacobsen, who was a member of Frankfort's expeditions to the Diyala sites, suggested that he might have been influenced by Pierre (Pinhas) Delougaz ideas concerning the ubiquitous bevelled ring bowls and their later substitutes, that these had contained a cheese-like substance resembling yoghurt. If Frankfort thought of cheese in bowls, he must have considered these bowls to have been seen from above in order to appear like rings on a mat. In view of the consistency with which vessels are represented in cylinders of the Agade Period as seen from the side, it seems unlikely that those containing yoghurt would have been represented differently. Objects represented as rings therefore probably were rings.

An alternative interpretation for the rings is that they are pot-stands. In fact, Frankfort (1969:32) himself described one on a stela from Khafaje. Two persons share the burden of carrying a pole, from which a large beer-jar is slung; one also carries in his hand a "circular pot-stand on which the pointed vessel will be placed." While the Khafaje stela is carved in the style of the Early Dynastic Period and the cylinders here shown belong to the time of the Dynasty of Agade, perhaps two centuries later, I see no reason to assume that pot-stands were less common in the Agade Period than before in view of the number of round or pointed-bodied vessels of Agade type known (see Hansen in Erich 1965:210).

In one of the relevant scenes on the cylinders (Figure 1b), however, the figures on either side of the large vessel seem to be using clay rings for its decoration, while in another scene a clay ring seems to be affixed to a large vessel as a handle (Boehmer 1965:abb. 703a). The possibility that the rings were made of clay and were prepared in readiness for vessel manufacture is strengthened by representations in seal impressions from Susa of the late Proto-historic Period, contemporary with the Jamdat Nasr style (Figure 1d). There, the handles of the vessel are indicated in such a way as to correspond to the circles in the seal designs of the later period.

Furthermore, several sealings from Susa show rings in association with vessels. In one scene (Figure 1e), two people seem to squat (to judge by the position of their preserved upper bodies) below a series of vessels which they may have already completed while continuing to work on others. The figure at the right seems to touch, smooth, or otherwise handle the neck of a very large vessel on the top of which a standing figure places its hand. Beside the vessel is a large ring. In a second scene (Figure 1f), a man busies himself with a very large vessel beside which is a ring. The vessel is so big that one may wonder whether it could have been turned on a wheel or whether, instead, it was built up by coils of clay. In such case, the ring beside the vessel would have been one example of a coil of clay ready for use.

We may return here to one of the cylinders of the Agade Period (Figure 1c), and point out that beside the rings appears a very large vat, which corresponds in its shape to one from Tell Asmar of the Proto-Imperial Period (immediately preceding the Dynasty of Agade). This vat might have been made of coils, but is not described as to its method of manufacture by Delougaz (1952).

In summarizing the pictorial evidence, I have to suggest that clay rings, probably of different sizes, were used for coiling, for adding handles, for pot-stands, and for feet of vessels. Careful study of comparatively minor details of art work can thus provide us with insights into the methods and techniques of ancient pottery manufacture that might otherwise have gone unnoticed.

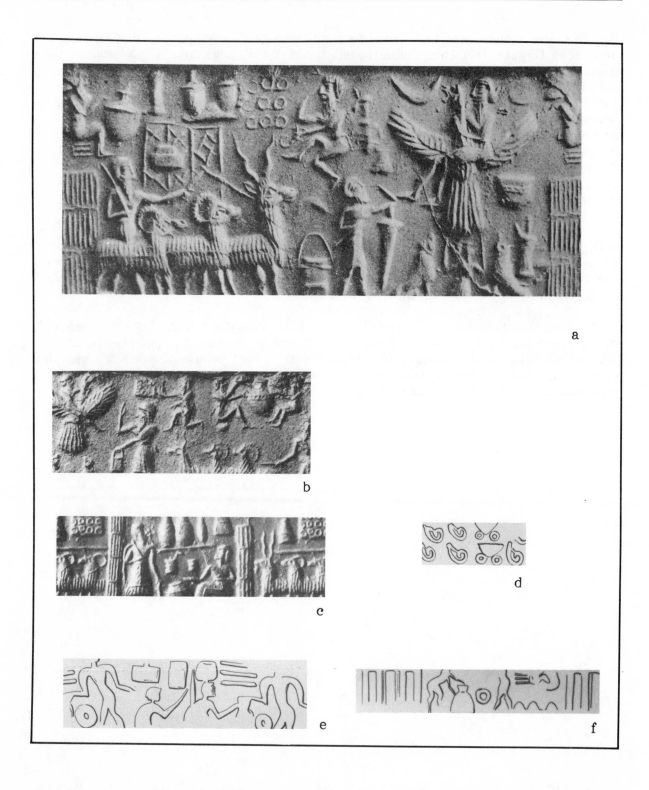

Figure 1.   Scenes and details from cylinder seal impressions showing pottery and pottery-making activities in early Mesopotamia. (a and b) Impressions of seals from the period of Agade, ca. 2300 to 2160 B.C. (c) An impression of a seal from Ur, dating to the same period. (d-f) Details from late Proto-historic period seals from Susa.

REFERENCES

Boehmer, R.M.
1965   Die Entwicklung der Glyptik wahrend der Akkad-zeit. Untersuchungen zur Assyriologie und Vorderasiatischen Archaologie, Neue Folge, Bd. 4, Berlin.

Delougaz, P.
1952   Pottery from the Diyala Region.   Oriental Institute Publications LXIII. Chicago: University of Chicago.

Ehrich, R.W.
1965   Chronologies in Old World Archaeology.   Chicago.

Frankfort, H.
1939   Cylinder Seals . . .   London.

1969   The Art and Architecture of the Ancient Orient.   4th rev. ed.   Baltimore: Penguin Books.

Pritchard, J.B.
1966   Ancient Near Eastern Texts.   Translation and commentary by E.A. Speiser. Princeton.

Chapter 3

Seasonal Pastoralism in Southern Greece:

A Consideration of the

Ecology of Neolithic Urfirnis Pottery

Thomas W. Jacobsen

The principal objectives of this contribution are two-fold. In the first place, an attempt will be made to explain the distribution (as presently understood) and the seemingly discrete regional concentration of a distinctive class of Greek Neolithic pottery known most commonly as "neolithic Urfirnis" (Weinberg 1970), or perhaps more accurately as "Corinthian Urfirnis" (French 1972). Second, this explanation will be based heavily upon ethnographic observations, and will aim at drawing attention to the potential importance of seasonal pastoralism ("transhumance," "pastoral nomadism") as a unifying mechanism and means of cultural exchange in Neolithic Greece. Before turning specifically to those matters, however, it will first be useful to summarize the problem and outline what is implied by the term "Neolithic Urfirnis."

NEOLITHIC URFIRNIS POTTERY

Although much remains to be done by way of technical analysis of this "ware," the broad definition of Neolithic Urfirnis is generally agreed upon by archaeologists working in Greece and the ware has been described in some detail (Weinberg 1970; Vitelli 1974). It is widely recognized as one of the most distinctive, best made, and most handsome manifestations of the prehistoric Aegean potter's craft. (It should not, however, be confused with a like-named ware characteristic of the Greek Early Bronze Age.) In addition to a repertory of distinctive shapes and similarities in paste, the most characteristic feature of this ware is its seemingly naturally lustrous slip (sometimes incorrectly called a "glaze" or "glaze paint") appearing either in patterns or monochrome on the vessel surfaces (Figure 1). It is this feature (which Matson calls a "vitrified slip"; personal communication) that led the German excavators at Orchomenos in central Greece to coin the term _Urfirnis_ to describe the surface treatment. Although efforts have been made to attribute the inspiration of this pottery and its distinctive surface treatment to superficially similar wares in the Near East (Weinberg 1970), it is safest at present to look for its roots in the earlier Neolithic of Greece itself (Howell 1970:104; Jacobsen 1973a).

Weinberg (1970) used what he took to be the relatively abrupt appearance and disappearance of Urfirnis pottery as the basis for his definition of the second major Neolithic horizon in southern and central Greece, his "Middle Neolithic" (M.N.). Although a chronological scheme for the Neolithic of southern Greece has not been determined, it now seems that the production of Neolithic Urfirnis pottery flourished for scarcely more than a few hundred years during the first half of the 5th millennium B.C. (in uncorrected radiocarbon years; Jacobsen 1977).

Yet one of the most interesting characteristics of this ware—indeed a characteristic fundamental to this paper—is its spatial distribution. Although found both in surface surveys and in excavations at a number of sites in central and southern Greece, Neolithic Urfirnis pottery seems to be most at home in the northeastern Peloponnese. Of the 21 well-documented or suspected sites in the Peloponnese with evidence of M.N. occupation, 19 are located in the northeastern third of the peninsula, i.e., in Corinthia, the Argolid, and eastern Arcadia (Jacobsen 1969:377, no. 46; French 1972:8, Fig. 6). Of these 19 sites, 15 have been subjected to some excavation, with two—Lerna (Figure 2, no. 7) and Franchthi Cave (Figure 2, no. 10)—producing the kinds of evidence that may eventually lead to a relatively complete picture of the lifeways of a southern Greek Neolithic settlement.

There exist, of course, inevitable local variations in workmanship and differing preferences for shapes and design composition within this area. Nevertheless, relatively detailed analysis of the abundant Urfirnis pottery from Lerna and Franchthi Cave, in comparison with a more general survey of related material from other sites in the region, has revealed considerable "shared information" and ceramic homogeneity over the geographical area in question (Vitelli 1974:212-215). The problem, as Vitelli has observed, is to understand the mechanisms of that interaction. To do so, we must first summarize the economic and geographical conditions of this region today, before turning to a consideration of Neolithic adaptations.

PASTORALISM AND THE HOMELAND OF NEOLITHIC URFIRNIS

The region under consideration, the northeastern Peloponnese, consists of the modern administrative units (nomoi) of the Corinthia, the Argolid, and (eastern) Arcadia (i.e., Arcadia roughly east of the Mainalon mountains) (Figure 2). It is an area of some 7000 sq. km. and represents about one third of the total land area of the Peloponnesian peninsula. The region is broadly dominated by physical features characteristic of limestone karst; this, combined with the role of the Mainalon range as the major divider between the wetter and drier parts of the Peloponnese, makes it one of the driest and most barren areas of the whole of Greece (Kayser and Thompson 1964). Although the introduction of irrigation by wells has come to render the area more agriculturally diversified (even allowing for the existence of flourishing citrus plantations today in several lowland districts), food production historically has depended in large measure upon animal husbandry and the cultivation of those crops (e.g., barley) most tolerant of warm and fairly dry climatic conditions. Such seems likely also to have been the case during the period which principally concerns us here.

This is not to suggest, however, that the northeastern Peloponnese is to be strictly regarded as an environmental unity. In terms of elevation and the complex of other factors contributing to the potential for food production, it may be divided into four distinct but interrelated ecological zones: zone 1, the higher mountains (>1000 m.); zone 2, the foothills and upland plains (600-1000 m.); zone 3, the rolling lowlands (200-600 m.); zone 4, the coastal belt (<200 m.). The area of highest mountains is largely restricted to the northwestern quadrant of the region. This area has for some time served as ideal summer pasture for flocks from the lowlands of eastern Corinthia and the Argolid, the seasonal movements of which covered distances up to 100 km. or more. These heights grade through a series of faulted and eroded terraces to the Isthmus and the alluvial coastal plain in the neighborhood of Corinth. Widely distributed herbaceous scrub vegetation serves as suitable pasture for the flocks of sheep and goats that are attracted to the fairly mild winter conditions of the Corinthia, and the meaning of the name of one of the major ancient sites in the district (Nemea, "pastures"; Figure 2, no. 2) testifies to the antiquity of this practice.

The other major upland area is that of eastern Arcadia, known since antiquity for its pastoralism (Georgoudi 1974). Among the industrial activities of this area today are carpet-making and tanning, crafts often associated with pastoralism, and a number of small settlements in the hills surrounding the upland basin are still devoted exclusively (or almost so) to seasonal pastoralism.

The lowlands and coastal belt of the Argolid are dry and largely devoid of natural vegetation other than scrub, especially in the area of the "Hermionid" at its southern extremity (Jameson 1976). Winter rain, plus the general mildness of the climate there, allows for an adequate growing season for cereal agriculture, and also provides areas of suitable grazing for local flocks, as well as those coming from some distance away (Bintliff 1977).

Seasonal Pastoralism in Modern Greece

By "seasonal pastoralism" I mean simply the movement of flocks under human guidance between winter pastures in the lowlands and summer grazing areas in the uplands. This is a basic form of pastoral adaptation in Greece and much of the circum-Mediterranean region (Braudel 1972; Grigg 1974), but there is considerable variation in its local manifestations. Those dimensions of seasonal pastoralism that are most significant here are the movements of people and their flocks throughout the region under consideration, and the several kinds of pastoral adaptations and the opportunities for cultural interaction which those movements help bring about.

Three pastoral groups (one local and two nonlocal) exploit the southern Argolid today (Koster 1976, 1977). The local group, the "Arvanites" (Hellenized Albanians), inhabits the area on a year-round basis and uses a fairly limited district. The Arvanites raise both sheep and goats as well as cultivate cereals, olives, and the vine, and thus practice a form of mixed food production. One nonlocal transhumant group that visits the area is the "Valtetsiotes," herders from the distant village of Valtetsi in eastern Arcadia. Some 60 families are now said to make the annual journey that begins in late October or early November and concludes with their return to their home village in late April or early May. The second nonlocal group of pastoralists who graze their flocks in the region during the winter are the Sarakatsani or "Roumeliotes" (Koster and Koster 1976). For much of their known history, the Sarakatsani have practiced an essentially nomadic existence, having no permanent home base and living merely in simple huts at their various seasonal encampments (Figure 3); it is only during this century that they have begun to settle in villages (normally near their upland, summer pastures) as a result of official encouragement by the Greek state (Campbell 1964).

This information, combined with such data as we have from other sources (Greece III 1945; Walker Kosmopoulos 1948), produces a picture of considerable pastoral activity and movement throughout our region in recent times. Koster (1977) has shown that three different ethnic groups of pastoralists, with three different kinds of pastoral adaptations, exploit the southern Argolid alone. A certain amount of interaction takes place among these groups, as well as between them and the sedentary agriculturalists in the same area (Koster and Koster 1976): the well-known "symbiosis" that exists between pastoralists and agriculturalists in general (Spooner 1973). Such interaction normally takes place during the course of the movement of the various groups from one grazing area to another in the spring and autumn and is illustrated by the partially reconstructed network of pastoral routes in Figure 2.

These interactions can and clearly do result in the exchange of both material goods and ideas as well as the development of kinship ties. Although present-day pastoralism exists within different political, technological, and socioeconomic circumstances from those in the past in Greece (Koster 1977:162-163), it is not unreasonable to assume that comparable interaction took place in earlier times (Hole 1978, 1979). It is a major proposition of this paper that seasonal pastoralism served as a significant mechanism of exchange in prehistoric Greece and contributed to interaction within and (very likely) between geographic regions.

The Antiquity of Seasonal Pastoralism in Greece

Although a number of scholars have argued that seasonal pastoralism has very deep roots in Greece, and its origins may reach back to the days of the mobile hunters of the Paleolithic period (Bintliff 1977; Campbell 1964; Hammond 1976; Higgs et al. 1967; Higgs and Jarman 1972), the direct evidence of early transhumance or pastoral nomadism in Greece is meager. Such strategies can be traced back fairly directly to the Classical period of Greek history (Georgoudi 1974; Höeg 1925; Mitchell 1957; White 1970), but what may be said about its role in prehistoric times?

Apart from the obvious absence of written documentation, this problem is extremely difficult to deal with (Hole 1978, 1979). Archaeologists active in Greece have generally neglected the question, until the studies of the late E.S. Higgs and his colleagues of the British Academy, working in northwest Greece, began to stimulate serious interest in the problem. Although at present our data from sites such as Lerna and Franchthi Cave are still in preliminary form and incomplete, I believe that there is enough information, when taken in consideration with the available archaeological, ethnographic, and environmental data (both ancient and modern), to make some inferences about the nature of M.N. adaptations in the northeastern Peloponnese. An underlying assumption in the following discussion is that there has been no substantial change in climate from that time to the present.

A Model of Pastoral Adaptation

Higgs (1976:160 ff.) has proposed a model to explain the means by which the resources of a given area are exploited. It consists of a series of three types of niche exploitation patterns—"sedentary," mobile cum sedentary," and "mobile." I would like to discuss this model in the context of prehistoric pastoralism in Greece, adding what I consider to be the expectable physical or archaeological manifestations of each economic niche, and then comparing those expectations with the archaeological realities of the northeastern Peloponnese.

a) **Niche I, sedentary.** This is a site that is "fully occupied all the year round," which, in marginal environments such as that under consideration here, would require maximized use of all local resources. Therefore we should expect some form of mixed food production, i.e., animal husbandry, agriculture, a certain amount of hunting and gathering of wild plants and animals, and, at suitable locations, fishing and shell collecting. Assuming adequate pasturage, flocks would be taken by a small group of herders to the grazing area on a daily basis and would not require (nor necessarily leave readily recognizable archaeological traces of) substantial physical facilities near the grazing area. The settlement itself should have some kind of "permanent" housing, evidence for the formal disposal of the dead (Jacobsen and Cullen, 1981), and pens for animals. There ought to be indications of a diversified assemblage of artifacts of stone, bone, clay, and other raw materials, artifacts appropriate to the various economic and symbolic activities carried out at the site.

b) **Niche II, mobile cum sedentary.** With reference to a pastoral economy, this would be an economic unit that farms the lowlands and pastures its flocks in the uplands; it represents more extensive pastoralism, probably on a seasonal basis. We should expect a segment of the population (the size of this group could vary considerably) to move with the flocks according to the season, while the rest of the population remains at "home base" year round. Thus there is a base settlement with facilities and equipment similar to those of the fully sedentary village; but there would also be the seasonal pastoral camp, the size of which would vary in accordance with the number of shepherds accompanying the flocks. The physical needs of the latter site presumably would be more limited than those of the former: less "permanent" housing; pens or folds for the animals would still be needed; perhaps less formal treatment of the dead (possibly only temporary interment of the corpse prior to final burial at the main site); and an artifactual assemblage of more restricted but specialized character. Sites such as this would obviously be more difficult to identify archaeologically, but very little effort has been expended in searching out such remains up to now. The location of this type of site could be expected to be near the pastures in the uplands, while that of the home base could be more flexible.

c) **Niche III, mobile.** The emphasis here is clearly upon seasonal mobility and may, as Higgs indicated, include groups of hunters and gatherers as well as pastoralists. We might think of seasonal movement between "impermanent" base camps, as in the traditional situation of the nomadic Sarakatsani. The equipment of these groups should be very much like that of the summer settlements of the mobile cum sedentary groups, but more in limited quantities. Indeed, when the Sarakatsan families of northern Greece made their seasonal moves, "they and their mules had little to carry except the poles (of their huts), the rugs, wooden and metal vessels, a few pottery cooking pots, and the implements for working wool and making homespun cloth

(Hammond 1976:48). We should expect that a number of "transit sites" (Higgs 1975:ix) were situated along the course of traditional routes. Such sites would have been occupied for short periods of time (possibly only a matter of hours and probably no more than a few days), but they would have been frequently visited over longer periods. They may be open sites, but caves would seem to serve as especially convenient shelters for that purpose. Some transit sites would appear to have become especially favored for a number of reasons, particularly if good water was available; they may eventually have come to be used by all groups passing through the vicinity, and could have played an important role in the exchange of goods and ideas among different mobile groups. These transit stations might also include burial sites for members of the group who died en route. Although very little has been written about the funerary practices of mobile pastoralists, it seems (Hole 1978) that their burial places are sometimes scattered along their migrational routes whether associated with camp sites or not (Jacobsen and Cullen 1981).

MIDDLE NEOLITHIC SITES IN NORTHEASTERN PELOPONNESE

Lerna and Franchti Cave seem to be the best candidates for M.N. settlements of Higgs' "sedentary" type. Both sites yielded evidence of stone structures with probable domestic functions and proper (normally secondary) human burials (if not formal cemeteries). Faunal remains point to the existence of animal husbandry, hunting and fishing, and the cultivation of cereals and legumes (Angel 1971; Payne 1975; Gejvall 1969; Hansen and Renfrew 1978; Jacobsen 1969, 1973a, 1973b, 1976, 1979). These sites thus seem to have practiced a mixed farming economy with herding an important activity, but we cannot rule out the possibility of a transhumant component at each site. Other sites, Argos (Figure 2, no. 12) and Tiryns (Figure 2, no. 13), may have been of the same type, but their remains are too scanty to warrant classification. Whether the Plain of Argos was as important agriculturally in the Neolithic as it has been in later times (Bintliff 1977), Figure 2 (area of nos. 7, 8, 12, 13) illustrates how significant this broad, flat expanse might have been for overland communication by mobile pastoralists at that time.

Old Corinth (Figure 2, no. 1) is one of the most extensively excavated sites in our region, but unfortunately those excavations have not produced the kinds of information necessary to establish its role in the economic life of the Neolithic (Weinberg 1970). The site, reasonably well-watered and located in a region of mild winters, overlooks the coastal plain of the Isthmus, and it has been suggested (Walker Kosmopoulos 1948) that it would have made an excellent winter station for pastoralist groups who summered elsewhere. Given the resources of the nearby coastal plain and the long history of human activity at the site, I would expect that it could have supported at least a small population year round and would therefore be better classified as a "mobile <u>cum</u> sedentary" if not fully sedentary settlement. Old Corinth, in any case, would have been a critical link between the pastoral networks of northeastern Peloponnese and central Greece; in fact, it may well have been that contacts of the kind implied by Sophocles in the <u>Oedipus</u> (Bintliff 1977:117) fostered the dispersal of goods and ideas between those regions. Such contacts, if projected back into prehistoric times could help explain the presence of quantities of Neolithic Urifirnis pottery at central Greek sites such as Elateia, Orchomenos, and Thespiai (French 1972).

Up to now we have no archaeological evidence of prehistoric pastoral sites (whether seasonal or not) in the highland regions of eastern Arcadia and western Corinthia (zone 1), but this may well be due to the lack of searching for them. Nor can the only excavated sites of zone 2--Asea (Figure 2, no. 15) and Ayioryitika (Figure 2, no. 16)--be readily classified according to the Higgs model. Published information about them is scanty, and it is possible that both could be fully sedentary villages.

Of those sites which almost certainly belong to Higgs' "mobile" niche (III), all are found at lower elevations. The cave of Kephalari (Figure 2, no. 8) is located a short distance to the northwest of Lerna and still within our coastal zone (zone 4). It has abundant water and would have provided small but good shelter for people as well as animals. Although its location near the margin of a potentially large grazing area might render it a suitable winter camp for Arcadian flocks, its small size and proximity to an ancient route connecting the Argolid with Arcadia might have made it a more likely transit station for pastoralists moving between the two regions. Still other likely transit sites are situated in the lowland zone (zone 3). One such site is Klenia Cave (Figure 2, no. 3), a fairly deep shelter with available water overlooking an alternate route between the Argolid and the Isthmus. Like Kephalari, this cavern seems to have been a shrine dedicated to the pastoral deity Pan in classical times. The Tsoungiza Cave (Figure 2, no. 2) was found in a collapsed state and is now not precisely locatable. It is situated above the Plain of Nemea with its great classical sanctuary of Zeus, an area which has long served as a rest-stop for pastoralists moving between the Argolid and western Corinthia (Koster 1976). The large collapsed cave or sinkhole near Didyma (Figure 2, no. 14) is spacious enough to accommodate a rather sizeable flock (as it still does today) and is located near the principal modern road leading northward from the southern Argolid. It could well have served, at the very least, as a temporary shelter for pastoral groups passing through this part of the Argolid in prehistoric times.

A final site deserving mention in this context is that at "Prosymna," near the ancient religious center at the Argive Heraeum (Figure 2, no. 9). The site has produced evidence of Neolithic activity at several points over an area of some 15 acres (Blegen 1937), but there are no clear indications of a settlement here; those remains which can be reasonably assigned to the M.N. consist of human burials in a cave-like hollow. The burials appear to be secondary, and many of the bones show signs of burning. There is also evidence of several fireplaces (campfires?) which the excavator suggests may have alternatively served as cremation pyres (Blegen 1937:24-25). This, together with the site's location along well-trod pastoral routes--not far from Koster's "bottleneck" on the eastern margin of the Plain of Argos (Koster 1976:24)--suggests that Prosymna was a transit station and may represent one of the best indications in Neolithic Greece of a transhumant burial ground.

If these interpretations are correct, it seems that the majority of the transit sites are in caves and most of them are located in the rolling country of our zone 3. It should perhaps be noted, however, that there is no reason to assume that at least some of the more sedentary settlements could not have accommodated a pastoral group in transit from time to time, especially if there were kin ties between members of both groups.

Pastoralists and Pottery

The question of the use of pottery by transhumant or nomadic peoples is obviously of some importance to the arguments of this paper, but it is a matter which--to my knowledge--has rarely been addressed in the ethnographic or archaeological literature. Containers of metal and wood are frequently mentioned in connection with modern transhumants and nomads, but pottery is usually not considered to be an important part of their equipment (Hole 1978). Metal objects are not as yet to be expected from M.N. contexts in Greece, but wooden vessels could well have been produced. None have been discovered up to now, but one fragment of a ceramic "box" from Franchthi Cave suggests to me that it was created in limitation of a wooden prototype (cf. Hammond [1976:40] who observed among the modern Vlachs of northern Greece that, "if one is given a souvenir plate or vase at Ioannina or at Tirana, it is usually painted of wood, skillfully carved to imitate pottery.") More to the point, Hammond also reports (1976:40, 48) that both the Vlachs and the Sarakatsani do use pottery, albeit normally a plain, coarse type of cooking ware.

A coarse variety of Urfirnis is known at most of the M.N. sites discussed in this paper (Vitelli 1974), but what use would mobile pastoralists have had for finer wares such as the best of the painted Neolithic Urfirnis? It is of course quite possible that they did not make significant use of it themselves but merely acted as the means of dispersal of those wares between one locality and another. Koster (personal communication) has observed the pastoralists often carry some luxury items, and archaeological support of this may be reflected by the situation among assumed Neolithic transhumants in western Yugoslavia (Sterud 1978). Many scholars (e.g., Wace and Thompson 1914; Hammond 1976) have acknowledged the traditional relationship between pastoralists and trade. Indeed, in our part of Greece, folk memory records the importance of transhumants as sources of goods as well as useful information of various kinds (Koster, personal communication).

To my knowledge, nothing is known about pastoralist potters today though there is no reason to assume that mobile pastoralists could not have produced their own pottery in the past (Hole 1978, 1979). Until we know more about this problem, however, I am inclined to think of Neolithic Urfirnis as something that seasonal pastoralists acquired from sedentary potters, and, whether or not they used it much themselves, it was they who were largely responsible for its dissemination (and eventual reproduction or imitation?) over a fairly large geographical area. Yet, as Higgs (1976:169) and others have suggested, this is a problem which clearly requires considerably more attention.

SUMMARY AND CONCLUSIONS

The primary purpose of this paper has been an attempt to draw attention to what appears to be a distinct regional concentration and distribution of a class of prehistoric Greek pottery known as Neolithic Urfirnis, and then to offer a possible explanation of this cultural unity by considering the paleoeconomic context to which it belongs. Distributional arguments at present suggest that the center of production of Urfirnis pottery may have been located somewhere in the northeastern part of the Peloponnesian peninsula of southern Greece, an area comprising the modern nomes of Corinthia, Argolid, and (eastern) Arcadia. It is proposed here that seasonal pastoralism was the mechanism principally (though perhaps not exclusively) responsible for historically unifying that region and thereby facilitating not only the creation of a regional "style" in ceramics but contributing to its dissemination beyond the limits of that region.

The northeastern Peloponnese is an area well suited to the practice of transhumance or nomadic pastoralism. Its agricultural productivity today is only marginal, and there is reason to believe that it was no better (if as good) in the Middle Neolithic. On the other hand, marked seasonal changes in the climatic regime and the relative proximity and accessibility of upland and lowland environmental zones combine to make reasonably good grazing areas readily available on a year-round basis.

Although rapidly disappearing throughout the Mediterranean world, seasonal pastoralism still plays a role in the economic life of the northeastern Peloponnese, and our historical evidence—though admittedly meager—suggests that its roots go back at least as far as classical antiquity. Its prehistoric past is more difficult to assess, but evidence from sites such as Lerna and Franchthi Cave indicate that the animals traditionally most suited to seasonal pastoralism in this area—sheep and goats—were the dominant species in the M.N. faunal assemblages. At the same time, the oft-cited venerability of transhumant routes is of interest, especially when the network of such routes today is compared with our present understanding of the pattern of M.N. settlements (Figure 2).

The specific nature of the interaction between these sites is admittedly a matter for speculation, but several reasonable possibilities are offered by ethnographic parallels. There would have been numerous opportunities for casual meetings between different pastoral groups while en route to their seasonal pastures or as a result of their utilization of common or at least adjacent grazing areas. Such meetings could have become more formalized as they were repeated year after year, perhaps even to the extent that certain locations came to have special significance to more than one group and became local ritual or trading centers (Bintliff 1977). The exchange of certain speciality products as well as information must also have taken place between the pastoralists and the more sedentary communities, and it is quite possible that the pastoralists' need for (ceramic) containers was satisfied in that manner. Under such circumstances, it is not difficult to imagine the development of kinship ties through intermarriage not only among the pastoralist groups themselves but between pastoralists and farmers. The extension and solidification of such ties would not only strengthen regional homogeneity but could lead to closer contact with other areas of southern and central Greece, thus explaining the distribution of Urfirnis pottery beyond the limits of its Peloponnesian homeland.

Finally, it should perhaps be stressed that, although emphasis is placed here upon pastoralism and its implications in the M.N. of southern Greece, there is no reason to believe that comparable phenomena could not have occurred both earlier and later in the Neolithic period. Indeed, it seems likely that some form of seasonal pastoralism was practiced throughout the Neolithic of southern Greece, and it is possible that it may have been even more intensified in the later stages of that period (Jacobsen 1978).[1]

NOTE

[1] This paper was completed in its present form in 1979 and is a substantially reduced version of an original written in 1978. The author wishes to thank F. Hole, H. Koster, S. Payne, and K. Vitelli for their valuable comments on the earlier manuscript. He would also like to recognize with gratitude the National Endowment for the Humanities whose support facilitated the completion of the original draft.

While circumstances have not permitted full updating of this paper, the author would like to draw attention to recent studies bearing upon issues raised above. Particularly noteworthy in connection with the physical remains of Greek pastoralist groups is Chang's (1981) study, which analyzes pastoral sites in the Greek Argolid and represents an important contribution to the development of an "archaeology of pastoralism."

The problem of "pastoralists and pottery" continues to be of interest to the author. While the production and use of pottery is still often regarded as "alien" to pastoralists (Orme 1981:269), a contemporary group making hand-made ceramics in southwestern Turkey is important:

> The Dont community is transhumant—i.e. in the spring the little group moves inland and up to the high valleys with their livestock where they spend about seven to eight months. Here the women produce a distinctive type of water jar with a vertical loop handle, and elongated neck on a gourd-shaped body, and a slightly cut-away pouring spout. They come in various sizes, sometimes painted with fugitive white paint. In the autumn the villagers leave the high valleys and return some 75-100 km to Dont on the coast with their store of pots which they sell during the autumn and winter in market towns like Fethiya, Mugla and Elmali.
>
> It is interesting that this pottery tradition, technologically the simplest of the four, is also the one in which the oldest pot shape is preserved, i.e. the characteristic prehistoric gourd-shaped form with cut-away spout (Birmingham 1974:47-48).

I regret to add that considerable efforts to learn more about this interesting group of potters from archaeological and anthropological colleagues working in Turkey have so far led nowhere.

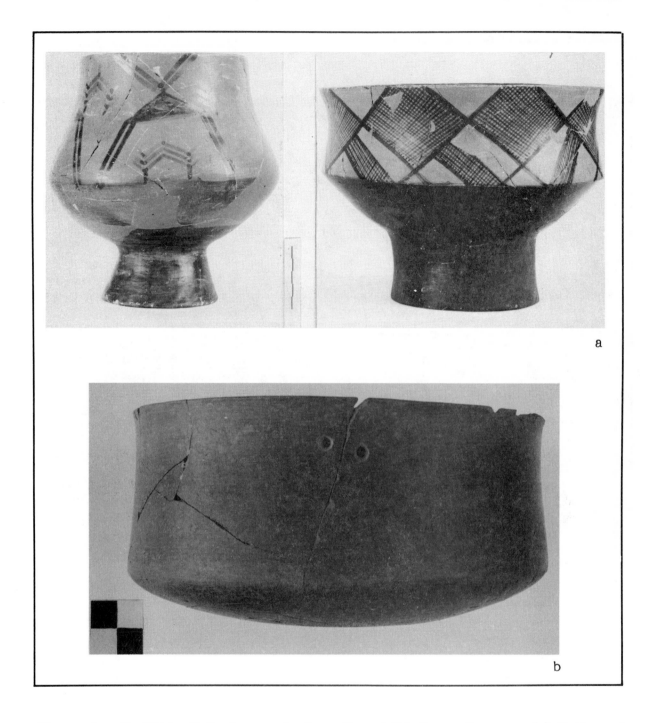

a

b

Figure 1. Neolithic Urfirnis vessels from Franchthi Cave, Greece. (a) Patterned vessels. (b) Monochrome bowl.

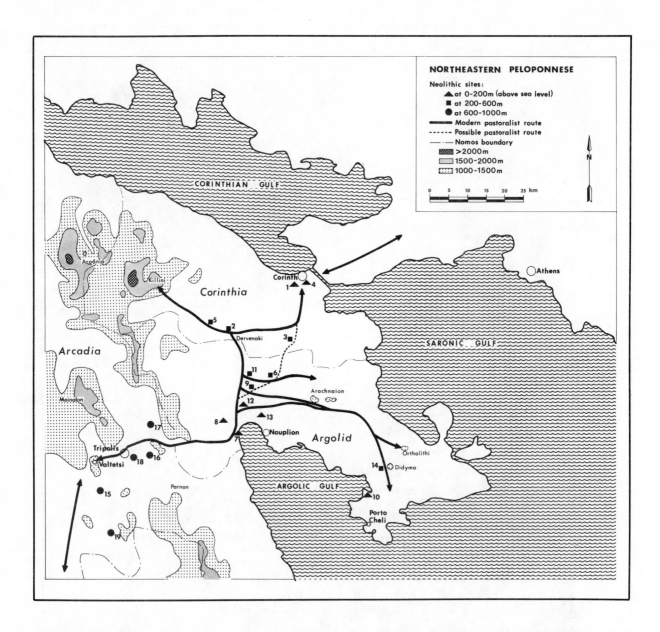

Figure 2. Map of the northeastern Peloponnese illustrating the relationship between Middle Neolithic sites and modern pastoralist routes. Locations in Corinthia: 1. Old Corinth; 2. Nemea (Tsoungiza) Cave; 3. Klenia (Pan) Cave; 4. Gonia; 5. Phlius. Locations in Argolid: 6. Berbati; 7. Lerna; 8. Kephalari (Dionysos and Pan) Cave; 9. Prosymna; 10. Franchthi Cave; 11. Mycenae; 12. Argos; 13; Tiryns; 14. Didyma Cave.* Locations in Arcadia: 15. Asea; 16. Ayioryitika; 17. Loukas-Rakhi t'Ambelia;* 18. Tzivas-Goumaradhes (?);* 19. Karyai-Derveni (?).* Asterisk (*) denotes unexcavated sites.

Figure 3. A Sarakatsan encampment on the Thessalian plain, 1968.

REFERENCES

Angel, J.
   1971   The People of Lerna.   Princeton: American School of Classical Studies, and Washington: Smithsonian Institution.

Bintliff, J.L.
   1977   Natural environment and human settlement in prehistoric Greece.   British Archaeological Reports 28(i–ii).

Birmingham, J.
   1974   Domestic Pottery in Greece and Turkey.   Sydney: The Macleay Museum.

Blegen, C.W.
   1937   Prosymna: The Helladic Settlement Preceding the Argive Heraeum.   Cambridge: Cambridge University Press.

Braudel, F.P.
   1972   The Mediterranean and the Mediterranean World.   New York: Harper and Row.

Campbell, J.K.
   1964   Honour, Family, and Patronage.   London: Oxford University Press.

Chang, C.
   1981   The Archaeology of Contemporary Herding Sites in Greece.   Unpublished Ph.D. dissertation, Department of Anthropology.   State University of New York at Binghamton.

French, D.H.
   1972   Notes on Prehistoric Pottery Groups from Central Greece.   Athens: Privately printed and circulated.

Gejvall, N.G.
   1972   Lerna.   Volume I: The Fauna.   Princeton: American School of Classical Studies.

Georgoudi, S.
   1974   Quelques problèmes de la transhumance dans la Grèce ancienne.   Revue des Etudes Grecques 87:155–185.

Greece
   1944–45 Geographical Handbook Series, 3 volumes.   London: Naval Intelligence Division, British Admiralty.

Grigg, D.B.
   1974   The Agricultural Systems of the World, an Evolutionary Approach.   London: Cambridge University Press.

Hammond, N.G.L.
  1976 Migration and Invasions in Greece and Adjacent Areas. Park Ridge, N.J.: Noyes.

Hansen, J. and J.M. Renfrew
  1978 Palaeolithic-Neolithic seed remains at Franchthi Cave, Greece. Nature 271:350-352.

Higgs, E.S. (ed.)
  1975 Palaeoeconomy. London: Cambridge University Press.

Higgs, E.S.
  1976 The history of European agriculture—the uplands. Philosophical Transactions of the Royal Society B. 275:159-173.

Higgs, E.S. and M.R. Jarman
  1972 The origins of animal and plant husbandry. In, Papers in Economic Prehistory, E.S. Higgs, ed. Pp.3-13. London: Cambridge University Press.

Higgs, E.S., C. Vita-Finzi, D.R. Harris, and A.E. Fagg
  1967 The climate, environment and industries of stone age Greece: part III. Proceedings of the Prehistoric Society 33:1-29.

Höeg, C.
  1925-26 Les Saracatsans, 3 volumes. France: Champion.

Hole, F.
  1978 Pastoral nomadism in western Iran. In, Explorations in Ethnoarchaeology, R.A. Gould, ed. Pp. 127-167. Albuquerque: University of Mexico.

  1979 Rediscovering the past in the present: ethnoarchaeology in Luristan, Iran. In, Ethnoarchaeology, C. Kramer, ed. Pp. 192-218. New York: Columbia University Press.

Howell, R.
  1970 A survey of eastern Arcadia in prehistory. The Annual of the British School of Archaeology at Athens 65:79-127.

Jacobsen, T.W.
  1969 Excavations at Porto Cheli and vicinity, preliminary report II: The Franchthi Cave. Hesperia 38-381.

  1973a Excavations in the Franchthi Cave, 1969-1971, part I. Hesperia 42:45-88.

  1973b Excavations in the Franchthi Cave, 1969-1971, part II. Hesperia 42:253-283.

  1976 17,000 years of Greek prehistory. Scientific American 234:76-87.

  1977 New radiocarbon dates from Franchthi Cave, Greece. Journal of Field Archaeology 4:367-368.

1978   Transhumance as a mechanism of exchange in Neolithic Greece. Abstracts, The Archaeological Institute of America 3:47.

1979   Excavations at Franchthi Cave, 1973-1974.   Archaiologikon Deltion (Chronika) 29:268-292.

Jacobsen, T.W. and T. Cullen
    1981   A consideration of mortuary practices in Neolithic Greece: burials from Franchthi Cave. In, Mortality and Immortality. The Anthropology and Archaeology of Death, S.C. Humphreys and H. King, eds. Pp. 79-101. London: Academic Press.

Jameson, H.
    1976   The southern Argolid: the setting for historical and cultural studies. In, Regional variation in modern Greece and Cyprus: towards a perspective on the ethnography of Greece, M. Dimen and E. Friedl, eds. Annals of the New York Academy of Sciences 268:74-91.

Kayser, B. and K. Thompson
    1964   Economic and Social Atlas of Greece. Athens: National Statistical Service of Greece.

Koster, H.A.
    1976   The thousand year road. Expedition 19:19-28.

    1977   The Ecology of Pastoralism in Relation to Changing Patterns of Land Use in the Northeast Peloponnese. Unpublished Ph.D. dissertation, Department of Anthropology, University of Pennsylvania.

Koster, H.A. and J.B. Koster
    1976   Competition or symbiosis?: pastoral adaptive strategies in the southern Argolid, Greece. In, Regional variation in modern Greece and Cyprus: toward a perspective on the ethnography of Greece, M. Dimen and E. Friedl, eds. Annals of the New York Academy of Sciences 268:275-285.

Michell, H.
    1957   The Economics of Ancient Greece. New York: Barnes and Noble.

Orme, B.
    1981   Anthropology for Archaeologists. Ithaca: Cornell University Press.

Payne, S.
    1975   Faunal change at Franchthi Cave from 20,000 B.C. to 3,000 B.C. In, Archaeozoological Studies, A.T. Clason ed. Pp. 120-131. New York: Elsevier.

Spooner, B.
1973   The cultural ecology of pastoral nomads.   Addison-Wesley Module in
       Anthropology 45.

Sterud, E.L.
1978   Prehistoric populations of the Dinaric Alps: an investigation of interregional
       interaction. In, Social Archaeology: Beyond Subsistence and Dating, C.L.
       Redman, et al., eds. Pp. 381-408. New York: Academic Press.

Vitelli, K.D.
1974   The Greek Neolithic Patterned Urfirnis Ware from the Franchthi Cave and
       Lerna. Unpublished Ph.D. dissertation, Department of Classical Archaeology,
       University of Pennsylvania.

Wace, A.B. and M.S. Thompson
1914   The Nomads of the Balkans. London: Methuen.

Walker Kosmopoulos, L.
1948   The Prehistoric Inhabitation of Corinth, I. Munich: Bruckmann.

Weinberg, S.S.
1970   The Stone Age in the Aegean. Cambridge Ancient History[2] I.I:557-618.

White, K.D.
1970   Roman Farming. Ithaca: Cornell University Press.

Chapter 4

The Archaeological Study of Specialized Pottery Production: Some Aspects of Method and Theory

Prudence M. Rice

The economic significance of potters and pottery in society is more and more becoming the subject of archaeological and ethnographic attention. Much of the archaeological work directly or indirectly concerned with the economic role of pottery has concentrated in inter- and intra-regional distribution and trade patterns (see Chapter 5, this volume), rather than on production. Many of these studies have drawn heavily on a variety of new, highly quantitative techniques of compositional analysis (see Part III of this volume). Although the methods of physicochemical analysis that are used to identify sources of raw material can logically provide a basis for a study of the manufacture of archaeological objects, such data have been primarily used to study trade. As a result, "provenience studies" have been largely concerned with "macroprovenience," that is, characterization of "local" versus "foreign" or "trade" materials on a regional level. "Microproveniencing" analyses, the kind that are necessary for study of production with a local area, are somewhat less common in archaeological analyses.

Ethnographic or ethnoarchaeological research, on the other hand, has often focused on production, using a variety of perspectives. Frequently these have emphasized manufacturing techniques or learning patterns. In general, however, correspondence has not been easy to achieve between the kinds of observables studied ethnographically, and the more limited range of behavioral data available to archaeologists, in the study of the organization of production. Additionally, it has been difficult to place production in an evolutionary perspective in order to understand how, through time, in some societies the manufacture of pottery evolved from what may have been a typical activity performed by self-sufficient households along with a variety of other tasks, to a specialized economic pursuit carried out by a small number of skilled practitioners who did little if anything else to earn a living.

An understanding of production, particularly specialist production, is not a single research objective but rather is predicated on a complex of closely interrelated theoretical and methodological questions. These questions have social, environmental, economic, organizational, and aesthetic components, all of which demand intensive research. This paper focuses on the role of resources in establishing the background against which the socioeconomic process of ceramic specialization takes place.

ENVIRONMENT AND SOCIOCULTURAL COMPLEXITY

The study of nonagricultural production provides a close look at the interaction of the social subsystem with its environment in terms of the resources used, the technology of production, and the social organization that defines the producing groups. Craft specialization generally accompanies the evolution of complex societies, but its existence has too frequently been inferred by archaeologists, rather than convincingly demonstrated. From an ecological perspective, both stratification and economic specialization symbolize the existing relationships between a human society and its environment. They reflect the underlying conditions of differential distribution of resources within a particular environment and the societal management of these resources. Occupational diversification, then, may be seen to arise as a response to two interacting sets of preconditions, environmental diversity and sociocultural diversity.

Environmental diversity, in terms of its bearing on the study of craft specialization, can be discussed through two components: (1) the environment itself—the resources available, their abundance or "scarcity," and their location; and (2) the culturally or historically prescribed patterns of access to or utilization of those resources, and changes in such patterns. Typically, analysis of environmental diversity focuses on the nonuniform distribution of "essential," "key," or "basic" resources necessary for the support and maintenance of human society. "Basic" resources are probably best considered relative rather than absolute, since among different societies or at different times in a culture's history the definition of a basic resource may vary "due to differences in geographical environment, technological equipment, and what may be called the historically determined perception of the exploitable environment" (Fried 1967:186).

Social processes of differentiation—ranking, stratification, segmentation—are generally accompanied by increasing differentiation of access to or use of resources (Fried 1967). This fact underscores the difficulty of defining resources as "basic". Although some resources are "basic" in ensuring subsistence for the society, others may be defined as essential in terms of symbolizing status or prestige for certain social segments, thereby helping maintain sociopolitical integration. In egalitarian societies, access to resources is largely unlimited. Divisions of labor on the basis of age or sex may be the only determinants by which an individual has any contact with a given kind of resource, and economies are characteristically oriented toward sufficiency. In ranked societies, with larger absolute population size and greater population density, some differentiation of resource access may be noted. Divisions of labor are still by age and sex, perhaps involving some low-level or incipient specialization ("artisanship") on the basis of skill, interest, or need. Reciprocal gift-giving is an important form of exchange among ethnographically known ranked societies, and prestige accrues to those who accumulate goods and dispose of them generously (Sahlins 1960). In complex stratified societies, division of labor is formalized and access to basic or productive resources is limited. Access can be restricted by assigning either direct or indirect use rights to particular individuals or groups, often in exchange for products of that resource.

The complexity of the relationship between an environment, and the cultural perception and exploitation of that environment, becomes increasingly significant. While environmental diversity provides conditions of uneven distribution or "scarcity" of resources (as a consequence of which we may think of "local" vs. "exotic" raw materials, for example), social organizations can also manipulate their relationships with their environments in terms of use and access, creating "social scarcity." With this perspective, a variety of economic interrelationships can be studied as correlates of the underlying conditions of differential distribution of resources within a particular environment, and the social management of those resources.

PROBLEMS IN DEFINING CRAFT SPECIALIZATION

Ethnographic researchers often identify economic specialists by the amount of time spent performing the occupation or craft, and/or by the proportion of subsistence obtained through a specialist's productive enterprise. Other considerations in defining craft specialization are the existence of "a recognized title, usually in the form of a native name for the specialty" or a "claim on society for some special treatment, e.g., payment of money, or gift in exchange" for the craft product (Tatje and Naroll 1973:773).

In contrast, archaeological definitions of craft specialization are poorly developed and not fully congruent with ethnographic ones. Criteria of occupational specialization in general or specialized craft production in particular are virtually impossible for archaeologists to correlate with the time, title, payment, or subsistence criteria that form the crux of ethnographic definitions. That this is so is not a crippling limitation, but the point is that some operational definition of craft production needs to be developed for archaeologists.

Rather than defining occupational specialization in terms of what it is, it may be more helpful for archaeologists to identify it in terms of what it does, thereby accentuating its functional role. Craft specialization is here considered to be one of the adaptive processes in the fluid interrelationships between a nonindustrialized society and its environment. Through this process behavioral and material variety in extractive and productive activities may be regulated or "regularized" via socially instituted mechanisms.

Thus, if craft specialization involves the regulation of use of resources within a particular group or groups of the society, it should have an effect on the products manufactured of those resources. That is, it may result in standardization or simplification (reduction in variety) in raw materials used for the products, techniques of manufacture, and product sizes, shapes, decorative styles, and so forth. On the other hand, such regulation may result in increased variety or elaboration, with producers, production means, and the products themselves reflecting the internal variety and complexity of a growing diverse social system. Different social segments will have different demands and different degrees of ability or means to satisfy them.

For pottery, there are a number of traditional lines of evidence for specialized production (Rice 1981) that hint at the utility of some of the above ideas. Some of the traditional indicators suggest simply that production was "specialized" in the sense of restricted to a small number of particularly skilled artisans. Observations on the apparent skill or proficiency of forming and/or decorating certain categories of vessels (e.g., Maya human-figure polychromes) or apparent mass production of masses of identical objects provided a basis for such conclusions. In addition, areas of production within a site have sometimes been inferred from localized concentrations of tools, raw materials, unfired vessels, or overfired "wasters." And regions of production have often been hypothesized on the basis of essentially age-area sorts of arguments: distribution patterns of design microstyles, or distinctive paste or technological characteristics.

In complex societies--civilizations or states--the socioeconomic differentiation was formalized to the extent that occupational barrios, wards, or shops can be found, as at Teotihuacan in Highland Mexico, for example. However, the proportion of state societies or urban centers with full-time specialists is relatively small compared to the number of other archaeologically known cultures, such as Halaf or Maya, where some degree of pottery specialization is likely but more difficult to recognize. Given the current interest in exchange in pottery and other craft products, there is clearly a need for more explicit archaeological indicators of occupational specialization. Two directions to guide development of such indicators and the path of future investigations of craft specialization may be suggested: (1) attention to the "ceramic environment" (kind and location of resources, etc.) and the technological study of clays and pottery; and (2) attention to relative degrees of variability or diversity, or "quality control," in technological and other properties of pottery through time and with increasing social complexity (Rice 1981).

The "Ceramic Environment"

Environmental considerations underscore the complexity of the ceramic craft specialization issue. Specialized production can only exist where the environment provides suitable resources for that specialization and where a sizeable and diverse social polity can support the craftsmen. With respect to ceramic craft specialization in particular, the matter of resources is complex, for clays or clayey soils are extremely widespread and their mere presence is not sufficient to give rise to specialization. Thus there are some general "preconditions" or "permissive factors" which set the stage for specialized manufacture of pottery. These include such considerations as availability and diversity of resources (not only clays, but temper, pigments, fuel for firing, tools for scraping, polishing, smoothing, compacting, etc.), and a suitable climate (a sufficient number of dry days throughout the year, or a dry season) to allow pottery to be dried and safely fired.

These factors allow for the existence of pottery-making in general, but for specialization to occur other permissive factors, which may also act as limiting and/or forcing situations, influence the interactions of human populations with their environment. The ethnographic literature is full of examples of ceramic-making communities being located only in certain parts of a region (e.g., the northern Valley of Guatemala, the perimeter of the Valley of Oaxaca), so that within a region certain factors are selecting for pottery-making as an economic activity in particular microenvironments as opposed to other economic alternatives. Locally, one community may specialize in one kind of ware and other communities in different wares. Obviously, a variety of complex historical factors operate to cause such specialization, but surely some "limiting" or "permissive" factors of environmental differentiation played a role as well.

One aspect of environmental zoning or microzoning likely to have been significant in the development and location of craft specialists in a region is the differential distribution of agriculturally good land and poor land. Such uneven distributions make agriculture less productive in some areas, and may stimulate a search for economic alternatives. Land which is considered poor for agriculture may be so because it is highly eroded and/or receives little (or unequally distributed) rainfall. However, either of these factors makes it more attractive to potters: erosion may serve to expose clays, and a greater number of rainfree days adds to the number of days per year in which pottery can be made, as Arnold (1975) has shown in highland Peru. Similar conditions obtain in the northern Valley of Guatemala. Land which is good for agriculture, on the other hand, can be farmed in such a way (intensively or extensively) as to ensure subsistence support for nonproducers in the society.

Yet another environmental factor that has been largely overlooked in consideration of the development and location of pottery craft specialists is the availability of fuel for firing pottery. Although a variety of fuels (coal, lignite, brush, reeds, grass, bark), including waste byproducts of animal (dung) or vegetal (straw, chaff) origin, are known to have been used, throughout the history of pottery-making the most common fuel appears to have been primarily wood. Wood was very much in demand as fuel for heating homes, cooking and baking, and metallurgy; for construction timbers and furniture; for vehicles (watercraft or carts); for shafts or handles on tools; and so forth. The availability of fuels, particularly wood, given this varied usage, was known to have been a problem both past and present, especially in areas of large and growing populations.

For example in contemporary Chamula, Mexico, Howry (1976:62) reports gradual deforestation, increasing scarcity of firewood, and its rising cost (which is the major financial outlay of potters for their resources) as bringing about changes in the location of successful pottery-making communities. Additional stresses on pottery production caused by the availability of firewood are reported in Mexico (Papousek 1981) and in the Philippines (Lawless 1978). It is not unreasonable to hypothesize that deforestation in antiquity, resulting from consumption of wood and from agricultural practices, led to similar problems, such as shortages, legal restrictions on manufacture and selling of firewood, taxes on domestic fuel, and changes in pottery itself. For example, Matson (1971) reported a decline in firing temperature of Seleucia figurines following a period of military and economic unrest which led to shortages of fuel. It is thus possible that a variety of otherwise inexplicable changes in techno-stylistic characteristics of pottery collections spanning a length of time may relate to changes in the availability of the local fuel supply for firing. Potters may have experienced the first "energy crunch."

To return to the subject of occupational specialization, future research will have to take into consideration the environmental constraints within which any kind of specialization is operative. In the case of pottery, there should be some attempt at defining the "effective ceramic environment" through analysis of the quantity and quality of available resources. Some awareness of their possible differential accessibility in the past (e.g., are they accessible now only because modern construction exposed them?) is also necessary, recognizing, of course, that the exact parameters may be unknowable.

The collection of clays, tempers, and other raw materials that could have been used by potters in the past is an important part of the study of the "effective ceramic environment" (see Chapter 9, this volume). This also is an essential step of "ceramic ecology" (Matson 1965; Arnold 1975; Rice 1976). Ceramic ecology may be considered a specialized aspect of general cultural ecology "which attempts to relate the raw materials and technologies that the local potter has available to the functions in his culture of the products he fashions" (Matson 1965:203). The fundamental procedures of ceramic ecology (Rice 1976) are:

1. Analysis of the ceramic environment and exploitative techniques, including identification and sampling of ceramic resources, and study of meteorological and/or climatological factors;

2. Analysis of the behavior patterns involved in pottery-making and use (e.g., is it restricted by age or sex? is it a household or class activity? how is it learned? what techniques are used? is it done individually or cooperatively in groups? how is it used? are broken vessels used?)

3. How is the behavior of making and using pottery affected by and how does it in turn affect other aspects of culture (settlement pattern, kinship structure, economic organization, ceremonial life, agricultural cycle, etc.)?

Ceramic technological studies, comprising observation and measurement of the range of variation in the properties of the raw materials, such as fired color, "stickiness," texture, shrinkage, etc., will help determine the boundary conditions within which ancient ceramic manufacture could have been carried out. Such determinations will give some idea of the variety of available resources for ceramic-making. They will also suggest the range in products likely to be made from them, and steps taken by potters to accommodate themselves to the resources or to modify them. Sticky, high-shrinkage clays will likely need large quantities of temper; coarse lean clays may not be suited to production of "fine wares" or thin-walled unusual forms; location in a limestone area may suggest that vessels, if calcite-bearing, will likely be comparatively low-fired (cf. Rye 1976). Varied kinds (colors, textures, etc.) of clays may suggest that a complex ceramic industry of varying degrees of specialization was possible, exhibiting elaboration in form, function, decoration, etc. Such observations establish the background, or the boundary conditions, within which specialization might have occurred. They also provide an intermediate step for inferences from ceramic data, since traditional attributes of ceramic analysis are thereby given behavioral or socioeconomic (as opposed to primarily chronological) significance.

This last point is an important one, for in relating material culture to extinct cultural systems, study of technological properties provides a basis for analysis of how patterning in material culture relates to patterning of resource management and access. However, as Thompson (1958:6-7) pointed out in his study of Yucatecan pottery-making, the analyst is responsible for establishing the significance of this relationship:

> The results of an analysis of the raw materials from which a group of artifacts is made are usually presented in terms of the properties of the materials. But the significance . . . is obscured unless the technological data are rephrased to emphasize some use which man makes of this . . . property. . . . This transition from a technological to a cultural orientation is a fundamental step in archaeological inferences because it establishes a cultural context. . . .

Ceramic craft specialization is one such cultural inference that can be approached through ceramic technological data. True, it cannot be known how the availability of specific clay resources or other raw materials for potting has changed through time, for example, by erosion or exhaustion of particular deposits. It is generally assumed for purposes of investigation that the clays available today (in river cuts, for example) or located near sites were also available in the past. The extent to which a ceramic occupational specialization developed and is archaeologically recognizable depends on the extent to which the potters perceived this range of resources, how they defined their effective ceramic environment, and how they optimized their relationship with this environment.

Variability

Earlier it was suggested that an appropriate strategy for the study of specialized pottery-making would involve two steps, study of the available resources for pottery and study of variability in the ceramic products. This latter topic is dealt with in greater detail in a separate paper (Rice 1981), but some of the essential points may be summarized here.

Some variability in preindustrial ceramic products exists for the same reasons variability exists in any other aspect of material culture: over time and space, replication of a "mental template" is never perfect. There are discrete and numerous producers with different skills, multiple incidents of production, multiple raw materials, and multiple procedures. Other kinds of variability result from any number of social and economic processes—different products for different consuming segments; class, ritual, or ethnic associations of decoration or form; different rates of production; etc.

Variability and innovation in material culture as a topic of archaeological or ethnographic study certainly has not been ignored up to the present, but attempts to put it into a theoretical framework have been relatively scarce (cf. Clarke 1968; Plog 1976; Rathje 1975; Barnett 1953). Clearly, variability (or its converse, standardization) may be observed and measured in all attributes of pottery, including color, form, dimensions, composition (kind, size, quantity of constituents), degree of firing, and a host of observations on manufacturing technique. In terms of recognizing the existence of craft specialization, some determination may be made of relative amounts of total variety or diversity within segments of an archaeological ceramic complex at any point in time. If specialization reflects, in part, restricted or regulated access to resources, then the products of such specialization should have a narrowly restricted or skewed range of variation in properties, reflecting the range inherent in those raw resources utilized in manufacture.

One example of this kind of inference is Johnson's (1975:300-301) study of the distribution of certain decorative attributes in Uruk pottery. A histogram of the distribution of values of horizontal line thickness in incised crosshatch bands on Uruk pottery was found to have regional significance, suggesting workshop areas east and west of the Dez River. Similar study of the distribution of mouth diameter measurements and wall thickness measurements by type and paste color in tripod dishes of Postclassic Maya pottery from Guatemala suggested a variety of locations of manufacture for the monochrome type, but that decorated types were less variable and probably were made at a smaller number of locations (Rice 1980). Rottlander plotted (1967) measurements of four major dimensions of Roman beakers and concluded, on the basis of consistent occurrence in whole and quarter subdivisions of a major Roman unit of linear measure (the digitus, and to a lesser extend the unciae), that manufacture of these vessels was standardized.

SUMMARY

Craft specialization is a process of gradual selection of (or restriction to) one occupational mode out of the alternative possibilities presented by environmental diversity or scarcity, and the culturally conditioned perceptions of that environment. It is an adjustment or regulation of socioeconomic interrelationships for the productive use of a society's environment. Such a view of craft specialization permits the joining of technological data on ceramic paste composition and firing with more traditional areas of ceramic analysis (form, decoration, typology, style) into a more complete understanding of the dynamics of a ceramic system.

Identification of ceramic resources and evidence for their exploitation may be obtained by study of variability in certain properties, such as amount of temper, hardness, degree of firing, color, mineralogy, or chemical composition. This identifies the standards or customs which potters recognized and more or less consistently adhered to through differential exploitation of raw materials and the skilled manipulation of those materials. Further, since many of these attributes may be related directly back to raw resources, comparable measurements on properties of raw clays and fired pottery can serve in trying to determine areas of manufacture by identifying the locations of the resources used.

REFERENCES

Arnold, D.E.
  1975 Ceramic ecology of the Ayacucho Basin, Peru: implications for prehistory. Current Anthropology 16:183-206.

Barnett, H.G.
  1953 Innovation, the Basis of Cultural Change. New York: McGraw-Hill.

Clarke, D.L.
  1968 Analytical Archaeology. London: Methuen.

Fried, M.H.
  1967 The Evolution of Political Society. New York: Random House.

Howry, J.C.
  1976 Fires on the Mountain: Ceramic Traditions and Marketing in the Highlands
        of Chiapas, Mexico.   Unpublished Ph.D. dissertation, Department of
        Anthropology, Harvard University.

Johnson, G.A.
  1975 Locational analysis and the investigation of Uruk local exchange systems.
        In, Ancient Civilization and Trade, J.A. Sabloff and C.C. Lamberg-
        Karlovsky, eds. Pp. 285-340. Albuquerque: University of New Mexico Press.

Lawless, R.
  1978 Deforestation and indigenous attitudes in Northern Luzon. Anthropology
        2:1-17.

Matson, F.R.
  1965 Ceramic ecology: an approach to the study of early cultures of the Near
        East. In, Ceramics and Man, F.R. Matson, ed. Pp. 202-217. Viking Fund
        Publication no. 41. Chicago: Aldine.

  1971 A study of temperatures used in firing ancient Mesopotamian pottery. In,
        Science and Archaeology, R.H. Brill, ed. Pp. 65-79. Cambridge: M.I.T.
        Press.

Papousek, D.A.
  1981 The Peasant-Potters of Los Pueblos. Van Gorcum.

Plog, F.
  1976 The Study of Prehistoric Change. New York: Academic Press.

Rathje, W.L.
  1975 The last tango in Mayapan: a tentative trajectory of production distribution
        systems. In, Ancient Civilization and Trade, J.A. Sabloff and C.C. Lamberg-
        Karlovsky, eds. Pp. 409-448. Albuquerque: University of New Mexico Press.

Rice, P.M.
  1976 Continuity and Change in the Valley of Guatemala: a Study of Whiteware
        Pottery Production.   Unpublished Ph.D. dissertation, Department of
        Anthropology, Pennsylvania State University.

  1980 Peten Postclassic pottery production and exchange: a view from Macanche.
        In, Models and Methods in Regional Exchange, R. Fry, ed. Society for
        American Archaeology Papers Series 1:67-82.

  1981 Evolution of specialized pottery production: a trial model. Current
        Anthropology 22:219-240.

Rottlander, R.C.A.
   1967   Is provincial Roman pottery standardized?   Archaeometry 9:76-91.

Rye, O.S.
   1976   Keeping your temper under control: materials and the manufacture of Papuan pottery. Archaeology and Physical Anthropology in Oceania XI:106-137.

Sahlins, M.D.
   1960   Political power and the economy in primitive society.   In, Essays in the Science of Culture, R. Carneiro and G. Dole, eds. New York: Crowell.

Tatje, T.A. and R. Naroll
   1973   Two measures of societal complexity: an empirical cross-cultural comparison.   In, A Handbook of Method in Cultural Anthropology, R. Naroll and R. Cohen, eds. Pp. 766-833.   New York: Columbia University Press.

Thompson, R.H.
   1958   Modern Yucatecan Maya Pottery Making.   Memoir No. 25 of the Society for American Archaeology.

Chapter 5

Pottery Manufacture:

Some Complications for the Study of Trade

Sander E. Van Der Leeuw

Trade in pottery has long been a subject of major interest to archaeologists and prehistorians. The typical evidence for trade consists of sherds found in one place that represent a pot thought to have been made in another. Techniques from the physical sciences (petrography, neutron activation analysis, X-ray diffraction, etc.) have been employed by archaeologists to characterize the paste of pottery and its inclusions. From these data, they then draw conclusions concerning the place of manufacture of the ceramics (see papers in Part III, this volume). Although these techniques enable us to determine provenience with much more certainty than did the older typological approach, neither gives any idea of the actual processes responsible for the distribution of the pottery we find.

This paper attempts to draw the first few lines of an approach which may in the long run solve some of the many questions. It argues that the manufacture and trade of pottery are subject to a finite, and actually fairly limited, set of variables. A processual systems model derived from ethnographic data is used to generate hypotheses about ceramic manufacture and trade in general, with some suggestions for the analysis of medieval European pottery specifically. My perspective in these matters derives from the technological study of pottery which has been developed by Shepard (1968), Matson (1965), and, above all, Franken (1974) and Franken and Kalsbeek (1969, 1975). As I will not be able to detail this approach within the narrow confines of this paper, I refer the reader to the above references, and to my dissertation (van der Leeuw 1976).

VARIABLES OF MANUFACTURE

Descriptions of various pottery-making techniques often leave the reader with the impression that there are almost as many techniques as potters, and that the matter is very complex.   In my opinion, this is due to the lack of order in such descriptions: we do not possess a set of concepts that effectively organize all this information.   A limited survey of ethnographical descriptions has, however, convinced me of the possibility of creating such a scheme in general, but nonetheless useful, terms.

As a first step (van der Leeuw 1977), it should be noted that it is not useful to extract phenomena observed in single instances from their context, "explain" them, and then generalize this explanation to situations with completely different contexts. Comparisons must be made more systematically.   Table 1 presents another, comparable, set of ethnographic data in much the same manner.

These data in Table 1 have been chosen for their applicability to a specific problem, i.e., the nature of the relation between methods of production and trade patterns in Northwestern Europe during the High Middle Ages.   This purpose requires us to make certain assumptions.

1. Four kinds of pottery occur especially frequently among the archaeological remains from the period:

   (a)   handmade pottery, built up in coils (e.g., "Eitöpfe", "Kugeltöpfe");

   (b)   pottery made on a small turntable (e.g., "Kugeltöpfe" with a turned/smoothed neck and rim);

   (c)   pottery made on a large potter's wheel (e.g., "Red-fired" ceramics as occur along the coasts of Holland, Belgium, Denmark, and France); and

   (d)   high-fired pottery made on a smaller (kick-) wheel with moderate momentum (e.g., Rhenish stoneware pottery).

2. The archaeological and ethnographic data used apply to comparable situations. To support this hypothesis, we have historical evidence for wheel-made pottery (cases 1c and 1d, above).   For case 1a, such evidence is lacking, and will be difficult to find in the future due to lack of documentation.   For case 1b, pottery made with a turntable, there is at most circumstantial evidence.   In all four cases, however, we can show that the technology used for the medieval pottery and the manufacturing methods described ethnographically are the same except for a few minor details.

3. The ethnographic descriptions are accurate.   This can be a problem because descriptions of pottery-making have been recorded by nonpotters—people who did not always know what to look for and what to describe.

I would like to use the data in Table 1 to argue in favor of a specific way to organize ceramic data and to model ceramic processes, i.e., for a systemic approach to pottery-making, -trading, -using, and -breaking.   I am not demonstrating but assuming, in this paper, that the available ethnographic data are best interpreted by considering each observed pottery technology and its concomitant marketing organization as a specific state of a "ceramic subsystem" in society. Space considerations do not permit me to go very deeply into the reasons for making that assumption, nor to sketch in any detail the systemic model used (an extensive publication on the subject is in preparation). The dynamic systems model used follows the lead presented by such studies as Miller's (1965), which has been used in archaeology by Yellen (1977), Jochim (1976), and Flannery (1972, 1976).

Figure 1 presents the way in which the ceramic system has been isolated from its environment, the main elements of which are climate, geology, human and physical geography, economy, and so forth. By implication, the constraints which these variables set are acknowledged, but are kept outside the bounds of detailed study for the moment (cf. Arnold 1978).

The entity "pot-making" is considered as the interplay between various subsystems, such as the raw materials, the tools, the potter, the customer, the weather, the social circumstances of the potter and those of his customers, etc. The relationships between these subsystems are relevant during the whole of the pot-making process, as well as during its individual steps. These steps include, for example: gathering the raw materials, paste preparation, shaping, drying, decorating, firing, and trading. Some of these also make themselves felt after the termination of manufacturing in a strict sense: for example, raw materials may influence the use of pottery (as is the case when special materials are used to make cooking pots). These relationships may be considered from various perspectives, both theoretical and operational. In principle these are innumerable but one might mention the material (technological), the energetic (work), and the informational (organization of the manufacturing process, for example) as common starting points for the study of pottery-manufacture. A consideration of the step of "pastemaking" may clarify these distinctions between subsystems, relationships and perspectives.

Pastemaking is the process by which the raw materials (the clay, temper, and water) are combined to form a paste which is subsequently used to shape pots. Thus, the raw materials are the input and the paste is the output. In the process, each of the materials is assessed in relation to the technique of manufacture to be used. Several matters have to be considered in order to decide how to prepare the raw materials for use (i.e., levigation, sieving, grinding of temper, etc.), how to mix them and in what proportions, and how to process the mixture.

This process of assessment is summarized in Figure 2. In this assessment, each of the raw materials is judged from various viewpoints. From the technological perspective, the potter will ask questions such as: how plastic is the clay? does it need to be reduced in plasticity by adding temper? how moist should the paste be? how much water should be added to achieve this? From the point of energetics, the potter will be concerned with the amount of work needed to collect the raw materials, to prepare them and to mix them, but also with the production losses inherent in using various pastes for the technique(s) available. He or she will assess the possibility of using another temper in a closer location, for example. From the organizational point of view, the potter will determine how to organize the process of gathering, storing, working the materials with a maximum of efficiency, without interruptions of the production process due to organizational problems, and so forth. Also, he or she will consider a minimum involvement to maintain production standards.

Looking at pottery in this manner means reconsidering the research to be devoted to pottery both in anthropological situations and from archaeological excavations.   It also means developing a completely new body of theory for archaeological ceramics.   Fortunately, anthropologists and ethnoarchaeologists have prepared the way with some recent, very effective studies (Hardin 1970; Plog 1980; Arnold 1975, 1978; David 1972; Papousek 1978; DeBoer 1975; DeBoer and Lathrap 1979).

Hardin's work is among the most illustrative.   Figure 3, which is drawn from her work (1977), synthesizes the decision-making procedure during the decorating of vessels in a Tarascan village in Mexico.   The potter has in mind a "decorative vocabulary" (a series of design elements) and a "decorative grammar" (a series of ways in which to combine decorative elements), as well as a "decorative syntax" which consists of general rules concerning the ways in which decoration should be executed on certain kinds of pots.   Given an undecorated pot, the potter divides the vessel by means of (mostly horizontal) lines into zones of decoration, which are further subdivided by primarily vertical lines into decorative areas.   Drawing upon his or her decorative vocabulary and grammar, (s)he then fills in the areas and critically examines the vessel when complete, and asks if the open spaces have been filled according to acceptable standards.   If so, the pot is considered ready; if not, the process starts anew.

One of the consequences of such a systemic approach is often that one is able to define certain states of the system which occur time and again, and which appear to be stable.   From that perspective, it is only to be expected that the ethnographic examples presented in Table 1 are very similar to the ones described earlier (van der Leeuw 1977), despite marked differences in time and area of occurrence.   The similarity should allow us to look for archaeological cases which may be described by these means with considerable confidence.   It also permits us, through the link provided by the technological analysis of pottery from excavations, to project ethnographic data concerning economic aspects of manufacture into the past.

ECONOMICS OF MANUFACTURE

The second half of this paper treats the economics of pottery-making, particularly the consequences of the above approach for that subject.   The discussion consists of two parts: first, a general consideration of some consequences for our study of the making and trading of pottery in the archaeological past; and second, a more pragmatic discussion of research possibilities in the case of a medieval town on the Baltic Sea.   The latter presupposes both a general model as used here as well as the existence of pottery workshops which show the characteristics summarized in the columns of Table 1.

General Considerations

An important point is that trade in pottery must be studied in conjunction with the manufacture of that pottery, the economic circumstances of the makers and users, the means of transportation, the physical and human geography of the area concerned, and the other elements of the environment of the pot-making system. The way in which a vessel is manufactured may give important clues as to the kind of market for which it may have been intended: coiled or hammer-and-anvil-made pottery tends to be associated with production for the local market; thrown pottery is made much faster and requires more investments in equipment, training, and manpower, thus needing a wider region to provide a larger and more rewarding market. Similarly, a workshop cannot be situated far from its clay and far from its temper and far from its fuel. Indeed, it is suggested that fuel is a much more important determinant for the location of pottery workshops than is clay at least up to the time in which fossil fuels were used and/or modern modes of transportation were available. Bulk seems to have been more of a limiting factor than weight.

A second, and hardly less important, point is that determining the provenience of pottery by means of typological categories is fallacious. A type is an a posteriori ideational category created by sorting a group of artifacts on the basis of similarity and dissimilarity. As such, it also is a group, and cannot be defined intrinsically (Dunnell 1972). The list of its attributes, however, is considered to be such an intrinsic definition that allows for later identification of new artifacts as members of the type. Logically, therefore, the type is handled as if it were a class (Dunnell 1972). One manifestation of the problem is Clarke's (1968:522) remark that it seems as if attributes are established by intuition and then used to define the group for which they are presumed the distinctive indicator. He correctly concludes that this is a circle of the most vicious nature (see also Hill and Evans 1972; van der Leeuw 1976:49-57).

Ceramic studies should begin with a thorough analysis and characterization of the materials from known production centers. Once these have been studied, the whole of the manufacturing process may be known, as well as a number of the idiosyncrasies of the potters in each workshop. This kind of approach gives us an idea of the nature and sizes of the products which belonged to the output of a workshop. It serves as a guide in determining gaps in the production scheme that may have been filled by other manufacturers. This is necessary because one cannot profitably study the distribution of any one product or set of products without considering all other products which may have fulfilled the same function in the region during the period under consideration. If this point is overlooked, one may never have an idea of the options open to a buyer at any one place, and thus one is never able to relate, for example, cost to distance from the manufacturing workshop. In that case, any conclusions drawn from distribution maps alone are a priori subject to severe criticism.

A Medieval Research Example

I have been developing a research design for the study of pottery from archaeological excavations in medieval Lübeck and its surroundings. For this study, the four kinds of pottery distinguished at the beginning of this essay are of particular importance. In addition, the data of Table 1, which present the technological and economic correlates of ethnographic situations of comparable levels of pottery-making, allow us to infer more of the social behavior involved in the production and use of this pottery, as well as realize limits to such interpretations.

The "Kugeltöpfe/Eitöpfe" were modelled by hand, by means of a combined hammer-and-anvil/coiling technique, or by means of some other technique using very simple tools, a variety of modified clays, and open, pit, or very simple kiln firing. Such variability in materials and manufacturing techniques suggests that meaningful differences between vessels may be difficult to find and harder yet to interpret. There is little likelihood of finding workshops where such pottery was made, either by excavation or by means of mineralogical identification of raw materials (except in the case of very localized minerals). One of the very rare possibilities for identifying areas of manufacture would be the discovery of unusual decorative stamps (or stamps with defects). Only in exceptional cases will we be able to distinguish marketing spheres for such products.

As a cooking pot, the "Kugeltöpfe" may well have been unsurpassable for a long time, due to the fact that its porosity and heat-conductive properties allow water to be brought to a boil much faster than in other vessels. Thus, it should be seen as hors concours when considering the products of other potteries. Technological analysis of this kind of pottery may explain some of the differences observed between individual products. However, analysis of rim form may be of doubtful value in view of such parallels with the Papago, where "no two rims made by the same potter are identical" (Fontana et al. 1962). Here, the rim is made with the surplus paste which sticks out very unevenly around the edge of the pot just before finishing it. The rim construction therefore depends strongly on the amount of surplus material, as well as on the shape of the pot, the position of the potter at the time of rim construction, the moisture of the paste, etc.

As for the pottery made on a small turntable (presumably the later "Kugeltöpfe" which have a smoothed upper part, as well as some of the Slav pottery [Hensel 1965:261 ff.]), the situation seems a bit more complex, and, above all, changed structurally through time. If we accept Hensel's basic thesis that pottery-making developed in Eastern Europe from household production to workshop industry without changing its fundamental technology, it becomes essential to develop a research design which will allow identification of possible production centers. Such a changeover from household production (i.e., working for the potter's household and close relatives and friends) to household industry (working for the village market and maybe that of a nearby town) may have been made possible by technological innovation (i.e., introduction of the turntable). Use of a turntable entails no more specific requirements for the paste than that of the hand-made pottery discussed above, as long as the device moves with interruptions.

On the other hand, smoothing the upper part with an uninterrupted rotary motion (and a wet cloth) favors the use of clays with relatively small nonplastic particles. This could have been achieved by careful selection of clay deposits to be used, but also would be possible by levigation of clays; thus selection of clays is no prerequisite for use of the turntable. Even if particular clays were selected, making it possible to distinguish different products via mineralogical or trace elemental analysis, the resultant mineral or chemical groups are not necessarily the products of individual potters or workshops. Often several potters use the same set of clay deposits (e.g., the Papago). In addition, there is the possibility of itinerant potters: the turntable is easy to carry, and can be used to work a variety of clays. The potter could therefore have gone from place to place, making pots with local clays.

Hensel's (1965) description of the later production of Slav pottery is similar to the Cypriot cases presented in Table 1 (Hampe and Winter 1962), where a whole village makes pots for the market. This entails technical modifications, because if the people are to live off their potting activities they have to produce fairly rapidly and efficiently. One may presume (semi-)permanent firing installations, and a shaping technique that exploits the rotary motion of the available turntable (or very small wheel) to the utmost. Technologically, this is easy to trace: the pots seem wheel-made, but upon closer examination show the traces of interruptions in the rotary motion of the clay during construction. What one sees is that the traces of either fingers or rib which were left during the shaping or finishing procedure are interrupted, so that they form short stretches, often not even as long as one circumference, instead of a long spiral.

How the adaptation of the turntable was effected is open to question: a helper could have turned the wheel continuously, or the potter could have added a lower wheel as is seen on many illustrations from the Slav countries. This wheel is rotated by foot, thus leaving the potter free to shape the clay (Rieth 1960). As on Cyprus, the sheer volume of clay to be used would require the exploitation of large outcrops, and hence a fairly consistent composition of the paste used in each workshop. As the paste has to be relatively fine to avoid "sanding" the potters' hands, there is a possibility that it was levigated. But many riverine or marine clay deposits would have been suitable as mined.

Because production must have been more or less standardized, it may be profitable to "fingerprint" production centers on the basis of idiosyncrasies, for example, by study of decorative technique. Such would require the reconstruction of the sequencing of application of the decorative elements. Such a sequence may then allow hypotheses concerning the decorative vocabulary and grammar of the decorator (who need not be the same as the potter). Another aspect of situations such as these would be the question of how far middlemen controlled the trade in pottery from such centers. This could considerably influence the area over which the pottery is marketed. Study of ethnographically known pottery-making centers has revealed difficulties in obtaining the necessary fuel for the firings. As mentioned above, access to fuel is a very limiting factor, and may give middlemen a profitable return cargo for their carts and/or ships.

Pottery made on a true potter's wheel can be distinguished from that previously discussed because the traces of rotation are continuous rather than interrupted. The output per workshop is much greater, and the trade volume of the two situations should never be compared directly. Relatively small numbers of potters can make such quantities and provide for whole cities. I suspect that in both the ancient and the present Near East, as well as in medieval Europe, each town had one or more potteries working in this manner (hence the series of discoveries of pottery workshops in Haarlem, Utrecht, Bergen-op-Zoom, Oslo, the Danish Isles, etc.). As the manufacture is more centralized, it should be relatively easy to distinguish production centers by way of mineralogical analyses, trace element analyses, potter's markets, or

TABLE 1

Technological and Economic Variables of Pottery-Making in 7 Ethnographic Cases

	Ethnographic Cases		
Variables	Early Jutish pottery[a]	Liberian pottery[b]	Papago pottery[c]
Raw Materials			
clay	"pleistocene loam"	unspecified stiff	unspecified
water	none	unspecified (any?)	many kinds
temper	any	any	any
fuel	peat	unspecified	various desert fuels
Tools			
digging	unspecified	unspecified	hoe, shovel
crushing	unspecified	unspecified (any?)	stick
transportation	unspecified	unspecified	bag
refining	unspecified (any?)	none	sieve
rotting	unspecified (any?)	none	unspecified (any?)
levigation	unspecified (any?)	none	unspecified (any?)
kneading	unspecified (any?)	none	unspecified (none?)
supporting	wooden disk or plank	grass ring or pad	turntable flat support
shaping	hammer/anvil	none	hammer/anvil, mould
additional	scraper,rag	rag or leather	rag; rag ring support
decorating	marl, pol. stone	bark knife,roulette	pol. stone
drying	in the house	open-air	no provisions
firing	open fire	open fire (?)	fire pit
Manuf. Technique			
shaping	ham/anv.,hollowing	coiling	ham/anv.,coils
decorating	polishing	incising	smoothing/polishing
firing	single brief firing	single brief firing	single brief firing
Products			
number	1 or 2	1	11
no. of sizes	unspecified (various?)	unspecified	unspecified
Econ. Variables			
provenience of raw materials	local	local (?)	local or regional
investments	none	none	none
market	own household	own household	local market
time per pot	a few hours	several hours	a few hours
Organization			
seasonality	occasional	unspecified	summer
part/full time	occasional	unspecified	part time
no. of workers	one	one	one
locality	sedentary	sedentary	sedentary
labor division	none	none	none
hired hands	none	none	none

[a] Elzinga 1964
[b] Donner 1940
[c] Fontana et al. 1962

TABLE 1 - (continued)

Ethnographic Cases

Later Jutish pottery[d]	Cypriot pottery[e]	S.Italian pottery[f]	Dutch pottery (15th cent)[g]
"pleistocene loam"	unspecified	unspecified,primary	unspecified, secondary
none	unspecified mineral	unspecified	sand,fine
any	any	any	any
peat	wood	brushwood	peat,brushwood
unspecified	unspecified	unspecified	unspecified
unspecified (any?)	unspecified	unspecified	unspecified (any?)
unspecified	truck	unspecified	ship
unspecified (any?)	unspecified (any?)	sieve	unspecified (any?)
unspecified (any?)	unspecified (any?)	unspecified (any?)	heap or pit
unspecified (any?)	unspecified (any?)	unspecified (any?)	unspecified (any?)
unspecified (any?)	pit	unspecified (any?)	table
wooden disk or plank	turntable	wheel	wheel
hammer/anvil	turntable	wheel	wheel
scraper; rag	scraper,string,knife	scraper,rib,string,pen	scraper,rib,string,knife
marl, pol. stone	unspecified (any?)	pen,glaze	rib,bar. horn,glaze
in the house	unspecified	unspecified	shed,stacks along kiln
open fire or pit	permanent kiln	permanent kiln	permanent kiln
ham/anv.,hollowing	hollowing,coiling	throwing in parts	throwing whole pots
polishing	unspecified (any?)	plastic,incision,glaze	plastic,incision,barb.
single brief firing	single long firing	long firing (twice?)	long firing (twice?)
5-10	10-25	10-25	10-25
unspecified	1-3	standard sizes,no.unk.	3-4
local	local,fuel regional	local/regional fuel farther away	local/regional
none	moderate	considerable	considerable
local market	local & distant	regional	regional & distant
a few hours	less than 1 hour	less than 1 hour	less than 1 hour
summer (?)	summer	all year	all year
part time	part time	full time	full time
one	one or two	family	several
sedentary/itinerant	sedentary	sedentary	sedentary
none	sex-linked	functional	functional
none	none	some	some

[d] Elzinga 1964
[e] Hampe and Winter 1962
[f] Hampe and Winter 1965
[g] Weijs 1972

"fingerprinting" of idiosyncracies.   The publication of the Utrecht and Haarlem kiln finds demonstrate clearly how much can be learned from the study of production wasters, both functionally (Bruijn 1979) and technologically (van der Leeuw 1976).

Because of the sheer complexity of the situation, it seems profitable to begin the study of trade patterns by first studying known kiln sites.   Combining the data from a number of these, one may proceed to map simultaneously available alternatives, and their relative frequencies of occurrence in other kinds of sites.   Computerized mapping can aid in such efforts; however, certain assumptions must be met: all source of manufacture (all kilns) must be known, and each object must be traced to its origin.   At present, we are not able to accomplish this for medieval pottery of the kind mentioned here, but systematic analysis of future kiln sites might one day bring us to that point.

The last situation to be considered is that of centers like the Rhenish, where large numbers of people are involved in mass-producing pots.   Unfortunately, most of the analysis of these ceramics is art-historic or typological, with very little understanding of technological issues and related socioeconomic ones.   Guild documents from the 16th century indicate that the units of production were small and that they were bound to strict rules concerning manufacturing techniques, firing techniques, and the status and number of wage-workers (Klinge 1972:10).   Manufacture occurred in large quantities, on a kickwheel, with specific clays which were obtained either by using the only material found in selected places, or by adding selected tempering materials.   There is a clear division of labor in the workshops, and a limited range of specific and characteristic products.   The shape of the product was in some cases clearly adapted to efficient stacking in the kiln, and to avoiding the laborious use of saggars (Bruijn 1963).

The distribution of Rhenish products expanded with the limits of the world known by, and explored by, traders from Western Europe (Reineking-von Bock 1980). The discrepancy between the size of the production units and the size of the trade in the products points to a division of labor between producers and traders, which might also have applied to the procurement of fuel.   Trade was probably modelled after the mercantile model, while production followed the rules of the (older) guild organization.   We know little about the interface: did the traders buy finished products?   did they own the kilns and provide the fuel for the potters to fire their green wares?   did they buy the green wares from the potters and have them fired by their own personnel?   We need systematic research on the products, their distribution and the historical documents available in order to solve these and many other questions.   In relation to the excavations at Lübeck, however, we may confidently point out that studying the patterns of trade in Rhenish wares along the Baltic would not allow us to reconstruct the history of the trade itself: the Baltic is a small area and reflects too little of the phenomenon under study.

Clearly, the study of prehistoric trade demands a better understanding of pottery production.   Such an understanding can only be achieved through better integration of ethnographic, technological, and archaeological data, and with a sensitivity toward behavioral correlates and differences between these lines of investigation.   An efficient model of pottery production to use in such an attempt would be a systemic model aimed at formulating variables which are valid in as many cases as possible.   The main problem which such a model leaves open is that of the study of transitions between system states (van der Leeuw 1981).

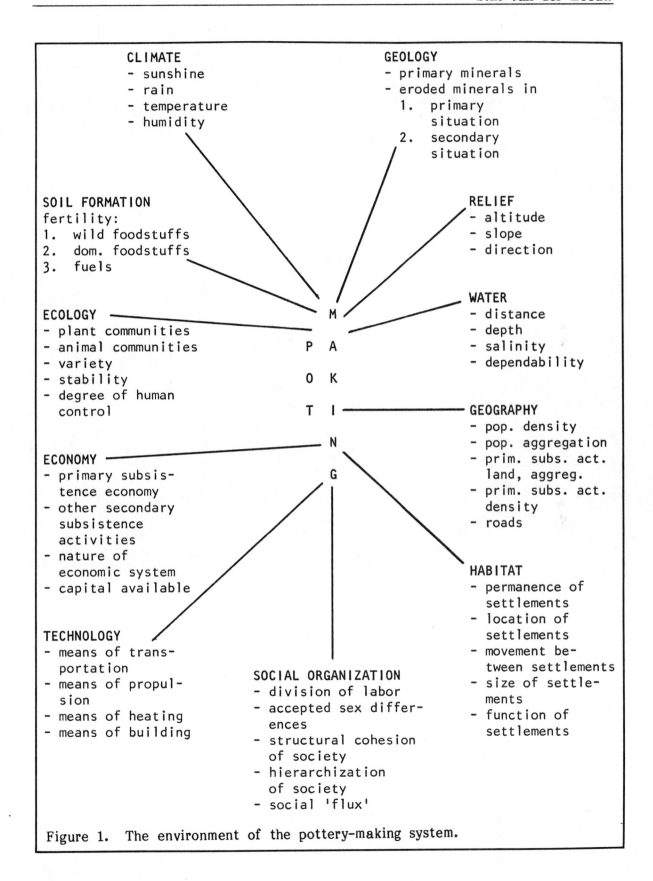

Figure 1. The environment of the pottery-making system.

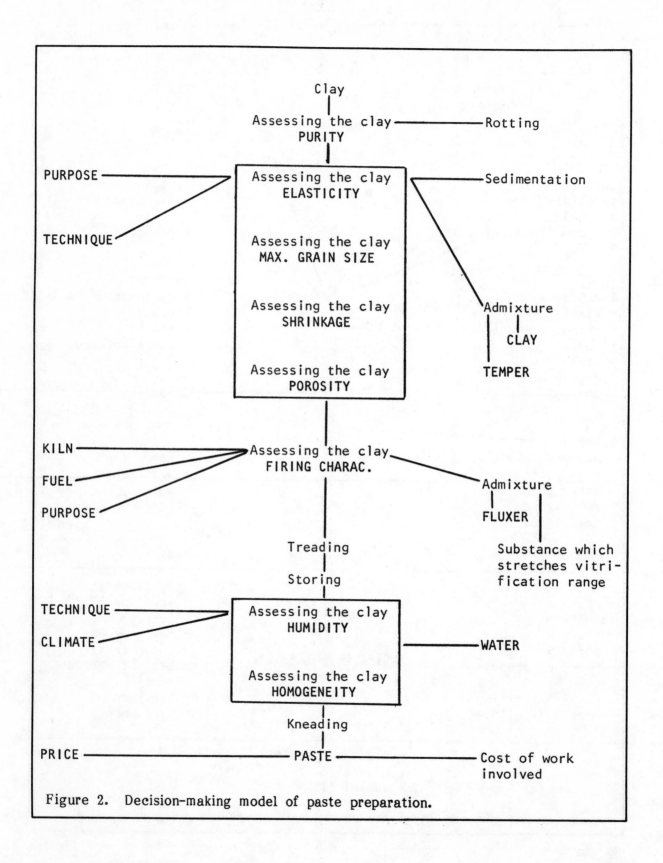

Figure 2.   Decision-making model of paste preparation.

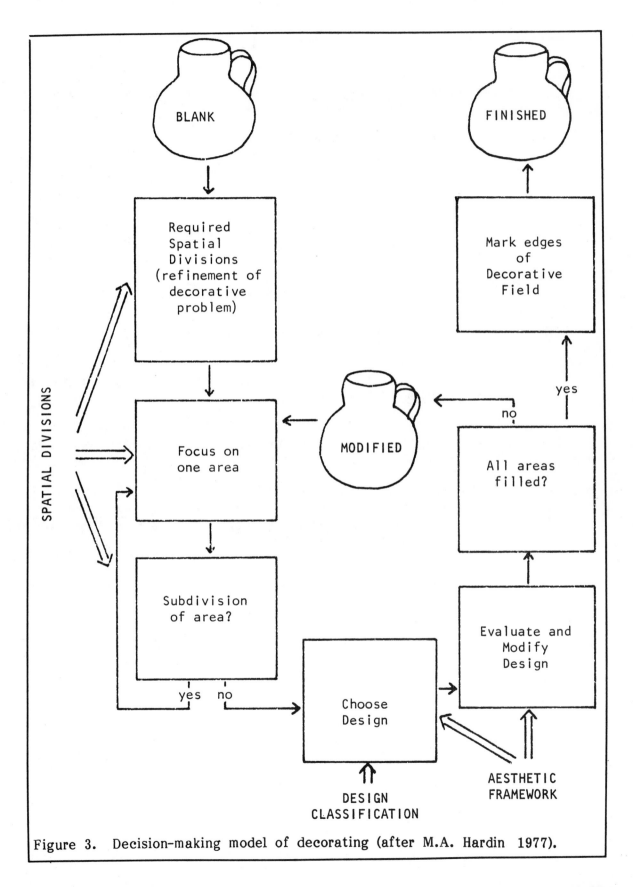

Figure 3.   Decision-making model of decorating (after M.A. Hardin 1977).

REFERENCES

Arnold, D.E.
  1975   Ceramic ecology of the Ayacucho Basin, Peru: implications for prehistory. Current Anthropology 16:183-205.

  1978   Ceramic variability, environment, and culture history among the Pokom in the Valley of Guatemala. In, The Spatial Organisation of Culture, I. Hodder, ed. Pp. 39-60. Pittsburgh: University of Pittsburgh Press.

Bruijn, A.

  1963   Die Mittelalterliche keramische Insdustrie in Sudlimburg. Berichten van de Rijksdienst voor het Oudheidkundig Modemonderzoek 12-13: 357-495.

  1979   Pottersvuren langs de Vecht. Rotterdam Papers III. Landbroek.

Clarke, D.L.
  1968   Analytical Archaelogy. London: Methuen.

David, N.
  1972   On the life span of pottery, type frequencies, and archaeological inference. American Antiquity 37:141-142.

DeBoer, W.
  1975   Aspects of trade and transport on the Ucayali River, Eastern Peru. Paper presented at CUNY Graduate Center.

DeBoer, W. and D.W. Lathrap
  1979   The making and breaking of Shipibo-Conibo ceramics. In, Ethnoarchaeology: Implications of Ethnography for Archaeology, C. Kramer, ed. Pp. 102-138. New York: Columbia University Press.

Donner, E.
  1940   Kunst and Handwerk in N-O Liberia. Baessler Archiv 23:45ff. Berlin.

Dunnell, R.C.
  1972   Systematics in Prehistory. New York.

Elzinga, G.
  1964   Deense "Jydepotten" uit Frieses bodem. It Beaken 26:306-326.

Flannery, K.V.
  1972   The cultural evolution of civilizations. Annual Review of Ecology and Systematics 3:399-426.

  1976   (ed.) The Early Mesoamerican Village. New York: Academic Press.

Fontana, B.L., W.J. Robinson, C.W. Cormack, and E.E. Leavitt, Jr.
1962   Papago Indian Pottery.   American Ethnological Society Monograph No. 37. Seattle.

Franken, H.J.
1974   In Search of the Jericho Potters.   Amsterdam.

Franken, H.J. and J. Kalsbeek
1969   The Excavations at Tell Deir Alla, vol. I.   Leiden.

1975   Potters of a Medieval Village in the Jordan Valley.   Amsterdam.

Hampe, R. and A. Winter
1962   Bei Topfern und Töpferinnen in Kreta, Messenien und Zypern.   Mainz/Bonn.

1965   Bei Töpfern und Zieglern in Suditalien und auf Sizilien.   Mainz/Bonn.

Hardin, M.A. (Friedrich)
1970   Design structure and social interaction.   American Antiquity 35:332-343.

1977   Individual style in San Jose pottery painting: the role of deliberate choice. In, The Individual in Prehistory, J.N. Hill and J. Gunn, eds.   Pp. 109-136. New York: Academic Press.

Hensel, W.
1965   Die Slawen im frühen Mittelalter.   Warszawa.

Hill, J.N. and R.K. Evans
1972   A model for classification and typology.   In, Models in Archaeology, D.L. Clarke, ed.   Pp. 231-273.   London: Methuen.

Jochim, M.
1976   Hunter-Gatherer Subsistence and Settlement: A Predictive Model.   New York: Academic Press.

Klinge, E.
1972   Siegburger Steinzeug.   Katalog des Hetjensmuseum.   Düsseldorf.

Matson, F.R. (ed.)
1965   Ceramics and Man.   Viking Fund Publication No. 41.   Chicago: Aldine.

Miller, J.G.
1965   Living systems: basic concepts.   Behavioral Science 10:193:237.

Papousek, D.A.
1978   Op eigen houtje . . .   (CEDLA Incidentele Publicaties, 10).   Amsterdam.

Plog, S.
1980   Stylistic Variation in Prehistoric Ceramics.   Cambridge: Cambridge University Press.

Reith, A.
1960   5000 Jahre Topferscheibe. Konstanz.

Shepard, A.O.
1968   Ceramics for the Archaeologist. Carnegie Institution of Washington, Pub. 609. Washington, D.C.

van der Leeuw, S.E.
1976   Studies in the Technology of Ancient Pottery, 2 vols. Amsterdam.

1977   Towards a study of the economics of pottery making. Ex Horreo, CINGULA IV:68-76. Amsterdam: IPP, University of Amsterdam.

1981   Ceramic exchange and manufacture: a "flow structure" approach. In Production and Distribution: A Ceramic Viewpoint, H. Howard and E. Morris, eds. BAR International Series 120:361-386.

Weijs, L.J.
1972   Techniek en producten van de Bergen-op-Zoomse potmakers. In Tussen Hete Vuren, L.J. Weijs, C.C.J. van de Watering, and C.J.F. Slootmans, eds., pp. 3-52. Tilburg.

Yellen, J.
1977   Archaeological Approaches to the Present. New York: Academic Press.

PART II
Ethnoarchaeological Studies

Part II

For studies of material culture in general, one of the most interesting of the relatively new hybrid subdisciplines in archaeology is that of ethnoarchaeology. Ethnoarchaeological research, in the sense of studying contemporary peoples for the purpose of obtaining insights into past behavior, is not a new field, but it is a rapidly growing one, especially since the early 1960s. Perhaps the major stimulus in this growth, at least in Americanist studies, is the emphasis in current archaeology on the development and testing of models of cultural processes on all levels, such as artifact manufacture, site formation, kinship systems, and regional settlement patterning, to name a few.

Ethnographic studies have long focused on potters and pottery-making communities. Even very early in the history of ethnographic observation of virtually any country or region in the world, mention can be found of ceramic crafts. This is particularly true since the last half of the 19th century, as the Western world adjusted to the presence of "primitive peoples" in its midst. The work of Holmes (1888) in Columbia, Mercer (1897) in Mexico, Steinen (1897) in Brazil, and Dobbs (1897) in India, are just a few examples of such early mention of the ceramic craft. Later ethnographic and ethnoarchaeological studies of pottery addressed themselves to a wide variety of issues above and beyond sheer description, explicitly calling attention to the interface of prehistoric and contemporary ceramic data.

One objective of more recent studies has been to trace contemporary pottery back into the archaeological past. Tschopik's (1950) study of Aymara (Peru) pottery revealed little change from pre-Columbian times to the present, despite "five hundred years of drastic acculturation" (1950:216). Shepard's (1963) look at contemporary pottery manufactured in Oaxaca, Mexico, concentrated on variables of paste, rather than decorative style or form, in comparison with locally known pre-Columbian pottery. She was able to identify many aspects of paste similarity between pottery from the prehistoric site of Monte Alban in Oaxaca, and the wares of modern potting communities in this general region. The work of Fontana and colleagues among the Papago in the Southwest United States (1962) attempted to trace the modern pottery back to the archaeologically known Hohokam cultures. Although its success in this objective was marginal, one of the significant contributions of the investigation was the demonstration that pottery is an appropriate place for ethnographic research to begin in the study of a culture.

Another objective of ethnographers working among potters has been to explore some of the variables that operate in the formation of archaeological assemblages or in interpretation of those assemblages. Foster (1960), David (1972), and DeBoer (1974) attempted to determine the use-life of different kinds (formal-functional categories) of pottery, and from that calculate the rate at which vessels enter the archaeological record through breakage. Foster (1965), Nicklin (1971), and Reina and Hill (1978) discussed the conservatism of potters, both toward changing their craft and in terms of a general dependence on "tradition" as a strong mechanism behind behavioral conformity in their lives. One of the more intriguing results of the Reina and Hill (1978) survey of contemporary Guatemalan pottery is that techniques of manufacture correlate strongly with language groups in the Guatemalan highlands.

Ethnographic and ethnoarchaeological ceramic research has greatly broadened archaeologists' understanding of the cultural role of pottery, moving far beyond the outmoded practice of identifying past cultures by their pottery, as "the incised pottery people" or "the red painted pottery culture." In addition to the above topics of interest, ethnographic studies have included observations on: potters' choices of raw materials and their processing; techniques of manufacture, decoration, and firing; patterns of learning; marketing and distribution patterns; status of potters within a community and attitudes toward their craft; and classificatory analyses and discrimination of the work of individual potters.

Many ethnoarchaeological studies involve, directly or indirectly, the use of analogies. Analogies are models about relationships, and in archaeology they usually extend the relationship between a material object and some aspect of behavior in its manufacture or use, from the present to the past. Unfortunately, such analogies have frequently been abused by archaeologists by being employed as "proofs" of such relationships: they were depended upon as "explanations" to such an extent that critics (Chang 1967; Binford 1968; Deetz 1968) observed that archaeologists acted as if they could say nothing about the past unless there existed a direct behavioral analogue in the present. Thus archaeology was not really fulfilling its promise in providing time depth behind cultural change for the discipline of anthropology as a whole (Freeman 1968).

In the context of this debate, two kinds of analogy may be identified. General comparative analogies between material objects can be observed cross-culturally, while direct historical analogies claim specific analogues in the past for behavior exhibited by known groups in the area in the ethnohistorical or ethnographic present. Much of the debate in the recent ethnoarchaeological literature centers on the proper use of these kinds of analogies, and was prompted by the use of direct historical analogy in the Southwestern United States to infer residence rules from pottery design element distributions at an archaeological site (Longacre 1964). This work and the many assumptions behind it (for example, the teaching of pottery-making from generation to generation) has been subsequently strongly criticized (Stanislawski 1969), as was the growing body of similar "ceramic sociology" studies (e.g., Deetz 1965; Whallon 1968). The end result of such critiques of analogue reasoning in ceramic ethnoarchaeology and other ethnoarchaeological studies has been greater restraint in the use of analogies.

The area of experimental archaeology has been particularly instructive for understanding variability in ceramic assemblages. Collection and testing of clays, experimental manipulation of firing variables, making of actual vessels, use of ancient tools to form, decorate, or fire test pieces—all have been productive in achieving a greater knowledge of ceramic materials and the range of techniques for adapting to them. An additional benefit of such experimental studies is that hypotheses about resource use, trade, and changes in ancient technologies can be formulated and tested, often by means of the physical, chemical, and mineralogical techniques discussed in the following section of this volume.

Some thought-provoking observations emerged from the diversity of interests and positions that exist within ethnoarchaeology.

One is that, in response to the hue and cry over the relevance of analogy in archaeological interpretations, many archaeologists feel that it is safer to use analogies with the ethnographic present as hypotheses to be tested with archaeological data. The analogues should not be considered "explanations" without such testing.

A second observation is that archaeologists can better draw analogues from or to small groups—e.g., task units involved in producing or using goods—than to societies as a whole. It has been pointed out that many terms used by ethnographers are themselves idealized abstractions or generalized observations about the cultural norm (e.g., matrilocal residence), and are not without their own range of variability within ethnographically known societies.

A third development is that there is a small group of archaeologists who feel that because of the necessary bias of archaeology toward material objects as its primary data base, archaeology should be considered to be the study of material culture, regardless of time or place (Leone 1972). The emphasis in this approach is on analyzing processes of formation of the archaeological record and generalizations about functional and locational relationships between material objects and behavior (Schiffer 1976). Thus, study of Coca Cola bottles, typewriters, and contemporary waste patterns are as much within the purview of archaeology as are potsherds and stone tools.

A fourth area of interest in ethnoarchaeology has been that of making contributions to the taxonomic concerns of traditional archaeological research (e.g., Arnold 1971). Such "ethnotaxonomic" or "folk taxonomic" studies are sometimes explicitly directed toward the creation of type categories whose "known cultural meaning, use, and function within a real society" is derived "from the viewpoint of the native peoples themselves" (Stanislawski 1975:21; see also Kempton 1981). Although the desirability of such quasi-universal type classes may be debatable, a major positive contribution of ethnoarchaeology has been to accentuate the need for common units of observation between archaeological and ethnographic research. For pottery, examination of the clay body, or paste, focuses on a number of such common units and has shown the value of research in which common analytical units can be compared over a very long time range. These technological studies of archaeological ceramics, ethnographic ceramics, and locally available resources have been of increasing importance and utility in the last years, demonstrating the ability to integrate into the ceramic ecological approach as well.

Positions on these and other related issues currently being argued may solidify in the future. Meanwhile, ethnoarchaeology is making solid contributions to the overall field of ceramic studies. Despite the many areas of debate and disagreement that have existed, and the occasional overly particularist "cautionary tale" approach, the capacity for joining archaeological and ethnographic method and theory, and the diversity of topics to which these may be directed, make ethnoarchaeology a fruitful area for future ceramic research. The papers in Part II of Pots and Potters cover many of these areas of ethnoarchaeological diversity, and serve in this volume as a bridge between the section of ceramic ecology and the more technical papers in Part III on technological analysis of pottery.

The first paper by Johnson, who is a potter himself, is an avowedly speculative study of the link between past and present in Guellala, where abandoned and functioning potters' workshops coexist. His observations on contemporary arrangements and activities suggest a long antiquity and conservatism in the organization of the craft and in potters' motor patterns.

Archaeology as well as ethnoarchaeology are covered in Solheim's paper, which reviews some of the problems and achievements of initial ceramic studies in Northeast Thailand. Archaeological studies of the pottery have included microanalysis of the contents of burial vessels from Non Nok Tha, while ethnoarchaeological studies have concentrated on form variations and the contemporary patterns of discard and re-use of vessels that, by extension into the past, were responsible for forming the archaeological record.

The next two papers fall into the realm of experimental archaeology. The first of these, treating the development of the potter's wheel in the Near East, reports a lack of success in attempts to use a pair of early Canaanite-Israelite wheels. However, study of a later Byzantine wheel suggested the addition of an upper wooden platform as the working surface, after which the assembly functioned successfully as a "slow wheel." The second experimental paper by Vitelli is a broad-based and wide-ranging discussion of the author's experiments with collecting clays and forming and firing vessels, much of that work being done in a classroom. Steps in finding and cleaning local clays, and building, finishing, and firing vessels are investigated, with generalizations drawn about potters' difficulties in dealing with the unknown in their craft. Specific references are made to replicating characteristics of Greek Neolithic Urfirnis ware (see Chapter 3, this volume).

Arnold's paper on design analysis is a contribution to the extensive literature that has related decorative styles to social organization in ethnological studies. Using four utilitarian vessel shapes made and sold in Quinua, Peru, Arnold elucidated the principles of design structure for these categories. The guiding premise of his study is that the arrangement of design on a vessel, rather than the independent design elements themselves, is more sensitive to social interaction patterns taking place within a community, and therefore more useful in defining communities of potters. In Quinua, design layout was found to be shape-specific, and different degrees of freedom or creativity permitted in design motif, symmetry, and layout also varied with vessel shape.

REFERENCES

Arnold, D.E.
  1971 Ethnomineralogy of Ticul, Yucatan potters: etics and emics. American Antiquity 36:20-40.

Binford, L.R.
  1968 Methodological considerations of the archaeological use of ethnographic data. In, Man the Hunter, R. Lee and I. Devore, eds. Pp. 268-273. Chicago: Aldine.

Chang, K.C.
  1967 Major aspects of the interrelationship of archaeology and ethnology. Current Anthropology 8:227-243.

David, N.
  1972 On the life span of pottery, type frequencies, and archaeological inference. American Antiquity 37:141-142.

DeBoer, W.R.
  1974 Ceramic longevity and archaeological interpretation: an example from the Upper Ucayali, Peru. American Antiquity 39:335-343.

Deetz, J.
  1965 The Dynamics of Stylistic Change in Arikara Ceramics. Illinois Studies in Anthropology, No. 4. Urbana: University of Illinois.

Dobbs, H.R.C.
  1897 The pottery and glass industries of the northwest provinces and Oudh. Journal of Indian Art 7:1-6.

  1968 The inference of residence and descent rules from archaeological data. In, New Perspectives in Archaeology, L. Binford and S. Binford, eds. Pp. 41-48. Chicago: Aldine.

Fontana, B.L., et al.
  1962 Papago Indian Pottery. Am. Ethnol. Soc. Monogr. 37. Seattle.

Foster, G.
  1960 Archaeological implications of the modern pottery of Acatlan, Puebla, Mexico. American Antiquity 26:205-214.

  1965 The sociology of pottery: questions and hypotheses arising from contemporary Mexican work. In, Ceramics and Man, F. Matson, ed. Pp. 43-61. Chicago: Aldine.

Freeman, L.G.
   1968   A theoretical framework for interpreting archaeological materials. In, Man the Hunter, R. Lee and I. Devore, eds.   Pp. 262-267.   Chicago: Aldine.

Holmes, W.H.
   1888   Ancient art of the province of Chiriqui, Columbia.   Bur. Am. Ethnol. 6th annual report, pp. 13-187.   Washington.

Kempton, W.
   1981   The Folk Classification of Ceramics, A Study of Cognitive Prototypes. New York: Academic Press.

Leone, M.P.
   1972   Issues in anthropological archaeology. In, Contemporary Archaeology, M. Leone, ed.   Pp. 14-27.   Carbondale: Southern Illinois University Press.

Longacre, W.A.
   1964   Sociological implications of the ceramic analysis.   In, The Prehistory of East Arizona, II, P. Martin et al., eds.   Fieldiana Anthropology 55:155-170.

Mercer, H.C.
   1897   The kabal or potter's wheel of Yucatan.   Bull. Mus. Sci. and Art, vol. 1, no. 2.   Philadelphia: University of Pennsylvania.

Nicklin, K.
   1971   Stability and innovation in pottery manufacture.   World Archaeology 3:13-48.

Reina, R. and R.M. Hill
   1978   The Traditional Pottery of Guatemala.   Austin: University of Texas Press.

Schiffer, M.
   1976   Behavioral Archaeology.   New York: Academic Press.

Shepard, A.O.
   1963   Beginnings of ceramic industrialization: an example from the Oaxaca valley.   Notes from a Ceramic Laboratory No. 2.   Carnegie Institution of Washington.

Stanislawski, M.B.
   1969   The ethno-archaeology of Hopi pottery making.   Plateau 42:27-33.

   1975   What you see is what you get: ethnoarchaeology and scientific model building.   Paper presented at the annual meeting of the Society for American Archaeology, Dallas.

Steinen, K. von den
   1897   Unter den Naturvolkern Zentral-Brasiliens.   Berlin: Dietrich Reimer.

Tschopik, H.
   1950   An Andean ceramic tradition in historical perspective.   American Antiquity 15:196-218.

Whallon, R. Jr.
    1968   Investigations of late prehistoric social organization in New York State.
    In, New Perspectives in Archaeology, L. Binford and S. Binford, eds.   Pp.
    223-244.   Chicago: Aldine.

Chapter 6

An Abandoned Pottery at Guellala on the
Island of Djerba, Tunisia:
A Hermeneutic Approach to Ethnoarchaeology

Robert H. Johnston

Archaeologists are always dealing with aspects of material culture in an attempt to reconstruct the history of a time past in as accurate a way as possible. Kathleen Kenyon states the real purpose of archaeological investigation in her book Beginning in Archaeology (1956:9): "To begin with, archaeology is not an end in itself, not just an abstract study. It is the method of finding out about the past of the human race in material aspects, and the study of the products of the past."

R.G. Collingwood (1962:282) ponders the question as to how the historian can reconstruct the past, since he was not an eyewitness and since it is totally gone as something to be experienced. Since many excavations deal with nonwritten material, civilizations must be reconstructed through inductive interpretation, or hermeneutics, on the basis of the artifacts and other archaeological remains left behind. The preponderance of ceramic materials at most major sites emphasizes the importance of Frederick Matson's ceramic ecological approach, which uses pottery as the starting point for an investigation of a total cultural complex that relates ethnographic and archaeological observations.

Working with Matson as a student for a number of years and being a staff member of fifteen expeditions to the Middle and Far East, I have had the privilege of combining the technical and analytical study of excavated ceramic material with the filming of village potters in many countries. I have been able to relate my own personal experiences as a professional potter to these studies. The potters I have studied live in remote areas in a number of countries, still somewhat untouched by the "rust of progress" (Nisbet 1976:115) of modern technology. The techniques they use have been handed down from one generation to another with little apparent change. My experiences may be summed up in Matson's own phrase, "witnessing the 'archaeological present'."

Although other technologies have undergone vast change or have been abandoned in many areas, the use of clay remains constant along with the tools and techniques used in the various processes. Tradition was the "essence of the craftsman's life" (Burford 1972:119), and it still is. Modern craftsmen still feel the links to the past and seem to want a different life from that of the usual member of our technocratic society. The craftsman's dislike of change probably had its roots in the past and in a fear of the unknown. The following attests to this attitude:

> The craftsman's boldness was tempered probably far more frequently than the surviving evidence indicates, by irrational fear of the incalculable. Particularly when he was using fire, he faced unpredictable forces, and steps must be taken to protect his work as far as possible from their effects. One of the best ways of doing so, apart from cluttering the place up with apotropaic charms, was to continue processing things in "the way we used to do them," the refrain which everyone in ancient society, but especially the farmer and the craftsman, was brought up (Burford 1972:122-123).

Potters are even more tradition bound than other craftsmen, as noted by George M. Foster in Traditional Cultures, and the Impact of Technological Change. Foster was part of a UNESCO project focused on a rural village in Mexico, where he observed the following:

> My recent research in Tzintzuntzan, Mexico, where about two-thirds of the families earn all or part of their living from pottery-making, shows that as a class potters are measurably more conservative than farmers or fishermen, who make up the remainder of the families. . . . There is a good deal of evidence to suggest that the conservatism of Tzintzuntzan reflects a basic conservatism in the psychological make up of potters in other parts of the world. As a rule-of-thumb guide to community development work, I would suggest that new community development programs avoid pottery-making villages (Foster 1962:143-144).

My own previous ethnographic studies in the Middle East and Far East related existing technical processes to the analytical and technical study of ceramic material from ancient archaeological sites. Today one hears the term "ethnoarchaeology" used in such studies "that observe relationships between human behavior and humans residing in contemporary societies" (Gould 1978:815). These relationships can be posited in a hermeneutic application to postulate behavior and technology in ancient civilization, an approach signalled by Lewis Binford: "the loss, breakage, and abandonment of implements and facilities at different locations, where groups of variable structures performed tasks, leave a 'fossil' record of the actual operation of an extinct society" (1964:425, quoted in Gould 1978:815). We are all involved, in technical and analytical studies, in explaining the interpreting phenomena and events through final cause and must involve ourselves in theory formulation as well.

THE POTTERY OF DJERBA

The Island of Djerba offers a unique opportunity to the ceramic scholar. Here exist potteries and potters that have direct links to the past. Their techniques, manufacturing methods, pottery shapes, kilns, and underground potteries are unique and tied to a long history. The Island of Djerba is located off the southeast coast of Tunisia in the Mediterranean Sea facing Libya to the east and the Gulf of Gabes to the north. The Island is noted at Latitude 34N and Longitude 11E (Oxford Regional Economic Atlas 1960:124). The notation of Djerba as a pottery center was first noted in my reading of Ceramique Punique. Pierre Cintas noted:

> Il est bien evident que l'on a fabrique partout. Des qu'une ville nouvelle s'organisait, comme a Utique ou a Carthage ou l'on a retrouve leurs fours, les potiers s'installaient. Hors de Carthage, une epitaphe de Motye mentionne un potier (531), et la presence d'argile presque partout le long des cotes de la Mediterranee favorisait l'industrie des potiers. Cette industrie est une des plus elementaires et il serait vraiment derausibbable d'imaginer que toutes les ceramiques puniques sont dues seulement a quelques grands centres producteurs. Comme aujourd'hui, en Tunisie, chaque bourgade de quelque importance dut avoir son four. Mais comme aujourd' hui aussi ou toute la production est centralisee a Jerba et a Nabeul, quelques grands centres specialises devaient pourtant suffire aux besoins majeurs du pays, en ce qui concerne les objets courants, tels que les grandes jarres ou les gargoulettes ordinaires, au moins (Cintas 1950:555).

The writer made several trips to Djerba and particularly to the region around the village of Guellala. Here there is an abundance of rich potter's clay and a long tradition of making giant storage pots along with a complete repertoire of pottery, including toys for children. Guellala is described as follows:

> Guellala! A six kilometres a l'Ouest de la chaussee qui desormais rattache Djerbe au continent, c'est un ensemble de villages qui constitue un des cheikhats les plus originaux du Sud-Ouest de l'ile. Guellala: les tourneurs d'argile; et le terme evoque deja l'artisanat de la poterie, car il n'est point de tourneur d'argile a s'arreter au stade de l'ebauche: tous ici pratiquent l'art du feu, voire le vernissage des pieces qu'ils confectionnent. El le fait deja que cet artisanat ait donne son nom a un village souligne son importance, sinon son anciennete (Combes et Louis 1967:3).

As one approaches Guellala and sees the fields of finished wares of all description standing all about, there is a feeling of familiarity with shapes and forms of the past—Etruscan, Roman, Phoenician—that are still being produced in the 20th century.

> Ressemblances avec les poteries egeennes, etrusques, pheniciennes, romaines, que tirer des comparaisons entre les formes pour resoudre le probleme de l'anciennete des techniques guellaliennes et de leur originalite? (Combes et Louis 1967:21).

As one enters the potter's quarter of Guellala one feels surrounded by ancient pottery (Figure 1). Potteries, kilns, and fired ware seem to be all round. The potteries and the kilns are mostly below ground so there is a feeling of a deserted area; there is little vegetation except for an occasional palm tree. Entrances to the underground kilns have stone arches holding overhead weight.

On a walk through one part of the work area, the writer came across an entire pottery area abandoned some unknown years ago. It was decided to study this area and make comparisons with the now working potteries to see how well one could reconstruct the present from the past. Here, truly was an example of the "archaeological present." Some of the parts of this abandoned area were still being used to prepare the clay while the pottery studios themselves lay all about in collapsed ruin.

It is hot at Guellala and the potters shield themselves and their clay from the ravages of the sun in cave-like workshops. The intense heat would quickly crack freshly made pots if they could not be protected from the sun. By working in dark, cool underground potteries the finished clay pieces can slowly and safely dry and the potter can work in comfort. The potters work on kick wheels and throw all manner of pottery. These range from small pitchers and jugs, thrown in one piece from a pug of clay prepared by an assistant, to large pithoi-like vessels that are made on different sized wheel heads, section by section, and later joined on the wheel to complete the piece. Broken vessels were noted in the walls and partitions of the underground potteries plastered with mud into the walls themselves. Combes and Louis described a studio interior as follows:

> L'atelier de Yamoun s'ouvre au vas du sol, entre le touffes de palmes et les collines de de'bris amonceles au long des siecles. C'est une cave om breise et fraiche. De grandes amphores manguees, fen dues a la cuisson, dresses comme de fascines, lein servent de toit, de muraille et de rempart contre les rages du soleil (Combes et Louis 1967:42).

The entrances of the potteries usually faced south and the buildings themselves oriented east and west with the drying areas for finished pottery facing north. This would provide a constant sun for even temperature. The potteries varied in size. They contained a throwing area, a general workshop area, an area for foot-treading clay to wedge it to remove air, and an area to store wedged clay ready for the potters, use. This arched area was separated from the storage-drying area by walls of broken pottery, stone, and clay. The work area was much smaller than the drying-storage area. One studio measured 25 feet by 16 feet. A similar-sized area described by Combes and Louis measured 8 meters by 4 meters.

As one enters the studio, the potters sit at their wheels to the left of the door. In front of the wheel is a slab of stone on which pugs of clay can be placed ready for throwing or pieces of finished ware waiting to be carried to the drying area by the assistant. Sitting near the door allows the potter to throw by good natural light and benefit by the fresh air coming through the open wooden door. The wheels are arranged singly or in groups of two or three wheels, side by side, in all the potteries we visited. The wheels are separated from the rest of the workshop by the stone slab mentioned above. One, two, or three potters can work at the same time with an assistant bringing pugs of wedged clay ready to throw, and to take away boards of finished ware or, in the case of larger vessels, to take away the thrown pots as fast as they are thrown.

The wheels used by the potters at Guellala, as well as the wheels found and studied in the abandoned potteries, were kick wheels. The wheels are made of wood and are fastened to wooden supports that are anchored in the wall of the pottery and to the stone slab wall in front of the potters. The upper throwing head (ca. 25 cm. diameter) is fastened to a wooden shaft which pierces the wooden kick wheel (ca. 75 cm. in diameter) and continues through to rest and turn in a stone socket buried in the studio floor. The main axle or shaft is secured to the supporting frame by cordage and a wedge to allow for adjustment. The shaft turns in an oiled pad of Esparto-grass which acts as a bushing to enable the wheel to turn easily. Wheels such as this are easily made in the potter's village and are very similar to simple wheels I have studied in other remote areas, including Afghanistan, Iran, and Jordan.

The potter sits or rests against a board seat angled upwards at the back by a small branch of wood. The wheel is usually kicked with the right foot in a counterclockwise rotation, although there are times when the potter reverses this direction in the finishing process. The potters fasten various fired-clay throwing bats to the upper wheel head to actually throw upon. The size of these bats is relative to the size of the finished, thrown piece. Some of the throwing bats are fastened to the wheel head with coils of wet clay.

Figure 2 was taken in a working pottery at Guellala showing one potter working at his kick wheel with an assistant wedging clay and preparing pugs of clay for the master potter. Figures 3 and 4 were taken nearby in the abandoned pottery area and portray what remains as the unused potteries disintegrate over years of disuse. One can note the collapsed roof, the fallen arch stones and the upturned potter's wheel. Remains of the stone slab table are still in place and various pieces of pottery are on the floor or still in place in the walls where they were used to construct the partition between the stone arches. The beauty of this study is the still existing direct relationships between the working potteries and the abandoned areas. One can study these photographs and form an accurate relationship with ancient potteries being excavated and find material guidelines to assist in the reconstruction of such areas. One feels the deep responsibility to record these data for others to see and use. Toynbee expresses this commitment to his discussion of the nature of history:

> My sensitiveness to the historic environment is part of living in
> the time dimension. It is the feeling for our ancestors and
> through our descendants, a feeling that we are trustees for the
> whole of human history (Toynbee and Urban 1974:51).

The ceiling/roof of the potteries are most interesting. The trunks of palm trees span the walls and arches over the potteries. The stone arches are made up of Roman-like arch stones. Some are mortared together while others are cut to fit together without mortar. On top of the beams formed by the palm tree trunks, there is a layer of palm fronds. Next, a dense layer of dried seaweed is placed over the palm fronds to seal in the large voids thus far. On top of this is placed a layer of clay which is rolled hard and flat. Eventually, grasses and weeds grow in the roof, holding the clay in place. This process make a tightly sealed roof and shades the pottery and the potter from the hot sun. It is the reason the potteries are hard to find since the roofs of the potteries look like any other grass- and weed-covered area. In fact you only know you are walking on the roof of a pottery when you notice the air holes sticking out of the ground at regular intervals. These are kept covered or uncovered depending on the desired temperature and humidity of the drying areas. One can see the fallen beams and the supporting arches in Figures 5 and 6. One should also note the unmortared arches, and collapsing beams, and the layered roof.

A comparative look at a working pottery shown in Figures 7 and 8 gives the reader some idea of how some of these spaces are used. Figure 7 indicates a drying area with pots at various stages of the drying process. It must be noted that freshly thrown pieces must dry very slowly, in a hot climate, to prevent cracking and warping. The clay used by the Guellala potters is an earthenware clay that is quite plastic. It has a fairly high degree of shrinkage; rough calculation would indicate a shrinkage of 20 to 25 percent between the freshly thrown piece and the same piece after air drying and firing. The pots are kept here for several weeks prior to firing until enough pieces have been made and dried for a firing. The pieces are then taken outside near the kiln to be fired where the hot sun can further dry the pieces prior to loading the kiln.

Other parts of the studio-drying areas are used to prepare the clay for the potter's use. Wet clay is brought in from the mixing pits and spread on the floor in a dark corner of the pottery. Here the potter's assistant foot-treads the clay to give it the proper consistency for the potter to wedge the clay, or drive the excess air from the clay. This excess air in the clay would form gas bubbles in the firing process and burst the finished piece. Sometimes air bubbles form in the raw clay during the throwing process, making it difficult for the potter to throw an even-walled piece. Figure 8 illustrates sections of foot-wedged clay waiting use by the master potter; Figure 9 provides the reader with a view of a Tunisian potter from Nabuel foot-treading clay in a manner like that observed at Guellala.

The clay used by the potters at Guellala is mined underground about two kilometers from the village. It is dug deep inside the hillside and hand-carried out through narrow hand-dug mine entrances. The clay is loaded on wagons and brought to the potters' quarters. A potter's assistant breaks up the lumps of hard mined clay with a hammer and the clay is shoveled into stone-lined mixing pits where water is added from a nearby well and the clay is mixed by foot-treading. In the abandoned potters' area we found a large column drum that was pulled over the raw clay to further crack the lumps prior to putting it into the mixing basin. The clay is mixed and allowed to settle; nothing is added to the now plastic material and it is bucketed to the potter's studio for foot wedging and ageing. Figure 10 gives the reader a look at the ancient column drum roller for crushing the raw clay. Close at hand was an abandoned dry well which at one time was used to provide water for the mixing area.

The firing at Guellala is done in large and small updraft kilns fueled with wood and palm fronds. The kilns stick out of the ground like large beehives and are fired from pits below ground level. The floors of the kilns are pierced to control the paths of the flame and to provide an even heat; the interiors of the kilns are constructed of local brick in a herringbone pattern in between straight rows of brick (Figure 11). Often broken and damaged pots are mortared into the exterior of the kiln to reinforce the structure and, in some cases, to provide draft holes for the firing (Figure 12). The tops of the kilns are domes with a covered opening. Kilns are fired slowly for twenty-four hours to remove the remaining moisture from the pottery, and for two more days and nights to reach the maximum temperature of about 850°C.

CONCLUSION

We may close by noting the relevance of such studies for archaeology. Ethnographic study of this abandoned potter's quarters has allowed us to draw out relationships between working potteries and those long ago put in disuse. An attempt has been made to note the disintegration of these potteries over a relatively short span of time. Such exact comparisons between past and present allow certain conclusions to be drawn.

The tradition of potters' techniques, potters' workshops, and pottery forms continues through time from generation to generation with little significant change, in some remote areas not yet affected with the move toward a technological society. The potter's tradition passes unbroken through time in these untouched or little-traveled areas like the links in a chain. Fathers teach sons and mothers teach daughters. If ethnoarchaeology is, in fact, the inclusion of information about function and disposal of ceramics as well as the manufacture of ceramic material, studies such as this should offer new insights to the field archaeologist in his attempt to reconstruct a civilization long since gone. In a hermeneutic method, the archaeologist must postulate and formulate ideational concepts about detailed life in an area, at times including the phenomenology of religion—an even more abstract concept. Contributions from technical studies, statistical studies, dimensional models constructed with the aid of computers, neutron activation analysis, and thermoluminescence all yield additional information for the field archaeologist to employ in his conclusions.

Time for ethnographic studies and studies relating to ethnoarchaeology is so terribly limited:

> The continued work of ceramics specialists combined with ethnographic studies and the study of excavated material should help add additional knowledge about the technology of ancient man and the ecological environment in which he lived. One feels a sense of urgency when making studies of village craftsmen in the Middle East and in Afghanistan. Modern technology is taking over in the making of goods and craftsmen are not teaching their sons and daughters to follow the old traditions. While we in America are in the post-technological phase and know too well the effects on living brought on by modern technology, most small nations in the Middle East are seeking technology to help them grow and provide much needed goods and services. Ethnographic studies of village potters will have to be made in the next 10 to 20 years. After that time, much of what we now study and record will have vanished (Johnston 1977:207).

Figure 1.   The potter's quarters at Guellala, Djerba, Tunisia, showing fired pots, vaulted entrances to underground kilns, and the mounded stone hills that cover the underground workshops.

Figure 2.   A potter working in a functioning workshop at Guellala.   While the potter works at his wheel, his assistant prepares pugs of clay.

Figure 3. Interior of an abandoned potter's studio at Guellala. Note fallen palm tree beams and sections of the stone table slab still in place.

Figure 4. Interior of an abandoned potter's studio at Guellala. Note partition constructed of broken pots behind the fallen potter's wheel.

Figure 5. Interior of an abandoned pottery at Guellala. Note the layered ceiling, broken pots used to form a partition, and fallen beams.

Figure 6. Interior of an abandoned pottery at Guellala, showing an area used for drying the formed vessels. Note the unmortared Roman arched vaults.

Figure 7. The drying area of a working underground pottery at Guellala.

Figure 8. The clay preparation area of an underground working pottery at Guellala, with foot-treaded clay in the center.

Figure 9. A Tunisian pottery from the city of Nabuel foot-treading clay in a manner like that observed at Guellala.

Figure 10. The ancient column drum roller for crushing the raw clay, lying outside the entrance to an underground pottery, together with a pile of freshly mined clay.

Figure 11. Interior of a large kiln at Guellala. Note rows of herringbone brick between rows of straight brick, the domed floor over the fire box, and the loading door leading into the firing chamber.

Figure 12. Exterior of a kiln at Guellala. Note the use of damaged pots mortared into the walls for reinforcement and draft.

REFERENCES

Burford, A.
   1972   Craftsmen in Greek and Roman Society.   London: Thames and Hudson.

Cintas, P.
   1950   Ceramique Punique.   Tunis: Publications De L'Institut Des Hautes Etudes
      De Tunis, Vol. III.

Collingwood, R.G.
   1962   The Idea of History.   London: Oxford University Press.

Combes, J.L. and A. Louis
   1967   Les Potiers De Djerba.   Tunis: Publication Du Centre Des Arts Et Traditions
      Populaires.

Foster, M.
   1962   Traditional Cultures: and the Impact of Technological Change.   New York:
      Harper and Row.

Gould, A.
   1978   The anthropology of human residues.   The American Anthropologist, 80(4)
      December 1978.   Washington, D.C.:   American Anthropological Association.

Johnston, H.
   1977   The development of the potter's wheel: an analytical and synthesizing
      study. In, Material Culture, H. Lechtman and R. Merrill, eds.   Pp. 169-
      210.   New York: West Publishing Co.

Kenyon, M.
   1956   Beginning in Archaeology.   New York: Frederick A. Praeger Inc.

Matson, F.R.
   1943   Technological notes on the pottery. In, The Excavations at Dura Europos,
      Toll, ed.   New Haven: Yale University Press.

Nisbet, R.
   1976   Sociology as an Art Form.   London: Oxford University Press.

Oxford Regional Economic Atlas
   1960   The Middle East and North Africa.   London: Oxford University Press.

Toynbee, J. and G.R. Urban
   1974   Toynbee on Toynbee.   New York: Oxford University Press.

Chapter 7

Pottery and the Prehistory of

Northeast Thailand

Wilhelm G. Solheim II

This paper is concerned with the quantity and variety of data on pottery from Northeastern Thailand and how these data are being and will be used in the reconstruction of the prehistory of the area. Northeastern Thailand is synonymous with the Khorat Plateau, and is bounded on the north and east by the Mekong River. The plateau has an average elevation of about 200 m. and is clearly bounded by sharp escarpments, which separate it from the central plains of Thailand on the west and the Cambodian plain on the south.

There has been no organized program of research on this pottery so the data available at this time are of a very random nature, resulting from a number of independent projects. The known present-day pottery manufactured on the Khorat Plateau appears very homogeneous from area to area, but it is different in form and decoration from any of the known prehistoric pottery traditions. The ethnohistory of the area is very poorly known and there is no explanation at present for the disappearance of pottery types made and used only 200 years ago. The problem is greater in early periods. At least five different pottery traditions can be identified in the period about 2000 years ago, and considering the areas of the plateau not yet surveyed, there are probably more. Over and above the early pottery (Bill 1975; Brown et al. 1977:33-38), these traditions include the Non Nok Tha, Ban Chiang (Van Esterik 1973; Krairikish 1973), Lam Pla Plerng (Solheim and Gorman 1966:116-123), Phimai black (Solheim 1965a; Solheim and Ayres 1979:68-76), and the Roi Et (Higham 1977:113-134). I will not attempt to discuss here the relationships of these traditions; this is one of the long-term objectives of pottery studies on the plateau.

ARCHAEOLOGICAL RESEARCH

Research into the prehistoric archaeology of northeastern Thailand started in 1963 with the beginning of the archaeological salvage program sponsored jointly by the Fine Arts Department of Thailand and the University of Hawaii (Solheim 1963, 1964a, 1966; Solheim and Gorman 1966). In 1965 the University of Otago joined this program and in the early 1970s the University of Pennsylvania began a program with the Fine Arts Department. Since the 1970s, the Fine Arts Department of Thailand has been actively continuing this research with their own independent programs (Rutnin 1979). These efforts have resulted in at least seven independent surveys and excavations at two major sites have been completed. Non Nok Tha (at First Nam Pong 7), was the first of these sites to be discovered (Solheim and Gorman 1966:176-177), with hundreds of whole and restorable whole vessels recovered from burials (Bayard 1970, 1971). The second major site is Ban Chiang (Charoenwongsa 1973; You-di 1975; Gorman and Charoenwongsa 1976), particularly famous for its painted pottery dating from the 4th and 5th millennia B.C. (Bronson and Han 1972; Patanne 1972, 1973; Griffin 1973).

Non Nok Tha, a low mound in an area of rice paddy fields (Bayard 1970:111), is located about 65 km. west-northwest of Khon Kaen, in northeastern Thailand. The site was discovered in April 1964 (Solheim and Gorman 1966: 13-15), tested in January 1965 (Solheim, Parker, and Bayard 1966:77-81), first excavated in January to April 1966 (Solheim, Parker, and Bayard 1966), and excavated again in 1968 (Bayard 1970, 1971). While there is controversy over the interpretation of our more than 30 radiocarbon and thermoluminescence dates from the site, we subdivide the site into an Early Period from about 3500 to 2500 B.C., a Middle Period from 2500 B.C. to A.D. 200, and after a gap, a Late Period from A.D. 1000 to about 200 years ago (Bayard 1977:64-65). The inhabitants of the site were probably semisedentary agriculturalists who lived at the site for 15 or 20 years, moved to other sites, and in time, reoccupied the site many different times. They were growing rice and making pottery from the start of occupation, and they manufactured bronze tools from at least the beginning of the Middle Period (Solheim 1968) and probably from the beginning of the Early Period. The areas excavated were predominantly funereal. There is considerable variety in the pottery associated with the 205 burials recovered, and much change is evident through time. At least two distinctive forms of small cord-marked cups, and larger cord-marked jars with low ring supports, found with burials from the bottom layer, are recognizable with the cremation burials of the top layer (Solheim 1967a:Plate Ib). The extended burials were rarely without pottery but ordinarily had vessels placed by the head or feet or both (Bayard 1970:Plate IIIb; Solheim 1967a:Plate II, IIIa).

Most burials at Non Nok Tha had from two to four or more pottery vessels associated with them, at least some of which were probably placed with the burials as containers of food items. Many of these vessels, when found relatively intact, were brought back to Hawaii with their soil contents undisturbed. As I felt that the pots may have contained something, such as food, at the time of the burial, we examined the contents of these vessels carefully. All soil, after mechanical disaggregation and dry examination, was washed through a fine screen. Initial sortings of the material revealed that in the soil of some of the pots there were a number of very small bones, apparently fish bones, plus a number of small granules which could have been very small seeds; a grain of carbonized rice was also found in one of the pots. The small fish bones suggested that some vessels contained a fish paste, used everywhere in Thailand today as a condiment and concentrated source of protein and minerals. Douglas Yen, an ethnobotanist at the Bishop Museum, found a number of seeds, some definitely rice, but most, if not all, unidentifiable further because of abrasion from the screening. Millet seeds would have been expected in these vessel contents, but millet seeds are very small spheres and none could be identified.

Chemical analysis of soils revealed not only that the contents of the jars were different from the cemetery soil outside the jars, and this in turn was quite distinct from the soil outside the site (Nelson 1970a, 1970b), but also that there were differences between jars (Streck 1976; McNeill 1978). Other analyses of the Non Nok Tha pottery and vessel contents included pollen analysis (not yet completed) and thermoluminescence tests on sherds to check for different clay sources. Fired pottery, made of clay from a single source, may produce a distinctive thermoluminescence curve or signature that is different from the curve of clay from any other source (Welch 1977). If this is so, this method can be used to investigate questions of local versus nonlocal pottery manufacture at Non Nok Tha, and eventually contribute to the reconstruction of trade patterns in Northeastern Thailand. From some of the excavation strata sherds were recovered that were obviously not the common local pottery—being tempered variously with rice husk, sand, laterite, ground potsherds, prepared fired clay, and combinations of all these—so there must have been trade in pottery in much the same way as there is today (Solheim 1964b).

ETHNOARCHAEOLOGICAL RESEARCH

I have always felt that a knowledge of the present-day pottery manufacture and use in an area can be of much value in understanding and interpreting the prehistoric pottery of the region (Solheim 1965b). For that reason when doing archaeological fieldwork I attempt to get at least a preliminary, simple description of pottery manufacture whenever possible, and I encourage my students and others to go into greater depth on this and related ethnographic matters. The reports that follow were independent studies, and unfortunately no comprehensive analysis has been made of the present-day pottery manufacture of Northeastern Thailand as a whole. Data from Laos are included here as the pottery manufacture there is similar to that observed in Northeastern Thailand. Much more needs to be done before the total area can be dealt with, however.

The earliest ethnoarchaeological study in Northeastern Thailand was concerned with the method of surface treatment of earthenware pottery with a carved paddle, as seen in a village of eastern Laos (Colani 1931). Here a slow wheel is used with an axle inserted into a hole in the bottom of a circular disk and apparently set tight to the dish with wedges; the axle turns in a section of bamboo set into the ground. The description of the formation of the pot is incomplete, but my own observations in Luang Prabang, Laos (Solheim 1967b) have illuminated the procedure. A thick clay cylinder is placed on the wheel and first the rim is formed by finger pressure while turning, then the upper two-thirds of the pot is formed by paddle and anvil while turning on the wheel. The bottom third is completed after some drying, using the paddle and anvil to close the open lower end and form the bottom, with the vessel held in the potter's lap.

Another study of ethnographic pottery manufacture revealed a different technique. At a village near Khon Kaen in Northeastern Thailand (Solheim 1964b) no slow wheel was used. A hollow clay cylinder was formed by rolling the cylinder on a mat with an even, smooth stick inside. This is then placed vertically on a wooden stump and the rim formed by finger pressure while the potter walks around the stump, thus turning the person around the vessel. The body is formed and the hole in the bottom closed while working with a paddle and anvil, holding the vessel in the lap.

Rim Form Variation

Questions of production and the problem of identifying individual potters was explored by study of variations in rim form. Most potters who make pottery by hand seem to feel they can recognize the pottery that they have made themselves as well as the work of other potters. A student investigated this question in the village of Ban Don Boom, studying variation of any kind as found in the work of one potter working from morning to night over several weeks, and variation in making the same type of vessel among several different potters. The student's diary (Burke 1970) gives insight into some of the problems involved in such a study:

When I asked [the potters] if they could tell the difference between their pots and other potters' pots they all said yes. But it was not so easy to get them to explain how they were able to do this.

Nang Wang was the most specific when she explained how she could tell from the inside of the rim. She even showed me how she could measure it with her thumb. Since they all hold their thumbs in a certain position while walking backwards around the pot, to make the rim, then only their thumb will fit in that groove on their pots. With that explanation, Nang Wang proceeded to show me how her thumb in that position would not fit in her neighbor's pot. That sounded wonderful . . . but having had some experience with contradictory responses I decided to ask another potter who had not been present at the time of this declaration.

Nang Geen, can you tell the difference between your pot and someone else's? Yes, I can. Can you tell from the rim? Yes, I can. Which part of the rim? (Oh no, I thought, as she pointed to the <u>outside</u> of the rim!) You mean, Nang Geen, the height of the part between the body and the rim is different for each potter? Yes, it is. What about the inside of the rim? It is always the same. Can you tell which potter made a pot from the outside of the rim? Yes, I can. Can you tell from the inside? No. Is there any other way you can tell your pot from your neighbor's? The shape of the body. You mean the shape of your <u>aan-nams</u> are different from the other potters'? Yes. Can you show where it is different? (She walked toward the rows of upside-down pots drying under her house and patted the side of one near the bottom.) You mean, Nang Wong's aan-nams are different in this particular spot? Yes. . . . Is the outside of the rim different too? Yes. Is the inside of the rim different? No, it is the same.

I bought a mor kang from Nang Geen and Suwan and I took it over to Nang Yuan, her neighbor. I asked her if she could tell who made this pot. Yes, it came from Nang Geen's house. But who made it? It was Nang Wong. How did you decide that? It looks like hers. What part? The shape. Is the rim like Nang Wong's too? Yes, it is. The outside or inside of the rim? Both. Are you sure it is Nang Wong's mor kang? Yes, it came from that house.

Next I took it to Nang Wang's house who is Nang Yuan's neighbor. Nang Wang, can you tell me who made this pot? Yes, it was Nang Yuan. What part of this pot made you decide it was made by Nang Yuan? The inside of the rim. Anything else? And the shape. Anything else? The inside of the pot and the bottom and where the body joins the rim. Anything else? The shape.

I think the truth herein, is not that they can tell who made a pot, but just if it is theirs or not.

And on the subject of the measurements in general:

I made detailed measurements of the inside and outside of rims, [restricting] myself to aan-nams since everyone made them regularly. I took two measurements on the inside of "the groove" made by the potter's thumb and three measurements on the outside. My purpose was to see if there was a [meaningful] measurable variable or not. My conclusions on that score are that the rim in Ban Don Boom is pretty standard, in fact almost machine-like. . . . One potter was visibly or rather measurably different by about 1 mm.

Even height and circumference of the aan-nams are often exactly the same give or take 1 or 2 mm. The biggest difference was in circumference. The smallest measurement I made was 1.29 m. and the largest was 1.55 m. But there are so many overlapping measurements that even circumference is no criterion for proving which potter made which pot.

Measurements can become an obsession. I found the more I made the more I saw I had to make. For example—the rim. I started measuring the lip, the groove made by the thumb and the shoulder joint. I ended up measuring eight different points on the inside and outside until I realized that this was ridiculous because the potters could see what I was trying to measure but I couldn't see. . . . .

The difference was that the potters were striving for uniformity and I was looking for variation. In other words, I was trying to beat them at their game, playing their rules on their homeground. Naturally I was slightly frustrated and only vaguely successful in my search for . . . what I wanted—a measurable variable.

Site Formation Processes

Another ethnoarchaeological study was undertaken from March to June 1970 in the village of Ban Koeng Nau (Calder 1972). Although this village obtains its pottery from a pottery-making village nearby, rather than making its own, the village was the site of a study of the cultural context of breakage and distribution patterns. The investigation proceeded in two steps (Calder 1972:39):

Firstly, a questionnaire technique was used to elicit information on pottery types, usage, storage, breakage, and the future of pot fragments and sherds. Also a catalogue of each type of pot was compiled. Secondly, hypotheses concerning the probable distribution of sherds in a recently abandoned house floor and in refuse and footpath areas of the village were constructed and tested by excavation. The sherds recovered were analyzed and the results tabulated. From the overall data obtained conclusions were drawn concerning factors involved in breakage, patterns of sherd distribution, and relationships between sherd distribution and household activities.

Ethnographic data suggest that sherd disposal, at least in living areas, was related to the storage of pots and their function. Consequently fragments found within a house floor should assist in the reconstruction of the layout of that house (Calder 1972:73-76):

The vessel survey revealed some twenty-nine different types of pots, each having a specific name, function, and storage area. Cooking vessels, predominantly earthenwares, are located and used in the kitchen areas of the house. Storage vessels, which are predominantly stonewares, are kept near the portal or the side of the house to catch rainfall runoff, or under the central area of the building where they are sometimes used for storing dry commodities. Porcelains and celadons, being prestigious items, are kept in the least frequented area of the house, the sleeping quarters; however when in use they can be found in the kitchen. The range of breakage modes is extensive, although the majority of pots are broken by water pressure, aging, and souring, or children accidentally knocking them over. Earthenware pots, when broken, have a variety of secondary functions: as frying 'pans', dry storage containers, water troughs, or as children's playthings. The rims are often inverted and used as pot stands. In contrast stoneware vessels have few secondary functions, and porcelain and celadon wares none.

Unusable sherds are generally left where they fall, unless they are large and/or sharp, in which case they tend to be moved to infrequently used areas where they will not constitute a danger to bare feet. No single area is designated for their deposition. Apart from the purposeful movement of sherds by people, they are also disturbed to a lesser extent in the course of children's games, flooding and animal activities.

With the introduction of more extensive communications some pottery types have been replaced by metal, glass and plastic items. The rate of change, though difficult to gauge accurately because of the villagers' relative rather than absolute concept of time, is only slowly gaining momentum in Ban Koeng. Trading practices do not appear to have altered greatly over the last generation, and trading links with the pottery village of Ban Mo are still strong.

These ethnographic facts indicate that sherds are likely to be found in relation to their functions within the house floor areas, and with no correlation to function outside house floors. This was tested by excavation.

The excavation revealed that the distribution of sherds was distinct for each area excavated. The paths and rubbish area contained relatively regular concentrations of sherds, although the average size and number recovered from the rubbish area were greater than for the paths. In contrast, the sherds found in the house floor tended to cluster in specific areas. They also tended to occur in typological groups. For example, sherds from cooking vessels predominated in two areas, on the south-east and south-west corners of the excavation; porcelain and celadon fragments occurred with these groups and to the north side of the site as well. Stoneware sherds occurred most frequently on the south-west, south, and south-east sides of the house floor, and within the central squares of the excavation. The house floor extension also contained a large number of stoneware fragments.

From the distribution patterns a basic house plan was inferred. Those porcelain fragments not found with sherds from cooking vessels lay under the sleeping quarters. The concentration of stoneware sherds, predominantly small and worn, was near the portal area, while larger stoneware sherds not found in the cooking vessels areas, demarcated the storage area in the centre of the site. The two areas of highest sherd concentration contained fragments of pots associated with cooking and eating. These were interpreted as kitchen areas. The initial conundrum of two kitchen areas within one house was later explained by closer inspection of the area to the east of the site, which indicated that another earlier dwelling had overlapped the excavated site. From sherd distribution patterns the hypotheses concerning the house layout were thus validated. The house plan and the overlapping of both the earlier and later buildings were confirmed by the previous occupants of the recently abandoned house site.

Sherds with no known secondary function predominated in the paths and the rubbish area and there was no distinctive clustering of functional types. In contrast to the rubbish area the paths contained a high proportion of small well-worn sherds, indicating wear by traffic, whereas sherds in the refuse area tended to be much larger. Unlike the house floor, neither the path nor the rubbish site evidenced structural features. The rubbish and house floor sites were the only areas to exhibit any nonceramic artifacts, but those in the house floor resulted from specialized activities such as animal husbandry, fishing, and cooking. Sherd distribution patterns and the house floor-plan in relation to this information, implied a variety of cultural activities undertaken by the family of the later house when the site was occupied.

HISTORICAL OVERVIEW

The pottery made in the Khorat Plateau today is not closely related to the pottery that was made in the northern half of the plateau only about 200 years ago. The very close sharing of the methods of pottery manufacture used among potting villages in the northern half today is most probably because they all appear to have been started by immigrants from the southern portion of the plateau between 30 and 80 years ago. Unfortunately, little is known of the history of the movement of the Khorat potters into the northern area of the plateau. The method of manufacture in the northern plateau differs somewhat from that reported from the two locations in Laos: the use of the slow wheel in place of walking around the pot while making the rim, appears to be the primary difference.

Moving back in time 2000 years, I mentioned the existence of at least five distinct pottery traditions. Unlike some other scholars, I do not see the Non Nok Tha pottery as an outpost variant of the Ban Chiang pottery, though there are some obvious relationships. There is relatively little similarity in the forms of the two pottery traditions, and the painted pottery, so rare at Non Nok Tha, shows little resemblance to that of Non Nok Tha of the same time period (3rd millennium B.C.). There are similarities in the methods of decoration of the earliest pottery at both sites, but the total patterns and forms do not overlap. It would seem likely that the peoples making the five different pottery traditions were living similar lives and in contact with each other for hundreds if not thousands of years, but they continued to make clearly distinctive pottery. I suspect this distinctiveness in their pottery was part of their maintenance of separate identities.

We have the tools and the materials to work out trade relationships in the pottery from five or six thousand years ago to the present. Through these techniques, combined with data on the associated bronze technology and manufacture, we should be able to work out the large scale changes in social and intercommunity organization. There is much left to be done, but I feel that on the Khorat Plateau we have a good start in utilizing the wealth of available pottery data in reconstructing the prehistory of Southeast Asia.

REFERENCES

Bayard, D.
1970   Excavation at Non Nok Tha, northeastern Thailand, 1968 an interim report. Asian Perspectives 13:109-143.

1971   Non Nok Tha: the 1968 excavation: Procedure, Stratification and a summary of the evidence. Dunedin, New Zealand: University of Otago Studies in Prehistoric Anthropology 4.

1977   Phu Wiang pottery and the prehistory of northeastern Thailand. Modern Quaternary Research in Southeast Asia 3:57-102.

Bill, J.
1975   Ban Chieng, prähistorische keramik aus nordostthailand aus schweizer privatbesitz.   Zurich: Museum   Bellerive   Sammlung   des Kunstgewerbemuseums.

Bronson, B. and M. Han
1976   A thermoluminescence series from Thailand. Antiquity 46:332-326.

Brown, R.M., O. Karow, P.W. Meister, and H.W. Siegel
1977   Legend and Reality Early Ceramics from Southeast Asia. Oxford in Asia Studies in Ceramics. Kuala Lumpur: Oxford University Press.

Burke, M.
1970   Dan Don Boom Diary: a study of pottery manufacture in a Northeast Thai village. Final report on project, ms., files of the author.

Calder, A.M.
1972   Cracked pots and rubbish tips: an ethnoarchaeological investigation of vessel and sherd distribution in a Thai-Lao village. Unpublished M.A. thesis, University of Otago, Dunedin, New Zealand.

Charoenwongsa, P.
1973   Ban Chiang. Bangkok: Silpakon University.

Colani, M.
1931   Procedes de decoration d'un potier de village (Cammon-Laos). Bulletin de l'Ecole Francaise d'Extreme Orient 31:499-501.

Griffin, R.S.
1973   Thailand's Ban Chiang: the birthplace of civilization? Arts of Asia Nov.-Dec.:31-34.

Gorman, C.F. and P. Charoenwongsa
1976 Ban Chiang: a mosaic of impressions from the first two years. Expedition 18:14-26

Higham, C.F.W
1977 The prehistory of the southern Khorat Plateau, north east Thailand with particular reference to Roi Et Province. Modern Quaternary Research in Southeast Asia 3:103-141.

Krairikish, P.
1973 Provisional classification of painted pottery from Ban Chieng. Artibus Asiae 35:145-162.

McNeill, J.R.
1978 An investigation of the possibilities of computer analysis of burial vessel associated soil samples. Ms., Department of Anthropology, University of Hawaii, Honolulu.

Nelson, M.L.
1970a Soil analysis and archaeology: analysis of soil samples from Non Nok Tha, Thailand, preliminary report. Ms., files of the author.

1970b Analysis of soil from archaeological sites using Hellige-Troug soil testing kit. Ms., files of the author.

Patanne, E.P.
1972 Rediscovery of Southeast Asia. Orientations 3:39-46.

1973 Potter's art of the Southeast Asian Neolithic. Orientations 4:35-44.

Rutnin, S.
1979 A Pottery Sequence from Non Chai, Northeast Thailand. Unpublished M.A. thesis, University of Otago, Dunedin, New Zealand.

Solheim, W.G. II
1963 Salvage archaeology in Thailand. Bulletin of the International Committee on Urgent Anthropological and Ethnological Research 6:39.

1964a Thailand and prehistory. Silpakon Journal 8:42-77.

1964b Pottery manufacture in Sting Mor and Ban Nong Sua Kin Ma, Thailand. Journal of the Siam Society 52:151-161.

1965a A preliminary report on a new pottery complex in northeastern Thailand. In, Felicitation Volumes of Southeast-Asian Studies II:249-254. Bangkok: The Siam Society.

1965b The functions of pottery in Southeast Asia--from the present to the past. In, Ceramics and Man, F. Matson, ed. Pp. 254-273. Chicago: Aldine Press.

1966 Prehistoric archaeology in Thailand. Antiquity 40:8-16.

1967a Recent archaeological discoveries in Thailand. In, <u>Archaeology at the Eighth Pacific Science Congress</u>, W.G. Solheim II, ed. Asian & Pacific Archaeology Series No. 1, pp. 47-54. University of Hawaii, Social Science Research Institute.

1976b Notes on pottery manufacture near Luang Prabang, Laos. <u>Journal of the Siam Society</u> 55:81-84.

1968 Early bronze in northeastern Thailand. <u>Current Anthropology</u> 9(1):59-62.

Solheim, W.G. II and M. Ayres
1979 The late prehistoric and early historic pottery of the Khorat Plateau with special reference to Phimai. In, <u>Early South East Asia</u>, R.B. Smith and W. Watson, eds. Pp. 63-77. New York: Oxford University Press.

Solheim, W.G. II, R.H. Parker, and D.T. Baynard
1966 Archaeological survey and excavation in Northern Thailand. Preliminary Reports on Excavations at Ban Nadi, Ban Sao Lao, Pimai no. 1. Mimeographed, University of Hawaii, Honolulu.

Solheim, W.G. II and C.F. Gorman
1966 Archaeological salvage program; northeastern Thailand, first season. <u>Journal of the Siam Society</u> 44:111-210.

Streck, C.F., Jr.
1976 Analysis of soil samples from burial-associated pottery in a prehistoric site: Non Nok Tha, Northeastern Thailand. Ms., files of the author.

Van Esterik, P.
1973 A preliminary analysis of Ban Chiang Painted pottery, northeastern Thailand. <u>Asian Perspectives</u> 16(2):174-194.

Welch, D.J.
1977 Artificial thermoluminescence of Phimai pottery: potential for determing clay sources. Ms., Dept. of Anthropology, University of Hawaii, Honolulu.

You-di, C.
1975 <u>Ban Chiang Prehistoric Cultures.</u> Bangkok, Fine Arts Department.

Chapter 8

Experiments with an Ancient Potter's Wheel

Ruth Amiran and Dodo Shenhav

Anthropologists as well as archaeologists have devoted a great deal of attention to the potter's wheel, since the solution of the historical problems involved in the distribution and development of this tool are likely to shed light on human technological abilities in various cultures and periods. Much literature has accumulated on the question of the beginning of this tool. We should mention the work of Foster (1959), in which the various aspects of this subject were analyzed and summarized from a sociological starting point. Until now there have been two answers to the question of the origin of this tool: (1) the invention of the potter's wheel is based on the principle of the cart wheel and follows its invention; (2) the potter's wheel is a tool that developed slowly and gradually, and it is possible to show its continuity in the stages of development. Foster is inclined to the second answer, and since in our opinion also it seems the more reasonable interpretation, we hoped to acquire evidence of its validity (Amiran 1956).

In this brief paper our principal intention is to describe the experiments which we carried out with a pair of ancient Canaanite–Israelite potter's wheels[1] (Figures 1a and 1b). These experiments may clarify many uncertainties and answer questions not asked before.

One question in this particular study was the most basic one: how is this pair of stones put into operation? The surfaces of the two stones, one pivoted and one socketed, are worn smooth and shiny by the rotary motion they underwent. Before we started experimenting, we "lived" with the assumption that the potter's work was done straight upon the upper stone itself. But with the first step of the experiment we realized that this assumption must be incorrect. Experimentation revealed that the rotary motion of the upper stone ceased the moment the potter's hands began their work and any measure of pressure was exerted upon the upper stone. Also, the very moving of the upper stone by the apprentice was nearly impossible because the upper stone is so small that there was no room to work on it at the same time that it is being rotated. Finally, the small dimensions of the upper stone did not permit continuous momentum.

We tried two ways of overcoming these obstacles. In one, we poured water, then soap, and lastly thick oil into the socket in the lower stone, and these lubricants did increase the rotary speed of the upper stone. We also gave the apprentice a leather strap or rope which we wrapped around the upper stone, thus enabling him to move the upper stone from a distance. Both modifications were unsatisfactory for long-term practical use of the stones, and we concluded that this pair of stones alone is not the complete potter's wheel. One important section of the tool must have disappeared with time.

The solution we propose for the completion of the tool is based on logic and on various analogues, but principally on the observation we made accidentally on the side of the upper stone of a Byzantine potter's wheel,[2] shown here in Figures 2a and 2b. There we discovered traces of iron rust, which appear to be evidence for a device which was attached by an iron belt. We incline to think that the device was a wooden board of a much larger diameter than that of the upper stone which would be placed on top of the upper stone. The iron belt would be in the shape of an upside-down "L" in cross section, the vertical part fastened around the upper stone, the horizontal part nailed to the underside of the wooden board. This reconstruction suits the Byzantine potter's wheel.

On this basis we concluded that a wooden board was also placed on the upper stone of the Canaanite-Israelite potter's wheel of the type of the one shown in Figures 1a and 1b. Figure 3 shows the reconstruction of our specimen in its entirety, with the wooden board on top now exhibited in the Pottery Museum, Tel Aviv. Our experiments showed that a board of 60 cm. in diameter would be the right size for both the potter and his assistant, and that it generates enough momentum so that the potter will have sufficient time for his creating. The maximum speed we have attained on this tool is 60 rpm—a good speed for throwing small pottery vessels. It is slower than the usual speed in the first stages of today's pottery manufacture, i.e., shaping (150 rpm) and opening (100 rpm) the egg-shaped lump of clay. Figure 4 shows the potter (Shenhav) at work on the reconstructed ancient pair of wheels, while the hand of a helper is charging the momentum. Both the potter and his help have room to do their functions. Several small vessels were successfully produced upon this reconstructed wheel.

We should note that the way the wooden board would be attached to the upper stone would differ from period to period. We should not assume that iron belts would be used in the Canaanite-Israelite type of pair of stones, similar to the one experimented with in this study. Perhaps the domed upper surface of the upper stone can be fitted to the board by a simple depression in the wooden board, using a fixative such as mud or some other substance. We also should note that most of the wheels found in the various excavations in this area [3] have a flat, not a convex, top. This phenomenon too should be restudied.

We have termed the pre-Byzantine type of potter's wheel as Canaanite-Israelite, simply to distinguish between the tools of these two long periods. Much more research is needed on this subject of the potter's tools. Such studies are important not only for the history of technology, they have ramifications and inferences for other fields of archaeology as well.

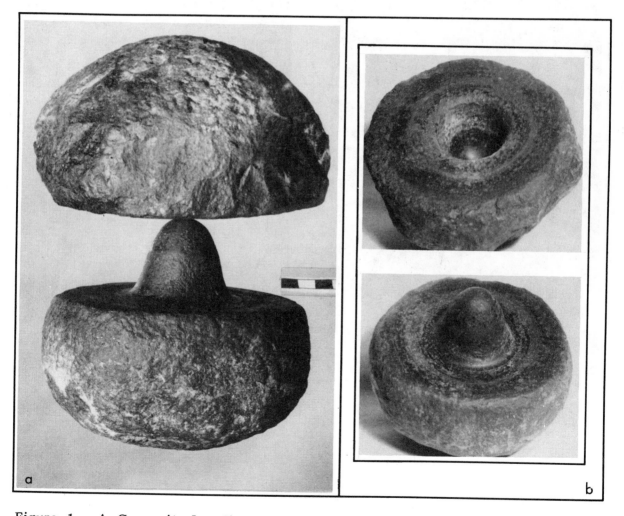

Figure 1. A Canaanite-Israelite potter's wheel, made of two stones, one pivoted and one socketed. Note wear patterns in 1b. (See note 1.)

Figure 2. Pivoted and socketed stones of a Byzantine potter's wheel. (See note 2.)

Figure 3. Reconstruction of an ancient potter's wheel as it looked in use, a wooden board attached to the top of the Canaanite-Israelite wheel shown in Figure 1.

Figure 4. The potter (Shenhav) working at the reconstructed wheel, with an assistant maintaining its rotation.

NOTES

1 These experiments were inspired by the symposium "Ceramics and Man" originated by Matson on behalf of the Wenner-Gren Foundation for Anthropological Research in 1961, at Burg Wartenstein. The potter's wheel belongs to the Pottery Museum of the Museum Haaretz, in Tel Aviv. Inv. No. 16861. Its provenience is unknown. The photographs are of Bettina Oppenheimer.

2 This pair was found in the Byzantine site at Mefalsim, and is now in the Museum "Adam ve-Amalo" in Tel Aviv.

3 Cf., for example, Hazor II, plate 127:22, of the Late Bronze Age.

REFERENCES

Amiran, R.
  1956   Millstones and the potter's wheel. Eretz-Isreal 4:46-49. (Hebrew with English summary)

Foster, G.M.
  1959   The potter's wheel—an analysis of idea and artifact in invention. Southwestern Journal of Anthropology 15:99-119.

Chapter 9

Greek Neolithic Pottery by Experiment

Karen D. Vitelli

Fred Matson happened to be working on experiments with local clays and shrinkage bars outside the dig house the first day that I ever attempted to inventory an object from the Franchthi Cave excavations. As I turned the clay figurine around and around, I repeatedly went outside to pester him with questions: How important is it to describe the clay? What should I write about the color? What should I say? As answers, I received lessons and demonstrations of how different clays behave. I continue to turn to Matson's work for lively ceramic questions. I have adapted his approach of working with clays in my current research on the Neolithic pottery from excavations at the Southern Greek sites of Franchthi Cave (Jacobsen 1969, 1973, 1976) and Lerna (Caskey 1954, 1955, 1956, 1957, 1958, 1959).

There are a number of works published on the technology involved in making ceramic objects. Many, such as Anna Shepard's Ceramics for the Archaeologist (1968), speak specifically to the questions and in the language of archaeologists. Yet written accounts must reflect the author's general interests and experiences with the pottery-making process and can never include, much less pursue, all the implications of every conceivable variable. By also attempting to build pots ourselves, we inevitably become impressed with the complexities of the medium. We experience the range of emotions which accompany a potter's successes and failures. We learn which steps are essential in the process and which may be elaborated or omitted at the discretion of the potter. We learn to recognize the subtle marks of a potter's procedure and can use these to understand and explain how and why one archaeological object, or group of objects, is different from another. As we become more accurate in our descriptions of the nature of ceramic change, we may expect also to become more proficient in understanding and explaining why change in ceramic artifacts took place. Comparing the results of our experiments with those of the ancient potters helps us identify the Neolithic potters' tools and integrate pottery with the other artifacts and environmental evidence from excavations.

Many students have joined me in pot-making and have contributed to the experiments and discoveries. The rules of our experimentation are simple: use only the materials, tools, and techniques which would have been available to the prehistoric potter. The rules are frequently broken. We work inside heated buildings in the winter, we dig from clay beds which were not exposed or did not exist in antiquity, we use matches to start our fires, etc. Whenever a rule is broken, however, we try to suggest ancient substitutes and to explore the theoretical consequences.

THE PROCESS

Finding Clays

The first step in our experiments is to locate clay. In Nauplion, Greece; Baltimore, Maryland; and Bloomington, Indiana, this has never presented a problem. Even "city kids" raised in an asphalt and cement world and initially baffled by the assignment soon headed for the country, asked around for clay sources, or just looked for places where "dirt" was exposed. They all quickly reinvented the age-old test of wetting a handful of dirt and trying to shape it. If it cracked and crumbled, they moved on. If it allowed itself to be shaped and held the shape without cracking, they began looking around for tools to dig with and a container with which to carry the clay back to the work area. No one brought aplastic earth back to the workshop more than once.

Digging tools are seldom hard to find. Sharp rocks, sticks, and shells may be slower than picks and shovels, but they work. In fact, for the entire pot-making process two strong hands are the best and the only essential tools. A good sharp rock, however, and something in which to put the clay speed up the digging process considerably. We generally use plastic bags and buckets to transport the clay, substituting these for ancient pots, baskets, wood, skin or textile containers, or even large flat rocks. The Pueblo Indians in Guthe's day carried their clay home in a shawl or gunnysack (Guthe 1925:19).

In our experience, after the first assignment in which students often went far afield to find clay, they developed sharp eyes for recognizing clay, compared notes on each others sources and the quality of the clay, and very soon were all using the same one or two nearby sources. One was at a construction site, where the mound of clay excavated by a steamshovel was gradually eroded away by Baltimore's rains and deposited in puddles at our feet. When the rains stopped, the clay settled out, coarse grains at the bottom and the finest clay, naturally levigated, on top. This was our first observation of a possible seasonal cycle to the ancient potting routine. If in antiquity "puddle clay" had been collected and set aside wet to age—in the bothroi or pits found at some sites—it would have simplified the preparation process when the dry potting season came around.

Convenience is not the only reason for loyalty to a clay source. For the last six summers in Nauplion, Greece, a small group of the Franchthi staff has been making pots after museum closing hours. We continue to use that source exclusively, although it means carrying the heavy clay on a long trip home. Another disadvantage is that the clay has a high salt content--more so in recent summers which followed dry springs, than in the first two years that we used the clay from the same place--which interferes with the color and burnish of the pots. Additionally, the clay contains many difficult-to-remove, tiny, smelly bivalve molluscs, which have caused more than one pot to explode in the fire. We are aware that there are other clay sources closer to home that might not have these disadvantages, yet even we display this aspect of the potters' conservatism reported by Foster (1965:49 and passim). It takes a while to get used to a new clay, to learn how it will allow itself to be prepared and worked, what shapes it may be teased into, and how it has to be dried and fired to result in an intact pot. Each new clay is different and can require considerable readjustment by the potter to be able to achieve a successful product. This is, no doubt, why the migrant potters mentioned by Ravines (1975:200) take their clay with them, in spite of its weight and the strong possibility that clays could be found along their route. It also suggests why the clays used by the Franchthi potters show so little variation over the millennia of production.

On the other hand, from our experiences in locating clays, I find it hard to believe that a potter would be forced to abandon potting simply because the accustomed clay source was, for whatever reasons, no longer accessible. The potter would have to adjust procedures to accommodate a new clay and the resulting products would be correspondingly different from earlier ones, but a potter who wanted to continue potting would be able to do so.

Preparation

Having collected our clay, each of us was, at least the first time, anxious to begin building with a minimum of time spent in preparation. We added enough water to make the clay plastic and began extracting any large pebbles or inclusions that our fingers encountered in the course of building. A few days after one of our first building sessions, I walked into the studio to find 20 outraged students who were convinced that a vandal had been at work. A large number of our first pots lay in shattered piles; others had big cracks and looked on the verge of collapse. The "vandal" was shrinkage, and prompted our first concerted attempts to understand the structure of clays.

When water is added to dry clay to make it plastic, the tiny particles of clay, each measured in microns, or thousandths of a millimeter, both absorb water into the particles and are coated with a thin film of water (Rhodes 1957:8-9). During drying and firing, this water is removed and the clay body shrinks in proportion to the amount of water which leaves it. Any solid nonclay material which is included with the clay particles, because of its greater size, serves a primary function of reducing the amount of water absorbed, and therefore, also reduces the amount of subsequent shrinkage. These nonplastic particles, called temper when they have been intentionally added by the potter, also promote a more even drying of the clay body by providing passages for the movement of water from the interior of the object to the surfaces where evaporation occurs (for a detailed discussion of clay structures, see Lawrence 1972:33-60; Searle and Grimshaw 1959:505-519). The goal is an homogeneous clay body which will react uniformly to drying and firing. If some part of a pot shrinks or expands more than another part of the same vessel, the tension within the pot will produce cracks.

Our vandal had been selective. Some of our pots had been made with naturally gritty, homogeneous clays that required no preparation. These pots had dried intact. Other pots had cracked around large impurities or undissolved lumps of clay, which promoted uneven drying. These clays should have been cleaned before use by a process such as levigation, which separates "materials of different particle size by allowing them to settle in water" (Shepard 1968:182), as had happened naturally to our "puddle clay." A faster method, though requiring greater input of energy, for cleaning dry clay is to grind it to a fine powder using the same tools and movements used in grinding flour.

Our most severely damaged pots had been made with naturally clean clays, with nonplastics that were few and tiny. These clays required a substantial amount of water to become plastic, shrank proportionately when that water evaporated, and finally self-destructed. There were other factors involved as well. The extent of the damage resulting from the use of clean clay also depended on how the clay had been worked (see "Particle orientation"; Lawrence 1972:102-110), the shape it had been worked into, the thickness of the walls, and the rate and means of drying. No clay process is simple. With clean clays, our main problems, magnified when combined with direct firing (see below) could be solved by adding temper. This is clear both from our analysis of our own initial successes and failures and from examination of the Neolithic sherds, most of which have substantial percentages of nonplastics visible in the biscuits.

Nonplastics

We have found a number of ways to produce an effective clay body. Naturally gritty but aplastic clays may be combined with clean plastic clays to produce a workable blend. Mixing clays is standard procedure in contemporary ceramics studios (Rhodes 1957:22 and passim) and is documented in the ethnographic literature (DeBoer and Lathrap 1979:116-117). The practice should be taken into consideration in archaeological analyses aimed at determining clay sources exploited in antiquity.

We are still experimenting with different kinds and quantities of temper. Organic tempers—straw, hair, cattail fluff, and bird seed are among those we have tried—have the advantage of needing little preparation. Each has its own effect on the workability of the clay. All serve the purpose of reducing shrinkage. The disadvantage of organic tempers, for certain intended vessel functions, is that organic tempers burn out during firing leaving small—or, in the case of bird seed, large—holes which make the finished vessel quite porous.

Inorganic tempers, to judge from the sherds, were more widely used in the Greek Neolithic. Of the inorganic tempers we have used, sand is the easiest, requiring essentially no preparation. Sand is commonly found in the Greek Neolithic "biscuit" wares. So far we have not been able to think of a way to determine whether it was naturally occurring in the clays or added by the potters.

Some of the earliest Neolithic pottery from the Franchthi Cave (C^{14} dates ca. 6000 B.C.; see Jacobsen 1969:375) has a wide variety of nonplastics, irregular in size, shape, and mineral makeup and distribution throughout a single vessel or sherd. This variety is comparable to what we observed in our modern sherds from vessels made with untreated, naturally occurring gritty clays. Somewhat later in the Franchthi sequence we find sherds which have, along with other scattered mineral inclusions, a preponderance of crushed calcite particles up to 3 mm. in diameter. According to Charles Vitaliano, Professor of Petrology at Indiana University, the shape of the calcite crystals in these sherds appears to be the product of manual crushing rather than natural weathering. We may thus describe the Neolithic calcite inclusions as temper, intentionally added by the potters who had learned their lessons about working with pure clays.

I have tried grinding calcite ($CaCO_3$), which is the one reasonably sure temper added by the Franchthi potters, and which occurs frequently in outcrops around the cave. It has a Mohs Scale hardness of three and is quickly crushed into sparkling crystals 1-2 mm. in diameter. These small crystals are easily ground into a fine powder.

Calcite and other forms of calcium carbonate (limestone and shell are other potential sources) frequently occur naturally in the Greek clays that we have dug and are present in most of the Southern Greek Neolithic sherds. They usually appear as white or gray grains, of varying sizes, and effervesce when exposed to even a dilute solution of hydrochloric acid at room temperature. In addition to reducing shrinkage, the calcium carbonate has other effects on the potter's work. A standard book of clays (Rhodes 1957:47) for contemporary potters indicates:

> Lime or bits of limestone cannot be tolerated in a clay, because when lime is fired it is altered from calcium carbonate to calcium oxide. Calcium oxide is an unstable oxide in the atmosphere, because it takes on water or hydrates. This hydration, which will go on slowly even in a small lump of limestone buried in a fired clay object, causes the lime to swell. The swelling exerts an irresistible pressure against the fired clay which surrounds the bit of lime and the piece will break, or a flake of clay will break off, revealing the troublesome impurity.

The Greek Neolithic potters, although probably aware of the problem (Figure 1) were not overly concerned, since the hydration does not start until the lime has been exposed to temperatures in the range of 700-800°C. That these temperatures can be reached in a simple open fire I learned from one of my shell-tempered pots, which came from the fire intact, but two weeks later developed surface spalling from expanding lime (Figure 2). The ancient potters usually kept the time and temperature range of their fires below the danger point. The unhydrated lime in their pots provides the archaeologist with a maximum temperature range for these Neolithic firings.

Some of the Franchthi pottery stands out from the rest because of the absence of lime, and, more striking, the large (2-4 mm.) flecks of biotite (black mica which weathers to gold). Accompanying the biotite are sharp shiny black particles of hornblende and dull white particles of quartz or feldspar. This combination of minerals reminded Curtis Runnels, of Indiana University, of the composition of the andesitic lava used for many of the millstones from Franchthi. Runnels has shown

(1981:71) that specific andesite sources, much as obsidian sources, can be distinguished by petrographic analyses. This suggests the possibility of identifying the specific source of the andesitic nonplastics in our Neolithic pots. The source of the andesite, however, need not be the source of the clays or of the pots, since we still would not know if the nonplastics were natural inclusions in the clay, temper added at the andesite source by potters whose pots were then transported to Franchthi, or whether the temper, perhaps in the form of millstones, or the clay was transported and worked into pots at some site distant from the andesite source. Since andesite was demonstrably being brought to Franchthi for millstones and since it shows up as temper throughout our sequence in a variety of different wares, I am rather tempted by the idea that Franchthi potters, wasting nothing, ground down their broken millstones and/or the residue from the manufacture and sharpening of millstones for use as temper, attracted both by the ease of crushing it and the glitter of the gold mica.

Whatever the tempering material used, the result is a clay which behaves differently from an untempered clean clay and it requires relearning on the part of a potter accustomed to working with a clean clay. For example, plasticity is reduced by the addition of temper, and the clay dries out more quickly even while it is being worked. Although it does not affect our handbuilding work, it is worth noting for colleagues concerned with later periods that heavily tempered clays are rarely suitable for throwing on the wheel both because of loss of plasticity and the tearing, sandpaper effect of sharp nonplastic particles on the potter's hands.

Inorganic tempers do not burn out during firing, although, as in the example of calcium carbonate, they do have an effect on the firing process. Nonplastics may act as fluxes, reducing the melting point of silica in the clay, and thus are responsible for producing low-firing clays which will mature in temperatures reached in primitive solid fuel fires (Shepard 1968:22-23; Green 1971:66).

All this suggests that the nonplastics in ancient clay vessels played a considerable role in their creation and function. It is likely that early potters, especially those who did not have the advantage of firing in a kiln, spent a substantial amount of time removing unwanted and dangerous inclusions in the natural clays, and in acquiring, preparing, and adding the chosen temper in the appropriate amount. It also suggests that archaeologists might discover new dimensions of information in their potsherds if they were to devote more attention to the kind, size, and quantity of nonplastic inclusions in their sherds.

Building

Beginners usually ask how they should build a pot. I try to resist making suggestions in the hope that their imaginations will come up with new ideas. Pinching, coiling, and molding are the best known and most frequently used methods, alone or in combination, but pots can also be carved, or built up piecemeal, from the bottom or from the lip, in an almost endless variety of ways. Variations of paddles and anvils are useful in shaping and thinning vessels: one student put a tennis ball inside a small pinch pot and idly circled the room chatting, spinning the ball inside the pot until he had a thin, symmetrical piece.

A common mistake of beginners is to start out with a mental image of the finished pot they would like to produce. They try to proceed in one step to that finished shape, using lots of water (Berensohn 1972:27) to make the surfaces smooth and neat, and making the lower part of the vessel in its final, thin-walled form. Then they discover that the walls are too weak to support any further addition of clay—and we end up with a large collection of ashtrays. After several attempts through the entire process from preparing clays through building and firing, they learn the patience of timing, the pitfalls and the processes. Never in our experience has a determined student failed to produce a respectable pot. Patience is the prime requisite, and can make up for lack of artistic skill.

It is necessary for the archaeologist to make frequent reference to the ancient sherds while working in clay to learn to recognize the marks and surface qualities produced by various procedures and tools. By constant reference back and forth from the Neolithic pots to our own sherds, I have been able to reconstruct some of the work habits of different Neolithic potters. Some built their pots with coils. The evidence for this is not, as I had originally imagined, to be felt in the undulating walls of the pot. While leaving the coils visible may be decorative, it was rarely done by early potters (for exceptions, see Amiran 1965:245; Guthe 1925:Plate 2), I suspect, because the unsmoothed coil joints are too fragile to survive readily the uneven heat in a primitive fire. Rather, the Greek Neolithic potters used coils much as do contemporary Pueblo potters (LeFree 1975:Fig. 16), applying the coil not directly on top of, but inside or outside the previously built wall (Figure 3). After applying the coil the clay is smeared up and/or down to cover and seal the juncture, eliminating any air pockets which might expand during firing and cause the pot to break at that point. Then the additional clay provided by the coil is pinched and pulled up in order to continue shaping the pot. Subsequent finishing eliminates all traces of the undulation or thick-thin areas of each coil joint. What remains, although rarely in Greek Neolithic sherds, to provide evidence of coil building is the smooth contact point between two coils preserved in the break of a sherd, with tails protruding on either side of the clay which was smeared up or down over the joint.

Whatever the potter's building method, as soon as a pot becomes larger than can be made in the hands at one sitting, it has to be set down on a surface. Once it is there, either the potter must move around it, or it must be turned to give equal attention to all surfaces. Some contemporary potters do walk around their pots (Newman 1974:42-46), however, it is more convenient and comfortable to turn the pot. If the pot itself is turned against its resting surface, the bottom of the pot is weakened by friction and may bend, warp or crack. A simple solution is to set the pot on a porous surface which may be rotated. Our students usually use newspaper. The mat impressions (Figure 4) on some Greek Final Neolithic pot bottoms suggest mats as reasonable alternatives to newspaper. A hard flat surface produces flat-bottomed pots. A large percentage of Greek Neolithic pots have rounded bottoms which would have required a concave resting surface. There are many such possibilities in a good Neolithic potting context (as opposed to an indoor modern ceramic studio where finding such a surface or container is difficult). One concave surface which could have been exploited by the Franchthi potters is common on our sherd tables: the base of a broken pot. Frequently the broken pot wall was intentionally chipped away to provide a regular shallow container. They are the perfect size, shape, and porosity to use as potters' turntables, and are the equivalent of the Pueblo "puki" (Guthe 1925:27).

119

One student built a series of small conical cups by securing fist-sized lumps of clay in bases of this sort, turning the base slowly and continuously with one hand while holding the other hand stationary over the lump of clay, applying pressure to shape the cup only with her fingers. This procedure produced fine parallel finger striations on the damp surfaces of the pot, striations which are indistinguishable from those produced when throwing pots on the wheel. The size of the cups made in this way is limited by the length of the potter's fingers, but larger pots, built with another technique, may be given a final shaping and smoothing by this method and will also have the fine finger striations if no further finishing is given the pot (Matson 1963:491). This should caution us against using the presence of parallel finger striations as conclusive evidence that a pot was thrown on the wheel. Additionally, it seems probable (contra Hodges 1977:65-67) that a turntable may have been employed by potters essentially since the beginning of pottery-making, simply to work on all surfaces of a pot without having to walk around it.

Finishing

One of the most common problems we have in finishing our pots is in producing a horizontal rim of uniform thickness. Our most successful solution to this problem is to pinch the lip as thin as possible and then fold it down all around the rim, later scraping away the evidence of the fold. The folding also reveals any large nonplastics which can be removed at this stage before they cause fatal cracks as the rim dries. The procedure was suggested by Neolithic sherds in which the fold was not completely covered by later scraping (Figure 5), or was poorly done, trapping air inside which caused the clay to pop off in firing (Figure 6).

To avoid the pitfalls of the novice, the walls of the pot under construction must be left thick enough to support the weight of the clay to be added. Later the walls are scraped down to the desired thinness. The scraping is best done before the pot dries to leather hard; it can be done later, but then it takes longer, requires more effort and a sharper tool, and leaves different marks on the vessel. Scraping around and around the pot wall thins the walls and, if done long and carefully enough, eliminates all the surface irregularities, finger depressions, coil undulations, etc., which are the mark of a handbuilt pot. Scraping contributes to the impressive symmetry and even thicknesses of most Greek Neolithic wares. I usually scrape my pots after they have dried to nearly leather hard. I tend to scrape less vigorously near the rim since there is danger that the pressure of scraping will cause the brittle rim to crack, and cracks at this stage are all but impossible to mend. Because of my timing, I regularly end up with a slightly thicker rim than body wall, comparable to the typical Middle Neolithic Urfirnis profile (Vitelli 1977:24-25, especially Fig. 12). The Final Neolithic potters at Franchthi and Lerna frequently scraped their pots only from the interior. The exteriors of their pots are often rough, providing good evidence for the earlier building steps. Such evidence is only preserved in the more carefully finished earlier wares.

My favorite tool for scraping the inside of a pot is a clam shell, the convex curve of which fits most interior vessel curves perfectly. For straight-sided vessels and exterior curves other tool(s) with straight and concave edges are desirable. Sherds with appropriate curves are excellent scraping tools, as are pieces of flint or other sharp-edged rocks. Obsidian does not work as well for scraping because it is too brittle and the tiny flakes that are removed when the edge encounters the hard nonplastics create a jagged edge which scores the vessel surface. Many of the variously shaped sticks and ribs which are available today in ceramic supply shops serve as effective scrapers and find their closest ancient parallels in polished bone tools.

The scraping process, on which I spend at least twice as much time as in the actual building, removes all or most surface traces of previous building processes. It also removes a considerable amount of clay, enough for a ring base or a lug or two, which can be added to the pot at this stage. I wonder if there was not even some superstition that once clay had been part of a vessel it should all be used, finally, in that pot. Some of the lugs and pellets on Neolithic pots might be explained in this way (Vitelli 1977:20).

That lugs and ring bases were added after the pot had been scraped can be demonstrated for the Middle Neolithic Urfirnis ware. Bases and lugs frequently break off from the body of the vessel at the point of attachment. The preserved surface under the lug or base is well smoothed in Urfirnis examples (see Jacobsen, this volume, Figure 1), contrasting with the rough, unscraped surface to which the handle of a Late Neolithic pot was added (Figure 7). We can deduce that the surface of the Late Neolithic vessel was scraped after the handle was added by comparing the painted surface with that preserved under the handle.

In Neolithic times, as now, cracks in the rim—in our case often caused by clumsy handling of a leather hard pot—were a source of frustration. After finding these rim cracks on a finished pot which may represent many hours of work, it is hard to resist attempting to mend it, even when experience has shown that the mend is rarely successful. I have tried smearing extra clay into and over a crack and managed to get the pot through a firing intact, but the patching clay always cracks and leaves an obvious, unsightly surface. All except my Middle Neolithic predecessors at Franchthi tried the same approach, with similar lack of success.

The longer we would-be potters have worked with clay, the more pots we have made, and the better the quality we are able to produce, the easier it is to bring ourselves to destroy a pot which does not come up to our self-imposed standards. I think of encounters I have had with contemporary production potters: some will sell their "seconds," or imperfect pieces, at reduced prices. Some will only give seconds to friends or use them in their own homes or workshops. Those with the highest standards destroy all imperfect pieces as soon as they are recognized as irreparably marred, either before or after firing. The Middle Neolithic Urfirnis potters, alone among the Franchthi potters, seem to fall into this last category. All the imperfections I have noticed in pieces of Urfirnis can be traced to firing errors, and these pots may have been rejected after firing.

This perfectionist attitude might be seen as a sign of professional pride and may be what inspires some archaeologists to assume that when ancient pottery is good it must have been made by specialists (Renfrew 1973:189; Arnold 1975:183). I do not accept the general idea that high quality pottery can only be made by specialists. With the right materials, which might accidentally be those available, a rank beginner can repeatedly produce high quality vessels in a limited range of size and shape. If, however, as in the case of the Urfirnis potters, a wide variety of sizes and shapes is consistently produced in quantity with apparent insistence on technical perfection, there may be reason to propose a degree of specialization by the potters.

Surface Treatment

Surface treatment, including decoration, is the final stage in finishing a pot before firing. It is also the aspect of ceramic analysis which has received most attention from archaeologists and has generated several terms whose use I often find confusing.

"Burnishing" is a process which involves rubbing the surface of a vessel with a hard, smooth tool such as a pebble, a smooth obsidian surface, a polished bone, a fingernail. I have frequently seen worn sherds described as "pot burnishers." In my experience few sherds are sufficiently fine grained to be useful burnishers. They usually will sand or remove clay from the surface rather than compact it and are more likely to have been used as scrapers. Burnishing tools leave shallow depressions or troughs in the surface of the vessel. The depth of the trough will depend on how dry the surface of the pot was when it was burnished; the width of the trough depends on the coincidence of the curvature of the burnisher and the vessel surface, rather than on the actual size and shape of the burnishing tool. If a smooth compacted surface, with or without luster (see Shepard 1968:123-124), is present on a pot but there are no detectable burnish troughs then the surface was probably polished with a soft yielding tool such as a piece of leather, a handful of fleece, or even a finger.

"Slip" is a "suspension of clay in water" (Shepard 1968:67) and its use "represents a definite refinement in ceramic technique" (Shepard 1968:191). The longer I work with clay processes the more frequently I find myself producing surfaces which I might once have described as slipped but which, in fact, are not. I find it exceedingly difficult to identify the presence of a slip, even on pots that I have made myself. Shepard (1968:191) and others suggest that a slip can be easily recognized when there is a prominent color contrast between the biscuit and the surface of a vessel. However, I have produced a prominent color contrast simply by burnishing a nearly dry surface, without adding a slip and without using water, which might have raise a "slip" from the clay body. Salts in the clay (or the fuel?) may rise and coat the surface of the vessel during drying and firing, producing a creamy or white deposit that stands in sharp contrast to the biscuit (Matson 1971:66, 68). Mineral pigments with or without the addition of clay may be used to create a color contrast. Firing conditions alone may produce a sharp color contrast between the surface and the biscuit.

Until the actual use of a slip has been confirmed through thin section or other analysis, it seems wiser to refrain from using the term. "Paint" is a neutral term implying only a mineral pigment, as distinct from a vegetal dye. The term paint includes the possibility of a slip having been used, and may be used accurately when it is clear that something has been added to the vessel surface.

Firing

Firing the pots is the ultimate test of the potter's skills and materials. I have seen an entire kiln load of pots made by a reasonably skilled contemporary potter come out cracked, warped, or in some way unserviceable, in spite of all the temperature controls, timing devices, and scientific formulae used with her modern electric kiln. Our own repeated and varied experimental attempts with direct firings, where the pots are in contact with the fuel, have taught us to be grateful for a 70 percent recovery of intact pots. The composition of the raw materials and every step in the building and drying process come into play with the timing and placement of pots within the fire, the kind, shape, and quantity of the fuel, the length of time and the temperatures within the fire and around each vessel, and the climate at the time of firing. There are so many variables that we despair of controlling them all. Kiln gods are still very much alive in contemporary ceramic studios and must have been around since the beginning of pottery-making (Vitelli 1977:29).

The Franchthi and Lerna Neolithic pots were fired in direct contact with the fuel in open, or direct fires, rather than in kilns with separate chambers for fuel and pots. This can be determined by the color variations, the firing clouds and firing circles which regularly appear on their surfaces. These markings are the result of the different temperatures and atmospheres which reach the different parts of a vessel depending on its contact points with pieces of fuel, ash, flames, and gases in the fire. This happens whether the fire is a simple open campfire or is provided with a heat-retaining wall.

Shrinkage caused by various reactions during the temperature changes in the fire again seems to be the primary cause of most of our firing failures. The pots must be completely dry (Riegger 1972:56) before they are exposed to sudden direct heat, or else the water remaining between the clay particles in the walls of the pot will suddenly turn to steam, expand, and explode the pot, or cause the surface to spall. Drying the pots completely is our biggest problem. Even in hot, dry Greek summer when the sun alone made the pots too hot to handle before they were put into the fire, we had trouble with spalling. In the humid climate of Baltimore or Bloomington, drying the pots completely is an almost overwhelming obstacle to successful primitive firing.

In attempting direct firings, we encounter again a seasonal aspect of pottery-making. A rainy season or a humid climate all but eliminates the possibility of successful direct firing (Arnold 1975:189). The humid climate of the Eastern U.S., together with the preponderance of high-firing clays, seems to be an important factor in explaining why the Eastern Woodland Indians never developed a ceramic tradition comparable to those in the Southwest. The Greek summers, on the other hand, coupled with the low-firing Greek clays provided great potential for ceramic development that was well exploited by the potters of antiquity.

Drying and warming can be encouraged by placing the pots next to rather than directly in the fire and turning them repeatedly for several hours before transferring them into the fire. Some kind of tongs--several long green sticks suffice--are necessary for this operation because the pots quickly become too hot to touch. They must also be moved delicately because they are extremely brittle at this stage, and it is all too easy to break a rim while attempting to turn or move a pot closer to the fire. I wonder, after trying to maneuver pots into the fire this way, if the various lugs and protrusions on Neolithic pots were not designed for lifting the hot pots into the fire?

Judging from our experiments, it is easier and more effective to move the fire around and closer to the pots, than to move the pots to the fire. If one part of a pot heats more rapidly than another the sudden spot shrinkage creates stress with the cooler part of the pot and will cause a crack. From this, it follows that larger pots and complex shapes, especially those with ring bases and pedestals or thick areas in an otherwise thin pot, are more difficult to dry and heat evenly and to recover intact from a direct firing. Our firings of pots over one foot in height/diameter, or with an attached base, have been most successful when we moved the fire rather than the pots.

In a true kiln, the pots can be heated slowly and evenly to complete the drying process. In enclosed chambers, they are protected from direct contact with the fuel, and from temperature and humidity differentials, and climate plays a less significant role (Arnold 1975:202). The need for temper in the clay is less vital since the rate of shrinkage is more controlled and regular, reducing the likelihood of shrinkage cracks. Not only can a higher recovery rate of intact pots from a kiln fire be anticipated, but the potters need not spend time in the earlier stages of pottery-making in collecting, preparing, and adding temper except for special function pots, such as very large vessels or cooking pots. The potter's wheel, which speeds production and requires very plastic clay, usually with few or very small nonplastics; and the kiln, which makes it possible to fire such a clay successfully, make the potter's life easier and permit a higher production rate for the same input of energy (contra Hodges 1977:67-69). If an archaeological ceramic assemblage shows clear use of these technological innovations I expect that it is an indication that the potters were commercially viable specialists.

Our firing methods, although we have tried a number of different ones, are still crude. We have tried different fuels and confirmed Shepard's comments about the complex role which they play (1968:215-216). Our most successful firings--100 percent recovery of small black-surfaced vessels--have been done with cow and horse dung. Salt-soaked driftwood has contributed, we think, to a white "bloom" on some of our homemade Greek pots. Straw sends out such billows of smoke that it is an undesirable fuel to use in a modern urban setting with the standard burning codes.

Even our most primitive open campfires have reached temperatures sufficient to decompose calcium carbonate, and therefore, presumably were hotter than the fires of the Neolithic potters firing their carbonate-rich clays. We have produced polychrome decoration in our primitive fires, using only pigments from various iron oxide rocks picked up in local Maryland gravel beds (contra Hodges 1977:65). If we could find a manganese source (Farnsworth and Simmons 1963:393-394), I expect that we can produce even more varied polychrome decoration, as the Greek Neolithic potters did, without using a kiln.

Our experiments have taught us that there is very little in the way of absolute statements that one can safely make about the way clay will or will not react. A heavily tempered clay will usually be too aplastic to throw on the wheel, but there are exceptions. Parallel striations and walls of even thickness are not necessarily proof of wheelmade construction. Lime-rich clays can be used quite successfully for pottery. A gray or black surface is not necessarily reduced (Shepard 1968: 220-221); fine clean clays can be successfully fired without a kiln; polychrome decoration can be produced without a kiln; etc. The number of variables which must be considered makes our archaeological deductions more difficult and emphasizes the need to understand and develop a respect for the complexities of the medium.

CERAMIC CHANGE

The complexity, in fact, is such that I sometimes wonder how we can discover such similarities in pottery from one place to another over long periods of time. In such contexts we in the Old World frequently resort to the use of the convenient but vague term "influence." The term suggests that one craftperson's work contributes in some way to the work of another, whether in the form of conscious imitation or unconscious suggestion.

Observing my own students working with their pottery experiments has suggested some questions about how the "Influence Process" works. Conscious imitation of another's work, especially if it constitutes a radical change from the way the person has worked before, implies an openness to the idea of change and the desirability of something new and different. Different social contexts provide differing degrees of susceptibility to change: not always will a new idea, even a very good one, be so perceived by all (for example, see Foster 1962:87-88). Balfet's work among others, suggests that where potters are concerned, a competitive commercial context provides more impetus to change, thus more susceptibility to innovative influence than does a noncommercial setting (Balfet 1965:170-171, and passim).

Watching my students over several semesters I have observed 25-30 novice potters go through stages in their own styles. They begin, as a group, with a variety of clays and approaches to pot-building. After a month or two of working together in a large room, all end up using the same one or two clays, tempers and pigments, as well as similar building techniques and designs. A remarkable similarity of products lines our shelves at the end of each semester, although individual idiosyncracies mark each person's work.

Out of curiosity, I made a final assignment each term for the students to study and research a handbuilt object in a museum or good publication, and to attempt to reproduce it using as closely as could be determined the same materials and techniques that had gone into the original. These intentional imitations were never more than superficial reproductions of the original. Obviously there are a number of reasons for this, not least of all the lack of experience and control of materials by the one-semester potters. The observations overall, however, suggest to me that "influence" is a many-legged animal. New World archaeologists prefer the term "interaction," which seems preferable because it recognizes the active human involvement necessary to result in a stylistic influence (Plog 1976:255; Hardin 1970:passim).

Some kinds of stylistic influence may result from the simple interaction of one craftperson with the product of another. Bunzel records that some Hopi women look for sherds at ancient sites to provide inspiration for their painting (Bunzel

1972:52). Hardin notes that design elements and design configurations "can diffuse easily even when there is minimal interaction between the painters" (1970:337). My students were more successful in reproducing designs than in any other aspect of their assignment to imitate an ancient object. With sufficient skill and motivation, they can copy design elements and composition, especially the geometric designs of most Neolithic pottery, from the object alone. The craftperson who is potentially open to the influence of another is, however, always limited by knowledge of the requisite technology and availability of materials.

I have seen, handled, studied, and drawn thousands of Urfirnis sherds. We have analyzed them for trace elements, mineral composition, firing temperatures, and firing atmospheres. I can come close to reproducing some of the typical Urfirnis shapes. I can paint them with typical Urfirnis designs. I cannot reproduce the lustrous glaze-like finish which distinguishes the ware from all others at Franchthi and Lerna. I can reproduce some of the Late Neolithic shapes and can paint the typical decoration of the Franchthi Matte Painted style. X-ray fluorescence spectrometry (done by Richard Jones at the Fitch Lab of the British School of Archaeology in Athens) has shown that some of the black pigment of this style was a manganese paint. Geologists have assured me that manganese occurs in the Southern Argolid and have described what I should look for in the field. So far, I have not recognized a manganese source. The several potential pigments that I tried fired white, not the brown-black pigments of manganese (Shepard 1968:41-42). Even knowing that the black patterns were drawn with manganese paint is not sufficient knowledge for me to be able to find and use the same paint for black patterns. The students who tried to reproduce museum objects repeatedly encountered similar technological stumbling blocks.

In pottery and other media there are a number of technological elements of style which do not necessarily reveal themselves directly to a would-be copier. Interaction with the creator of the product is necessary, unless the technique is successfully rediscovered, through possibly prolonged experimentation. In an archaeological context this suggests that if we find shared stylistic elements that depend on shared technological innovation we should understand interaction of craftspeople with each other, not just with each other's products. We must explain the interaction by movements of the people who make the pots, not just by movement of their products.

Archaeologists must be able to determine whether or not an innovation in an archaeological context is of a nature to require an encounter with the influencing craftsperson, or whether an example of the finished product would suffice to carry the needed information for the influence to take place. Only then can we understand the nature and the means of the influence and interaction for which we are looking. Such a determination requires that the archaeologist understand the technological processes and the relevant environmental resources and conditions of the ancient craftspeople whose work is being studied.

Even a brief and clumsy attempt at working in clay (or other medium) introduces the archaeologist to the complexities of that medium, to the range of understanding, experience, and pride of the ancient practitioner. By stumbling through the processes ourselves, making choices, responding to successes and failure, we learn the processes, but we also become more conscious of the people who made the objects which we excavate. It helps us remember that, in the end, it is these people whose lives we are trying to understand.

Figure 1. A Neolithic sherd from Greece, showing characteristic "lime popping" resulting from hydration and expansion of lime after firing to temperatures in the range of 700-800°C.

Figure 2. An experimental vessel, produced in the laboratory, tempered with shell and fired in an open fire. Surface spalling was caused by hydration and expansion of the shell.

Figure 3. Applying a coil of clay on the interior of the wall of a vessel to build its height.

4   5

Figure 4.   Impressions on the underside of vessels, such as the imprint of a mat on this Greek Final Neolithic pot, suggest that pots were built on surfaces that could be moved or rotated to make it convenient to turn the pot during handbuilding.

Figure 5.   Incomplete scraping of the rim fold of a Neolithic sherd.

6   7

Figure 6.   Careless finishing of a Neolithic folded rim, which resulted in trapped air that expanded in firing and caused the clay to pop off.

Figure 7.   Closeup of the surface of a Late Neolithic pot, showing the rough, unscraped surface underlying the point of attachment of its handle, which has broken off.

REFERENCES

Amiran, R.
   1965   The beginnings of pottery-making in the Near East.   In, <u>Ceramics and Man</u>, F.R. Matson, ed. Pp. 240-247. Chicago: Aldine.

Arnold, D.E.
   1975   Ceramic ecology of the Ayacucho Basin, Peru: implications for prehistory. <u>Current Anthropology</u> 16:183-204.

Balfet, H.
   1965   Ethnographic observations in North Africa and archaeological interpretation.   In, <u>Ceramics and Man,</u> R. Matson, ed.   Pp. 161-177. Chicago: Aldine.

Berensohn, P.
   1972   <u>Finding One's Way with Clay</u>. New York: Simon and Schuster.

Bunzel, R.
   1972   <u>The Pueblo Potter: A Study of Creative Imagination in Primitive Art</u>. New York: Dover Publications, Inc.

Caskey, J.L.
   1954   Excavations at Lerna, 1952-53. <u>Hesperia</u> 23:3-30.

   1955   Excavations at Lerna, 1954. <u>Hesperia</u> 24:25-49.

   1956   Excavations at Lerna, 1955. <u>Hesperia</u> 25:147-173.

   1957   Excavations at Lerna, 1956. <u>Hesperia</u> 26:142-162.

   1958   Excavations at Lerna, 1957. <u>Hesperia</u> 27:125-140.

   1959   Activities at Lerna, 1958-59. <u>Hesperia</u> 28:202-207.

DeBoer, W.R. and D.W. Lathrap
   1979   The making and breaking of Shipibo-Conibo ceramics. In, <u>Ethnoarchaeology. Implications of Ethnography for Archaeology</u>, C. Kramer, ed. Pp. 102-138. New York: Columbia University Press.

Farnsworth, M. and I. Simmons
   1963   Coloring agents for Greek glazes. <u>American Journal of Archaeology</u> 67:389-396.

Foster, G.M.
   1962   <u>Traditional Cultures and the Impact of Technological Change</u>. New York: Harper and Brothers.

   1965   The sociology of pottery: questions and hypotheses arising from contemporary Mexican work. In, <u>Ceramics and Man</u>, F. Matson, ed. Pp. 43-61. Chicago: Aldine.

Green, D.
1971   Experimenting with Pottery.   London: Faber and Faber.

Guthe, C.E.
1925   Pueblo Pottery Making.   New Haven: Yale University Press.

Hampe, R. and A. Winter
1965   Bei Töpfern und Zieglern in Süditalien, Sizilien, und Griechenland.   Mainz: Verlag des Römisch-Germanischen Zentralmuseums.

Hardin, M.A. (Friedrich)
1970   Design structure and social interaction: archaeological implications of an ethnographic analysis.   American Antiquity 35:332-343.

Hodges, H.
1977   Technology in the Ancient World.   New York: Alfred A. Knopf.

Jacobsen, T.W.
1969   Excavations at Porto Cheli and vicinity, preliminary report II: the Franchthi Cave, 1967-68.   Hesperia 38:343-381.

1973   Excavations in the Franchthi Cave, 1969-171, Part II.   Hesperia 42:253-283.

1976   17,000 years of Greek prehistory.   Scientific American June:76-87.

Lawrence, W.G.
1972   Ceramic Science for the Potter.   Radnor, Pennsylvania: Chilton Book Company.

LeFree, B.
1975   Santa Clara Pottery Today.   Albuquerque: University of New Mexico Press.

Matson, F.R.
1963   Some aspects of ceramic technology.   In, Science in Archaeology, D. Brothwell and E. Higgs, eds.   Pp. 489-498.   London: Thames and Hudson.

1965   Ceramics and Man.   (ed.) Viking Fund Publication no. 41. Chicago: Aldine.

1971   A study of temperatures used in firing ancient Mesopotamian pottery.   In, Science and Archaeology, R.H. Brill, ed.   Pp. 65-79.   Cambridge, Mass.: M.I.T. Press.

Newman, T.R.
1974   Contemporary African Arts and Crafts.   New York: Crown Publishers, Inc.

Plog, S.
1976   Measurement of Prehistoric Interaction between Communities.   In, The Early Mesoamerican Village, K.V. Flannery, ed.   Pp. 255-272.   New York: Academic Press.

Ravines, R.
1975   Comment.   In, Arnold, Ceramic ecology of the Ayacucho Basin, Peru:
        implications for prehistory." Current Anthropology 16:183-204, 199-200.

Renfrew, C.
1973   Trade and craft specialization. In, Neolithic Greece, D.R. Theochares, ed.
        Pp. 179-200. Athens: National Bank of Greece.

Rhodes, D.
1957   Clay and Glazes for the Potter. Philadelphia: Chilton Book Company.

Riegger, H.
1972   Primitive Pottery. New York: Van Nostrand Reinhold Company.

Runnels, C.N.
1981   A Diachronic Study and Economic Analysis of Millstones from the Argolid,
        Greece.   Unpublished Ph.D. dissertation, Department of Classical
        Archaeology, Indiana University.

Searle, A.B. and R.W. Grimshaw
1959   The Chemistry and Physics of Clays and Other Ceramic Materials. 3rd
        ed. New York: Interscience Publishers, Inc.
Shepard, A.O.
1968   Ceramics for the Archaeologist. Carnegie Institution of Washington,
        Publication 609. Washington.

Vitelli, K.D.
1977   Neolithic potter's marks from Lerna and the Franchthi cave. Journal of
        the Walters Art Gallery 36:17-30.

Photographs by Reg. Heron

Chapter 10

Social Interaction and Ceramic Design:

Community-wide Correlations in Quinua, Peru

Dean E. Arnold

Archaeologists traditionally have used ceramic design to formulate sequences of technological history and to develop chronologies. Since the development of systems archaeology in the 1960s and the pioneering work of Deetz (1965), Longacre (1970), and Hill (1970), archaeologists have had a great deal of interest in using ceramic design to reconstruct the social patterns of ancient societies.

These studies raise two important issues. First, how does ceramic design relate to the social structure? Allen and Richardson (1970) have shown that archaeologists' views of social structure are based upon Murdock's (1949) classification and are thus "ideal" statements of what descent and residence patterns should be rather than what they actually are in terms of "real" behavior. Related to this issue is whether patterns of learning pottery-making follow a descent and/or residence model and whether the subsequent interaction of potters reinforces these basic patterns. Stanislawski (1977, 1978; Stanislawski and Stanislawski 1978), however, has shown that the Hopi learning patterns do not correspond to any one social structural pattern (such as a descent, family, or clan model) that accounts for the transmission of the pottery-making skill from generation to generation.

A second and far more basic issue, however, concerns the nature of ceramic design itself. What is the nature of ceramic design? Bunzel (1929), Rowe (1959), Lathrap (1962), and Roe (1980) have all used the analogy of language to describe ceramic design. This analogy is a useful one because design, like language, is made up of units which are structured into higher level patterns. In language, these basic units are sounds which are structured into phonemes, syllables, morphemes, phrases, sentences and larger units of discourse like the paragraph. Similarly, in ceramic design, design elements are the basic units and are structured into sequences in a particular area of the pot and juxtaposed with other element sequences in other areas.

Some of the archaeological work dealing with ceramic design (e.g., Longacre 1970; Hill 1970) has focused on design elements and their frequencies as the aspect of the design which carries social information. Elements, however, are only one small part of the entire structure of the design. Like language, it is not the elements themselves but the way in which they are patterned and structured that carries information.

The potential of relating pottery design and social data does not lie in "ideal" patterns of social structure, but rather in the patterns of social interaction, as suggested in a pioneering paper by Hardin (1970). Like Bunzel (1929), she noted the importance of design structure on pottery and found that design structure reflects potters' interaction patterns and their intensity more than design elements. Hardin found that design elements and their configurations diffused through a community quickly with very little social interaction. Her work suggests that the structural analysis of both archaeological and ethnographic pottery design may reveal structural patterns which are products of the social interaction of groups of potters such as a family, extended family, barrio, or community.

If archaeology is to relate the structure of ceramic design to corporate groups that have regular social interaction, it is important to know the design correlates of these groups. One such social group is the community of potters. The community is particularly important to study because: (1) it is probably the largest group of potters with some social interaction, (2) it is probably small enough to have interaction often and regularly, and (3) it is a discrete entity in space: spatial discontinuity exists between different communities of potters. Structural similarities of pottery design in a community would not only be useful to identify ancient communities by direct historical analogy but, if such studies were extended geographically, they would provide the basis for a cross-cultural theory of ceramic design. This would relate kinds of design structures to particular social interactional groups and provide a guide for the design correlates of different levels of social interaction.

The purpose of this paper is to elucidate the etic design correlates of the community of potters in Quinua, Department of Ayacucho, Peru (see Arnold 1970, 1972a, 1972b, 1975a, 1975b; Mitchell 1976). Except for glosses in Quechua (the native language of Quinua) used to identify the vessel shapes in this paper, no emic data were used in the analysis. Rather, the data were compiled from detailed observations of pottery that was made and used in Quinua.

This study is based on a total of 172 examples of four vessel shapes which were observed during field work in the Quinua region from February-July 1967. These four vessel shapes include a low open bowl (plato-36 vessels) and three globular bottles: (1) A wide-necked bottle with a circular mouth (tachu-46 vessels). (2) A narrow-necked vessel with a small circular mouth (yukupuynu-44 vessels). (3) A narrow-necked vessel with a mouth molded into a pouring spout (puynu-46 vessels).

These shapes were selected for several reasons. First, all are utilitarian forms which were observed being used most frequently by the natives in Quinua. The tachu, puynu, and yukupuynu are all forms of a pitcher used for holding water or other liquids. Specifically, the tachu was observed to have the following uses: (1) carrying water from irrigation ditches to the house, (2) holding water for washing hands and dishes at roadside food vendors, and (3) transferring chicha (a maize beer) from a larger vessel into the cups of individual consumers at roadside vendors. The puynu has similar uses, but, in addition, smaller-sized puynus serve as individual containers from which people drink chicha at fiestas. The yukupuynu was observed only as a container for water used by market vendors. The plato is utilized as a container for holding hot food (like corn-on-the-cob) at roadside food vendors, but other uses are likely.

Second, Quinua potters produce the four utilitarian vessels almost exclusively for local use and consumption. These vessels occasionally find their way into the tourist market but this outlet for these vessels is a minor one. Potters who made objects for the tourist market made very few, if any, of these vessels although they probably knew how to make them. On the other hand, pottery vendors from Quinua were observed selling these four vessels, and only these vessels, in the local markets in Quinua, Ayacucho, Huanta, and Huamanguilla.

Third, these vessels are not made anywhere else in the valley except by potters around Quinua, thus they represent a unique product of Quinua potters sold to the populations in the valley. Since these vessels are made for utilitarian use and their production is aimed at the native population of the valley, they are more affected by the shared tradition of the community than by the changing responses of individual potters to the tourist market.

THE PRINCIPLES OF DESIGN

Quinua potters decorate their pottery according to a series of well-defined behavioral principles which have been abstracted from the present sample of vessels. These principles can be conveniently divided into four categories: (1) the preparation of the surface of a vessel, (2) the selection of the decorative space on the vessel and its subdivision into smaller units called "design zones," (3) the manner in which the designs are painted with regard to their fundamental units and the motions employed in their repetition (i.e., symmetry; see Shepard 1948:217; 1956:268), and (4) the pattern of association of each vessel shape with the repertoire of design zones and the designs placed in each zone.

First, several principles govern the preparation of the vessel surfaces for decoration. For the tachu, potters polish the body clay without applying any slip. For the puynu and yukupuynu, potters slip the vessel with red paint before polishing. For the plato, potters also place a red slip on one surface before polishing which then determines the treatment of the other surface. If the red slip is placed on the exterior of the vessel, then the interior is slipped white and polished; if the red slip is placed on the interior of the vessel, then the exterior is left unslipped and unpolished.

The second category of design principles consists of selecting the field of design on the vessels and subdividing this area into design zones. Each vessel shape utilizes a series of different design fields and subdivisions of those fields which together are referred to as "layout types": the tachu has three types, the yukupuynu and puynu have two types each, and the plato has five types.

The design space on the tachu occurs as one of three alternatives: the vessel may be entirely undecorated, the rim of the vessel may be painted white with the remainder of the vessel undecorated, or white stripes four to five centimeters wide may be painted on the vessel. These stripes define the design zones on the vessel and subsequent decoration is placed on these white stripes although sometimes the rim is also painted white.

When the potter elects the last alternative, he has three further options for the location of these stripes on the vessel. Most often, potters place them vertically from the rim to the base on the front of the handle, and directly opposite the handle (Layout Type A, Figure 1). There are two infrequent alternatives to this pattern, however. On one vessel, the potter placed them horizontally around the vessel at the point of the greatest circumference (Layout Type B, Figure 1). On another vessel, the potter placed them vertically from the rim to the base in three locations: one on the front of the handle and two others dividing the surface of the vessel into roughly three equal parts (Layout Type C, Figure 1).

The decorated space on the yukupuynu usually occurs on the upper part of the body of the vessel between the base of the neck and the vessel's greatest circumference and includes the rim and the handle. There are two layout types. For one (Layout Type A, Figure 2), all of the design zones within the field of decoration are horizontal bands which encircle the entire circumference of the vessel. First, a wide band (Zone A) covers much of the upper part of the body of the yukupuynu. A small band immediately below this zone marks the lower boundary of Zone A. Sometimes the potter places an upper boundary on this wide band in addition to the lower one. Second, potters may also add an additional band (Zone B) below the lower boundary of the wide band, and this is usually placed on or very near the point of the greatest circumference of the vessel. Third, if there is any space left between Zone B (at the point of greatest circumference) and the lower boundary of the wide band, then the potter may add another band (Zone C) between Zone B and the lower boundary of Zone A. Finally, if the potter wishes to add another band to the vessel, he places it below the point of greatest circumference (Zone D).

An additional type of design layout on the yukupuynu (Layout Type B, Figure 2) consists of a horizontal band located slightly above the point of greatest circumference and a vertical band of identical design opposite the handle extending downward from the rim and intersecting the horizontal band. The rim and handle are not decorated.

The decorative field on the puynu extends from the base of the vessel to the rim and includes the rim and handle. There are two design layouts on the puynu (Figure 3). For Layout Type A, the largest and most important zone (Zone A) occurs on all puynus in the sample, and consists of a series of three vertical panels placed around the upper body of the vessel (Figure 4). The center panel lies directly opposite the handle. This wide zone is bounded on the sides by the handle and on the bottom by a small band which forms the bottom boundary of the zone. Potters place it slightly above the greatest circumference of the vessel. The top boundary of these panels is not clearly defined, but may be the rim of the vessel. Other design zones elsewhere in this layout type are usually (but not always) bands which extend around the circumference on the vessel below the lower boundary of Zone A. Occasionally, a potter may also place a white band above this zone, but in the present sample, this practice is rare.

The second design layout type (Layout Type B) for the puynu uses an entirely different manner of laying out design space (Figure 3). On this type, the potter used two bands of design in a manner identical to that of Layout Type B of the yukupuynu shape (Figure 2).

The decorative space on the plato includes the rim and either the outside or the inside of the vessel. There are five types of design layout (Figure 5). Three types (A, A1, C) occur with white paint on the unslipped or red slipped interior. In Layout Type A, two design zones are bands which cross at right angles. A third zone occurs at the intersection of these bands in which a single finite motif (Shepard 1948:218, 1956:268) occurs. Layout Type A1 (Figure 5) consists of a variation of the same basic layout as Type A utilizing the basic structural division of the interior into fourths with a circular area in the center of the interior (Zone C). The primary difference between Type A and Type A1, however, lies in the difference in the design space. In Type A, two intersecting bands divide the vessel into fourths and the design space is within the bands. In Type A1, however, there is no band or line dividing the space into fourths, but only the quarter sections which form a design of alternating white and red painted sections both in the center zone and the outer portion of the interior of the vessel. A third type of layout (Type C) consists of two designs: a narrow circular band, and an area in the center of the decorative field of the vessel. A fourth layout type (Type D) consists of a red design on a white slipped interior. The layout consists of a single circular design zone in the center of the decorative field of the vessel. A fifth, and final design layout (Type B) uses white paint on a red-slipped exterior with a white slipped interior. This type consists of a single circular band around the exterior of the vessel.

The third category of design principles consists of patterns of symmetry or what some have called "pattern mathematics" (Zaslow 1977). Shepard treats symmetry as an important aspect of design and states that ". . . there is no other quality of design that lends itself as readily to precise definition as symmetry" (1965:167). She defines symmetry as the motion inherent in repetition and discusses it in relation to the three spatial categories of design: finite design, band patterns and surface patterns (Shepard 1948:217-226, 1956:168-169).

> Elements and motifs are symmetric with respect to a single axis (a line), or a point, or intersecting axes, and are referred to as finite designs. If a series of axes is taken to repeat the figure again and again along a straight line, a band pattern is produced.

> We can go further and repeat the fundamental part in two directions to form a surface or all-over pattern (Shepard 1956:268-269).

Not all of these spatial categories of design are relevant to an analysis of the Quinua style. Finite designs and band patterns are the only spatial categories used in Quinua. Although some of the finite designs are used alone, most of them are used as a portion of a band pattern.

The symmetry patterns of motifs and bands on the vessels in the sample were analyzed (Figure 6) using Shepard's classic work on applying principles of symmetry to pottery design (Shepard 1948, 1956:267-276). The analysis of symmetry first involves determining the fundamental unit (Shepard 1948:217, 1956:268-269) of the individual motif. The fundamental unit of a design:

> . . . may be unsymmetric area or part of an area of a segment of
> a line, but it is always the unique part of the pattern from
> which the entire composition can be generated by regular
> repetition of motion (Shepard 1956:268).

Second, when a design is repeated again and again along a straight line to form a band pattern (Shepard 1956:268), the analysis must also determine the fundamental unit of the band pattern as well as the motion of repetition.

Shepard (1956:275) points out that although perfectly symmetric designs are straightforward, asymmetry may be rendered imperfect because of the adaption of an essentially symmetric design to the curved surface of a pot, and a lack of skill or carelessness in the execution. Since virtually all of ceramic design needs to be applied to a curved surface in one way or another probably all the symmetry of ceramic design is imperfect, and the design on the Quinua pottery is no exception. Sloppiness of design execution also plays an important role in producing imperfect symmetry of Quinua design, but this aspect of the design will not be discussed here.

The tachu bands have no symmetry, but consist of a combination of three straight (S) or zigzag (Z), red (R) and/or black (B) lines drawn on top of the white stripe along its entire length. These band designs are produced according to the following principles: (1) the band must consist of three lines of red and/or black paint; (2) the center line must be framed by two lines which may be straight (most frequent) or zigzag; (3) the framing lines must mirror one another in color and shape; and (4) all straight lines must be parallel. A similar band of two white straight lines framing a white wavy line is used on all zones on Layout Type B of the puynu and yukupuynu.

The final principle of design consists of the interrelationship of slipping, design space, design layouts, and design repertoire on each of the four vessel shapes. These interrelationships are presented in diagram form (Figures 7-10) and model the collective design behavior of the potters that produced each vessel. They also illustrate much of the range of design behavior of potters in the sample. The diagrams thus represent each of the vessels (except in certain instances where data were missing) in a way that shows general community patterns of design on the one hand, and individual variation on the other.

In order to construct the diagrams, frequencies were calculated of each type of decoration, layout type, and decorative zone for each vessel shape. Each of these design characteristics was then arranged in hierarchical order with the highest frequencies to the top and lowest on the bottom. The frequencies for the fillers of each vertical class were then calculated and arranged horizontally from the highest frequencies on the left to the lowest on the right. Then the data from each vessel were mapped into the diagram by drawing lines connecting design numbers on each level. Considerable rearranging occurred at this stage of the analysis to avoid crossing lines, but each descending pathway represents a pattern found on an actual vessel in the sample. It is possible, then, to begin at the top of the diagram and trace each vessel in the sample through the diagram. Higher levels represent spatial units of design and their decorative contents which have a higher relative frequency in the sample than lower ones. As one moves down the diagram, one moves from the general design patterns of a given shape in the sample to more specific aspects of the design which exist on few vessels in the sample.

These diagrams do not represent the choices of individual potters, or the ways in which a potter actually paints a pot. Rather, these diagrams are etic behavioral composites of the design variability in the sample found on each vessel shape from high levels of generalization to low levels of generalization. The more frequent patterns of design lie at the upper left hand portion of the diagram whereas the less frequent patterns lie toward the lower right hand portion of the diagram. Assuming that the sample is representative of the pottery-making population in Quinua, movement down the diagram is from the general community-wide decorative patterns to the more idiosyncratic variation of the design behavior of individual potters.

Community Patterns of Design

From the analysis of the vessels in the sample, several design correlates of the community exist in Quinua (Table 1). First, surface preparation, slip and paint colors tend to be consistently similar on each vessel shape. On the puynu and yukupuynu, potters utilize a white paint on a polished red slip. The tachu is unslipped with a white band used as a base for red and/or black painted designs. The plato has more variety of paint and slip colors.

Second, certain ways of allocating and subdividing the design space on each vessel shape have high frequency in the sample. Layout Type A on the yukupuynu and the puynu represents 89 percent and 98 percent respectively of these vessels in the sample. For the tachu, no design (except for the rim) and Layout Type A occurred on most of the vessels of that shape. For the plato, most of the design layout is organized using Layout Type A, but the percentage is not as high as the predominant patterns of the layout types of the other three vessel shapes. The high frequency of these layout types in the sample suggests that they represent community-wide design conventions.

Third, there are certain design zones which are always present (obligatory zones) in the high frequency design layouts in the sample. On the yukupuynu, Zone A and its lower border are the two subareas of design which always occur in all of the sample of the Layout Type A vessels. The remainder of the zones on the yukupuynu may or may not be present (optional zones). For the puynu shape, the middle panel of Zone A and lower border of Zone A (Layout Type A) must be minimally present even though the left and right panels of Zone A are usually present as well. The remainder of the zones on the puynu are optional. On the plato, there

TABLE 1

Summary of Community-wide Behavioral Design Patterns in Quinua

Design Pattern	Vessel Shape			
	yukupuynu	puynu	tachu	plato
Surface preparation prior to decoration	Slipped red and polished	Slipped red and polished	Unslipped and polished	—
Paint color (primary)	White	White	White Zone	—
Layout of design	Type A	Type A	Rim and Type A	Type A
Obligatory Zones	Zone A, lower border Zone A	Middle Panel Zone A lower border Zone A	All	Zone A and B
Design associated with particular zones	Raised dot motif, (Zone A)	Three-stemmed plant (Zone A, Middle Panel)	Three lines of red and/or black	—
	—	Fern (Zone A, Left Right Panels)	—	—
Band symmetry	Vert. reflection, vert. and horiz. reflection	Vert. reflection, vert. and horiz. reflection	None	—
Motif symmetry	Bilateral	Bilateral	None	—
Zones with least variability in designs and symmetry	Lower border Zone A, Zone A	Zone A, lower border of Zone A	—	—

are also certain zones which always occur on each layout type. For Layout Type A, Zones A and B are obligatory zones whereas Zone C is optional. For Layout Type B, Zone A is obligatory; there are no other zones for this layout type. For Layout Type C, Zone A must be present on all vessels with this layout. Zone B is optional. On the tachu, each of the zones for each layout type is obligatory. There are no optional zones.

Fourth, certain designs are also associated with particular design zones on each shape. On the puynu shape, Zone A is divided into three panels, and the designs for each of these panels are finite designs (not bands) and are not placed in any other zone on the vessel. The design composition of each of these three panels is bilaterally symmetric with respect to a vertical axis passing through their centers. In terms of allocation of the designs in the entire zone, a line of symmetry directly opposite the handle runs vertically from the rim of the vessel to the bottom of the zone. The design space and the designs within this space are bilaterally symmetric with respect to this axis. Besides this characteristic of bilateral symmetry, however, each panel has a particular set of design characteristics. The middle panel is particularly unique by the fact that only one design is placed in this location, but no two are exactly alike.

All of the variation, however, conforms to a series of underlying behavioral principles. (1) The motif must be a plant with three stems. These stems must converge at the base of the plant, but may be joined or separated. (2) Individual leaves that are bilaterally symmetric along an oblique axis must be placed on the stems. (3) Flowers may or may not be added to the upper end of each of the three stems on the plant. If they occur, they must be a single large dot or a large dot with smaller dots around it. (4) A leaf motif that is bilaterally symmetric along a vertical axis may also be placed beside the central motif in the panel. The designs in the middle panel which do not conform to these principles are infrequent in the sample and can be partially explained as the incomplete application of them. On the yukupuynu, the raised dot motif consistently occurs in only one zone (Zone A). This motif or its variations never occur outside of Zone A. Since the plato has no clear community pattern of design layout, the designs associated with particular zones in those layouts cannot be described as community patterns of designs. For the tachu, the three line motif in red and/or black (on a solid white band) form never occurs in those colors on any other vessel.

Fifth, there are definite patterns of motif symmetry which had a relatively high frequency in the sample (Figure 11; Table 2). These symmetry patterns occur with three of the four vessel shapes (the designs on the tachu have no motif symmetry). In terms of the total repertoire and the total sample of design motifs, bilateral symmetry (most often along a vertical axis) was the repetitive motion of the highest frequency. This type of symmetry occurs most often on the puynu and yukupuynu shapes, with the plato having relatively equal percentage of bilateral and radial symmetries. Motifs with no symmetry also had a modest frequency in the sample.

Sixth, there was a high frequency of specific types of band symmetry in the sample. In relation to the total repertoire and total sample of band designs, vertical reflection and a combination of vertical and horizontal reflection provide the predominant type of repetitive motion used in the formation of bands (Figure 12; Table 3). These motions occurred with the highest frequency on the puynu and

TABLE 2

Symmetry Characteristics of All Motifs on All Vessels[*]

Vessel Shape	Rotational (Ro)	Radial (R)	Bilateral (B)	Motifs Without
Platos				
Total (25 motifs)	0	11(44)	12(48)	2(8)
Type A	0	8(32)	6(24)	0
Type B	0	0	3(12)	0
Type C	0	2(8)	3(12)	2(8)
Type D	0	1(4)	0	0
(Percent of total sample of motifs, all forms)	0	(5)	(6)	(1)
Puynu				
Total (105 motifs)	1(1)	13(12)	72(69)	19(18)
Type A	1(1)	13(12)	72(69)	19(18)
Type B	0	0	0	0(0)
(Percent of total sample of motifs, all forms)	(.05)	(6)	(34)	(9)
Yukupuynu				
Total (79 motifs)	0	11(14)	61(77)	7(9)
Type A	0	11(14)	61(77)	7(9)
Type B	0	0	0	0
(Percent of total sample of motifs, all forms)	0	(5)	(29)	(3)
Totals (from all vessels)				
Total sample of motifs (209 = 100%)	1(.05)	35(17)	145(69)	28(13)
Total repertoire of motifs; designs 1-30 (39 = 100%)	1(3)	12(31)	20(51)	5(13)

[*] Figures in parenthesis indicate percentage of sample within form categories.

Reprinted from Dorothy K. Washburn, editor, **Structure and Cognition in Art**, by permission of Cambridge University Press.

TABLE 3

Symmetry Classes on All Bands on All Vessels[*]

Vessel Shape	HR+T	VR	HR+VR	SR	BR	T	Without Symmetry
Platos							
Total (33 bands)	0	6(18)	8(24)	6(18)	0	0	13(39)
Type A	0	6(18)	6(18)	0	0	0	13(39)
Type B	0	0	0	3(9)	0	0	0
Type C	0	0	2(6)	3(9)	0	0	0
Type D	0	0	0	0	0	0	0
(Percent of total sample of bands, all forms)	0	(2)	(3)	(2)	0	0	(5)
Puynus							
Total (85 bands)	18(21)	5(6)	10(12)	0	1(1)	0	51(60)
Type A	18(21)	5(6)	10(12)	0	1(1)	0	41(48)
Type B	0	0	0	0	0	0	10(12)
(Percent of total sample of bands, all forms)	(7)	(2)	(4)	0	(.05)	0	(20)
Yukupuynus							
Total (134 bands)	6(4)	50(37)	8(6)	0	0	2(1)	68(51)
Type A	6(4)	50(37)	8(6)	0	0	2(1)	64(48)
Type B	0	0	0	0	0	0	4(3)
(Percent of total sample of bands, all forms)	(2)	(20)	(3)	0	0	(1)	(27)
Total (from all vessels)							
Total sample of bands (252=100%)	24(10)	61(24)	26(10)	6(2)	1(.05)	2(1)	132(52)
Total repertoire bands in designs 1-30 (22=100%)	1(5)	8(36)	8(36)	2(9)	1(5)	1(5)	1(5)

[*] Figures within parenthesis indicate percentage of sample within form categories.

yukupuynu. The plato had lower frequency of these motions and much more variability. Nonsymmetric bands of lines and solid colors also had a high frequency.

Finally, most of the variability in the sample occurs within the community-defined decorative space, but outside of the high frequency patterns of design. Nontypical, low frequency design layouts are associated with nontypical symmetry classes. When the frequencies of classes of motif symmetry are plotted with different layout types (Figure 13, based on Table 2), nontypical layout types are associated with nontypical classes of motif symmetry. When the band symmetry is plotted against the layout types (Figure 14, based on Table 3), vertical reflection and a combination of vertical and horizontal reflections are associated with high frequency layout types in the sample: Layout Type A in the puynu and yukupuynu and to a lesser extent on the plato. A considerable percentage of bands have no symmetry. Other layout types deviate from this pattern, suggesting that community patterns of band symmetry, like motif symmetry, are tied to definite layout types. Variation from these high frequency layout types also involves a variation from the associated symmetry class.

There is also a tendency toward greater variation in designs and symmetry classes in the optional zones on a vessel than in the obligatory zones (Table 4). This variation in symmetry occurs with both motif and band patterns and is related to the variability of the designs in the optional zones. For the yukupuynu (Table 5),

TABLE 4

Variation of Designs and Symmetry Classes on
Obligatory and Optional Design Zones

Vessel Shape	Obligatory (all zones combined)	Optional (all zones combined)
Puynu		
# of Designs	5	14
Kinds of Motif Symmetry	2	4
Kinds of Band Symmetry	1	5
Yukupuynu		
# of Designs	7	12
Kinds of Motif Symmetry	2	2
Kinds of Band Symmetry	2	4
Plato		
# of Designs	5	2
Kinds of Motif Symmetry	2	1
Kinds of Band Symmetry	3	0

TABLE 5

Variation in Designs and Symmetry Classes in Obligatory and Optional Design Zones on the yukupuynu

Decorative Feature	Obligatory Zones			Optional Zones		
	Zone A	Lower Border Zone A	Upper Border Zone A	Zone B	Zone C	Zone D
# of Designs	4	3	4	6	1	1
Motif Symmetry	B	R	B,R	B,R	B	0
Band Symmetry	VR VR+HR	VR+HR	VR VR+HR	VR VR+HR T HR+T	VR	0

the number of designs for the obligatory zones is similar to one optional zone, but Zone B shows far greater variability than the obligatory zones. Optional Zones C and D are too infrequent for generalization. For the puynu (Table 6), there is less variation in the obligatory zones than in the optional zones. Two of the optional zones (upper boundary of Zone A and Zone D) are too infrequent for generalization. For the tachu shape, there are no obligatory versus optional design zones. The principle of greater variation of design and classes of motif and band symmetry in optional design zones does not apply to the plato, however. For both Layout Type

TABLE 6

Variation of Designs and Symmetry Classes in Obligatory and Optional Design Zones on the puynu

Decorative Feature	Obligatory Zones			Optional Zones		
	Zone A	Lower Border Zone A	Upper Border Zone A	Zone B	Zone C	Zone D
# of Designs	2	3	1	7	3	3
Motif Symmetry	B	R	0	O,B,Ro,R	O,B,R	B
Band Symmetry	0	HR+VR	0	VR HR+T 0 BR HR+VR	VR+BR VR VR+HR	VR

A and C, the obligatory zones have greater variability in designs, motif and symmetry than in the optional zone (Table 7). Other plato layout types (Types B, A1, D) have too low a frequency to be considered a community pattern.

TABLE 7

Variation in Design and Symmetry Classes in Obligatory
and Optional Design Zones on the plato

Decorative Feature	Type A		
	(Obligatory Zones)		(Optional Zone)
	Zone A	Zone B	Zone C
# of Designs	5	5	2
Motif Symmetry	B,R	B,R	R
Band Symmetry	0	0	0
	VR	VR	
	VR+HR	VR+HR	

	Type C	
	(Obligatory Zone)	(Optional Zone)
# of Designs	3	2
Motif Symmetry	R,B	0
Band Symmetry	HR+VR	0
	SR	

Summary

This paper demonstrates that there are definite etic design correlates for an interacting community of potters. First of all, these correlates occur in several aspects of the design: the basic kinds of slipping and painting, the organization of the design space on the vessel, the high frequency of particular design zones, the association of particular designs in particular zones, and the use of particular patterns of motif and band symmetry. It is important to note that these correlates are not so much in the design itself or its elements, but rather in the structure of the design. While these community correlates have consistently high frequencies in the sample, these frequencies do not approach 100 percent and there is great variability in other aspects of the design. Some of this variability is defined by vessel shape; other kinds are defined by layout type and nonobligatory design zones. One kind of vessel, for example, may be more heterogeneous than another and simply may not reveal community patterns of design. Similarly, nontypical layouts or infrequent design zones are the most deviant with respect to their designs and symmetry types.

Most of this variability, however, occurs within the community-defined decorative space on the ceramic vessels and with designs which apparently reflect individual or group creativity. Some of the design variability (like Layout Type B on the puynu and yukupuynu) is individual because some of the vessels on which it occurs were sold by the same potter. Differentiation outside these community patterns is far greater than within the community patterns; one kind of variation co-varies with other kinds, and some is individual. Without further research, however, it is unclear whether the remainder of this variability is purely individual or whether it corresponds to social groups below the level of the community.

IMPLICATIONS FOR ARCHAEOLOGY

How are these conclusions related to the archaeological study of ceramics? This study suggests that the use of pottery design to reconstruct ancient patterns of social interaction must be done within the behavioral domain of particular vessel shapes, layout types, and design zones. Sherds, of course, represent only random and arbitrary subdivisions of the vessel shapes which do not represent discrete units of cultural behavior. They should not be used as ad hoc boundaries for defining design elements. Furthermore, sherds do not provide the structural data necessary for adequately describing design.

More importantly, however, the present study shows the kinds and amount of design variability produced by a community of potters is greatly affected by the vessel shape layout type and design zones; different vessel shapes have different kinds of design variability. The puynu and yukupuynu shapes in the present study, for example, have less variability in slip and design layout than the tachu and plato. In contrast, the plato and tachu have less variability in the number of designs than those designs used on puynu and yukupuynu. Similarly, there is less variability in the motif and band symmetry on the puynu and yukupuynu than the plato. Thus, the use of pottery design to reconstruct ancient patterns of social interaction must be done within the confines of particular vessel shapes. Using decorative and spatial units that cross-cut vessel shapes may give behaviorally spurious results.

This study also suggests that the community of potters has definite etic behavioral correlates in ceramic design that can be ascertained apart from emic design data. These design correlates are probably the product of consistent long-term interaction patterns in the community. Thus, if archaeologists are going to infer the social patterns of ancient communities from ceramic design then they must look to the patterns of social interaction and their etic design correlate that can be studied archaeologically rather than ideal patterns on social structure. While it would be expected that these design correlates may reflect corporate groups, such as kin groups or clan groups, it is quite possible that these interaction patterns in other societies may not reflect these social structural groupings.

Finally, this approach to ceramic design has great potential for the study of ancient groups of interacting potters. By controlling the variables of space and time in an archaeological context, it is possible to analyze a particular archaeological assemblage using the approach presented here. If one finds consistency in the high frequency of slip and paint combinations, types of design layout, use of designs in specific zones on these layouts, and use of symmetry types in these zones, it is

147

possible to infer that a particular community of potters produced these design characteristics. A similar approach focusing on symmetry has already been effectively utilized by Washburn (1977a, 1977b) and Zaslow and Dittert (1977). Thus, the use of symmetry in design analysis suggests that at least symmetry analysis is universal enough to serve as the basis of a design theory for inferring ancient social groups and their patterns of social interaction.

ACKNOWLEDGMENTS

This research was supported by a National Defense Foreign Language Fellowship and the Department of Anthropology of the University of Illinois, Urbana. The present manuscript is an extensively revised and condensed version of my Ph.D. dissertation (Arnold 1970). The raw data for this study can be found in the appendices of that report. I am especially grateful to R.T. Zuidema and D.W. Lathrap for their guidance, encouragement, and support which made this study possible. William P. Mitchell generously shared his facilities with me in Quinua. The Department of Sociology and Anthropology of Wheaton College, the Wheaton Alumni Faculty Development Fund, and a Wheaton Alumni Association grant all provided support for the preparation of the present manuscript. Rich Nickel made the drawings, and Greg Dolezal and Pauline Roelofs provided typing assistance.

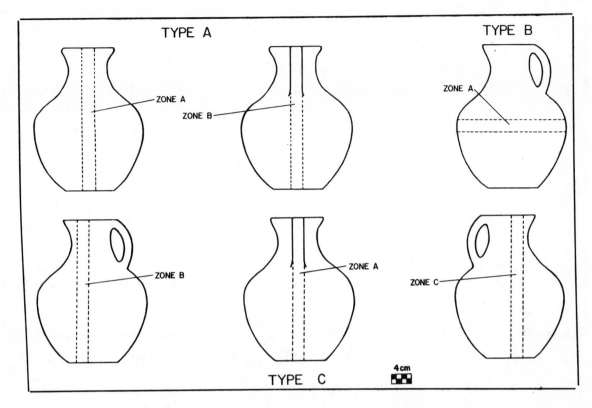

Figure 1. Design layouts for the <u>tachu</u>.

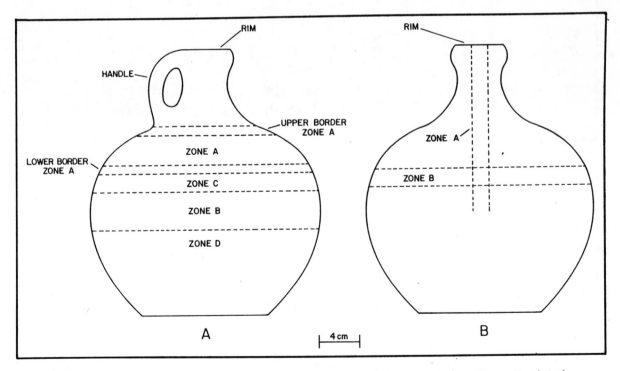

Figure 2. Design layouts for the <u>yukupuynu</u> (Type A left; Type B right).

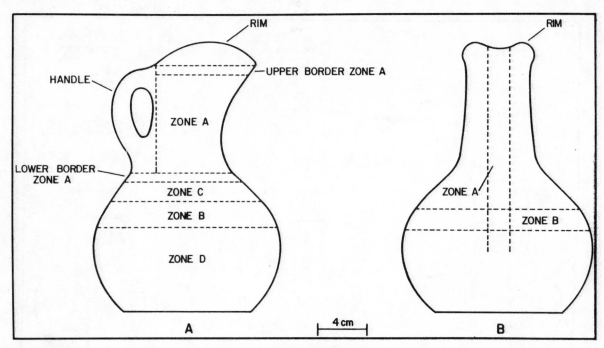

Figure 3. Design layouts for the puynu (Type A left; Type B right).

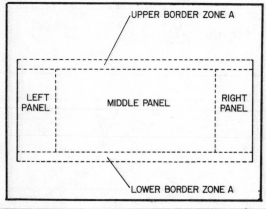

Figure 4.
Arrangement of vertical panels in Zone A of puynu layout Type A.

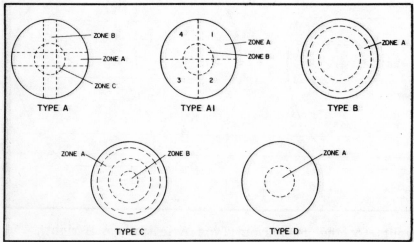

Figure 5.
Design layouts for the plato.

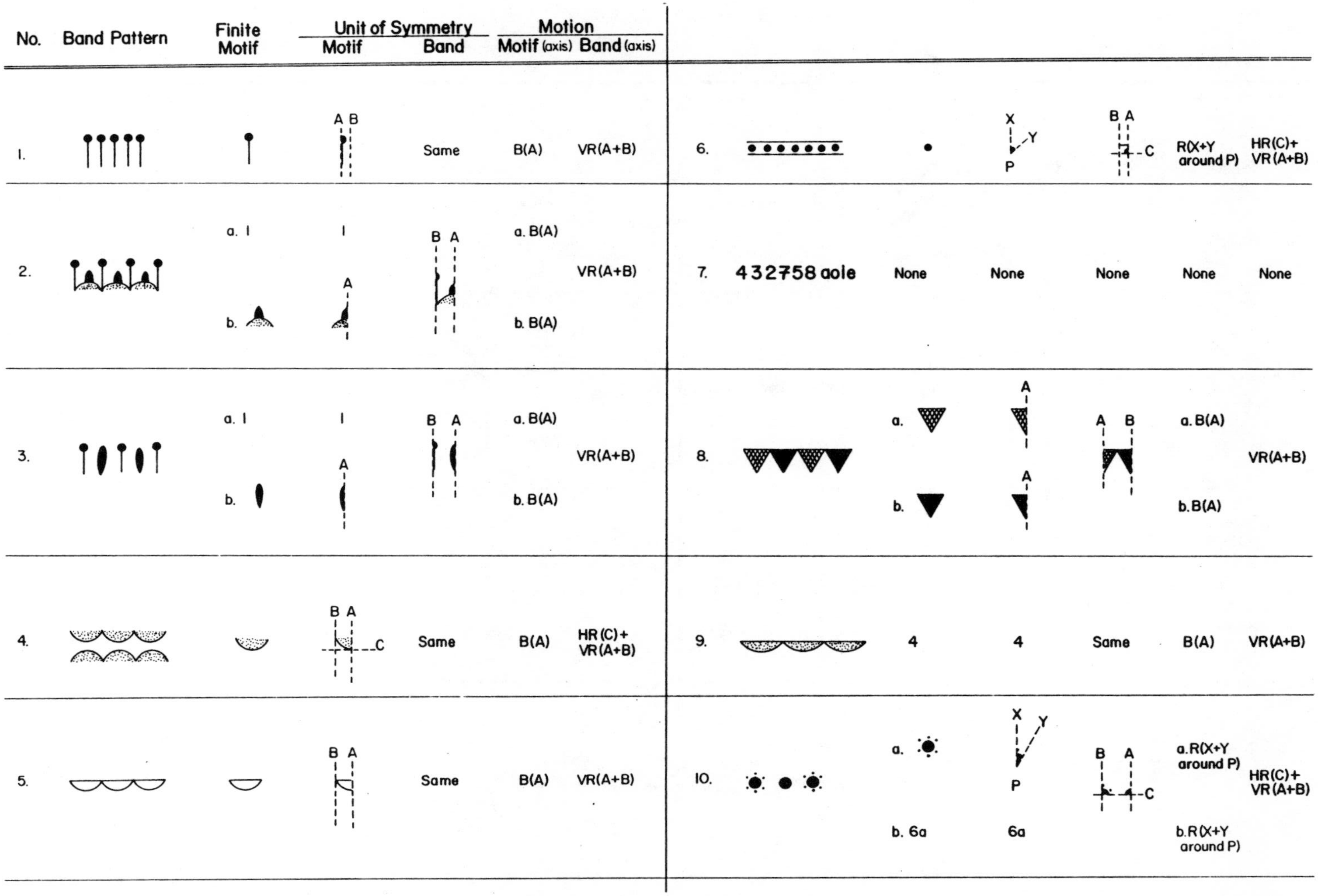

Figure 6. Symmetry of Quinua designs showing fundamental units and motions of finite motifs and band patterns. Motif symmetry types are bilateral (B), radial (R), and rotational (Ro). Band symmetry types are vertical reflection (VR), horizontal reflection (HR), translation (T), bifold rotation (BR), and slide reflection (SR). Letters in parentheses in symmetry columns refer to axes and points at which units of symmetry in the previous columns are repeated. Bands of solid color and straight or wavy lines were not included in this analysis.

Top row (16–20):

16.
a.   b. 6   6
R(X+Y around P)   R(X+Y around P)
HR(C)+ VR(A+B)

17.
a.   b.
a. B(A)   b. B(A)
VR(A+B)

18.
a. 10a   b. 6
10a   6
a. R(X+Y around P)   b. R(X+Y around P)
HR(C)+ VR(A+B)

19.
10a   10a
R(X+Y around P)
HR(C)+ VR(A+B)

20. None
None   None
B(A)
None

Bottom row (11–15):

11.
a. 10a   10a   3b, but on oblique axis
b. Same as 3b, but smaller
a. R(X+Y around P)   b. B(A)
T(A to B)

12.
None   None
None
HR(C)+ T(A to B)

13. None
None   None
Ro(P)
None

14.
a. 11b, but outline only   11b
b. 10a   10a
B(A)   R(X+Y around P)
BR(A+B)

15.
None   None
None
BR(P)+ VR(A+B)

21. None | None | None | B(A) | None

22. None | None | None | B(A) | None

23. None | None | None | B(A) | None

24. 6a | 6a | B A / C | R(X+Y around P) | HR(C)+ VR(A+B)

25. X Y P | B A / C | R(X+Y around P) | HR(C)+ VR(A+B)

26. None | X Y P | None | R(X+Y around P) | None

27. None | IIb | IIb | C B A — B(A) | SR(A to B along C)

28. None | None | None | None | None

29. None | None | None | None | None

30. None | IIb | IIb | A B C — B(A) | SR(A to B along C)

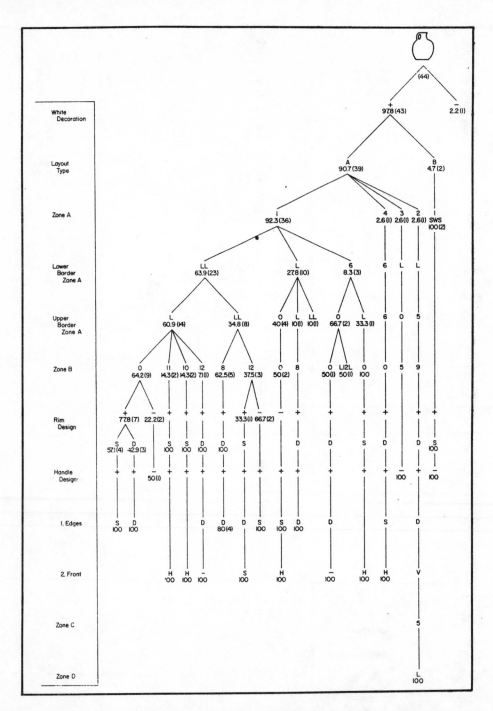

Figure 7. Interrelationship of patterns of design space and motifs for the yukupuynu. At any horizontal level, the symbol on the top line refers to the design in the design space on the left of the diagram, and to the repertoire of designs of Figure 6. The exceptions are single lines (L) or double lines (LL), solid color bands (S), or a band consisting of two parallel lines (SWS). On the second line, the first number refers to the percentage of items of the previous node on the diagram that have a particular design; the number in parenthesis refers to the actual number of vessels. Differences in figures result from missing data.

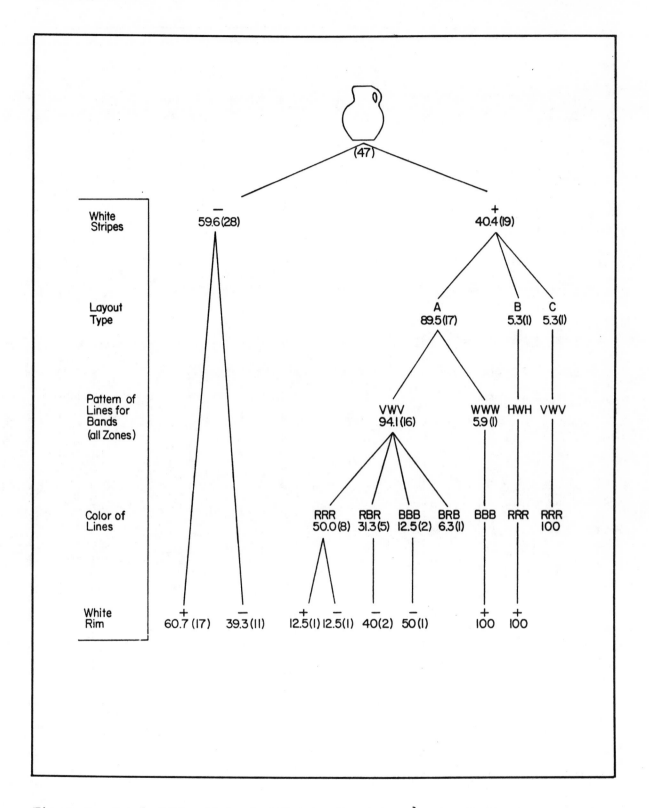

Figure 8. Interrelationships of patterns of design space and motifs for the tachu. See caption for Figure 7 for explanation.

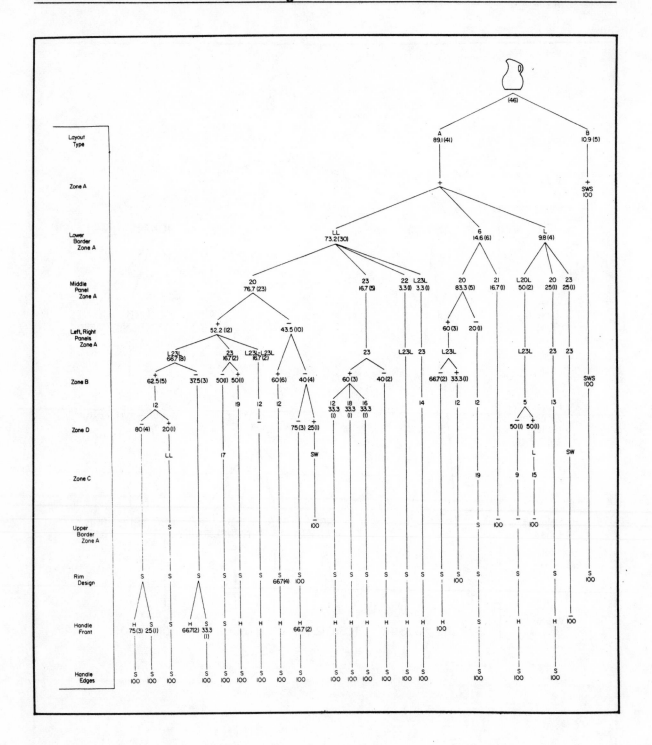

Figure 9. Interrelationships of patterns of design space and motifs for the _puynu_. See caption for Figure 7 for explanation.

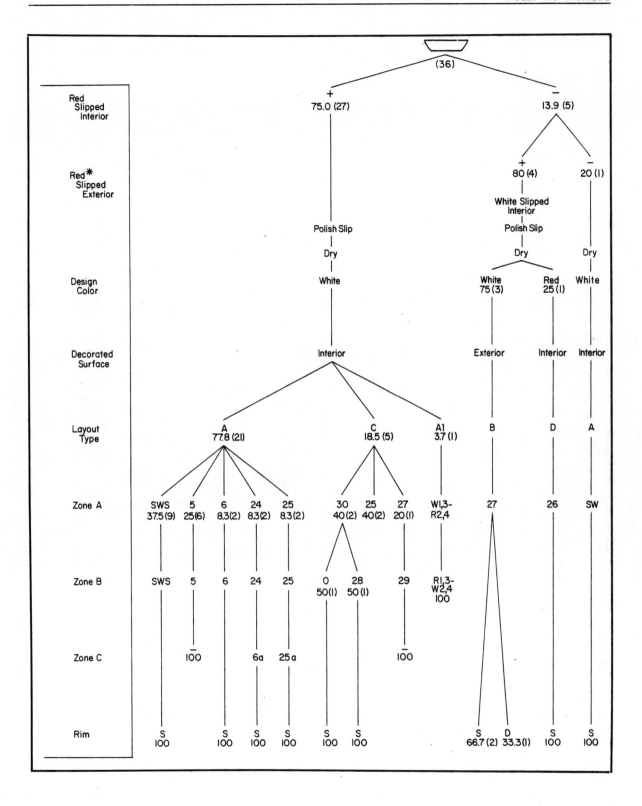

Figure 10. Interrelationships of patterns of design space and motifs for the plato. See caption for Figure 7 for explanation.

157

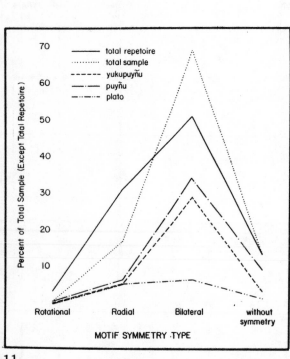

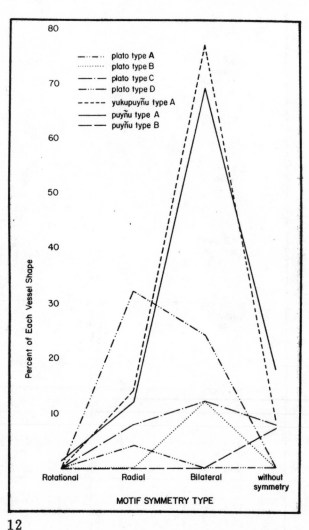

11   12

Figure 11. Percentages of each motif symmetry type in the total sample, each type in the total repertoire of designs, of the total sample of each motify symmetry type on each vessel shape (see Table 1). The total number of motifs in Figure 6 = 100%. Reprinted from Dorothy K. Washburn, editor, Structure and Cognition in Art, by permission of Cambridge University Press.

Figure 12. Percentage of each type of band symmetry (HR = horizontal reflection, VR = vertical reflection, SR = side reflection, BR = bifold rotation, T = translation) in the total sample, including percentage of each type in the total repertoire of the designs and percentage of the total sample of each band symmetry type found on each vessel shape (see Table 2). 100% equals the total number of band patterns in Figure 6. Reprinted from Dorothy K. Washburn, editor, Structure and Cognition in Art, by permission of Cambridge University Press.

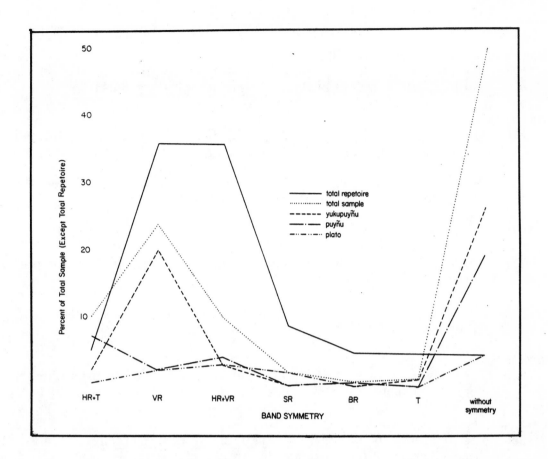

Figure 13.   Frequency of each motif symmetry type found on the layout type of each vessel shape.   Total motifs used on each vessel shape = 100%.   See Table 1.

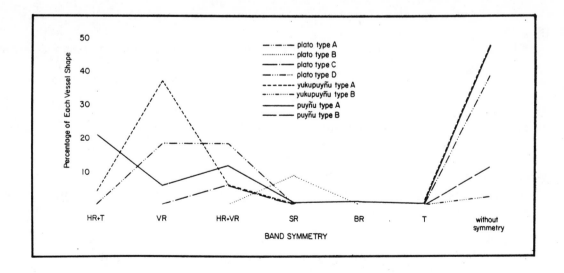

Figure 14.   Percent of each type of band symmetry found on the design layout of each vessel shape.   The total bands used on vessel shape = 100%.

REFERENCES

Allan, L. and J.B. Richardson III
   1971   The reconstruction of kinship from archaeological data: the concepts, the methods, and the feasibility. American Antiquity 36:41–53.

Arnold, D.E.
   1970   The Emics of Pottery Design from Quinua, Peru.   Unpublished Ph.D. dissertation, Department of Anthropology, University of Illinois, Urbana.

   1972a Mineralogical analyses of ceramic materials from Quinua, Department of Ayacucho, Peru. Archaeometry 14:93–101.

   1972b Native pottery-making in Quinua, Peru. Anthropos 67:858–872.

   1975a Ceramic ecology in the Ayacucho Basin, Peru: implications for prehistory. Current Anthropology 16:185–203.

   1975b Discussion and criticism: reply to Haaland and Browman.   Current Anthropology 16:637–640.

Bunzel, R.L.
   1929   The Pueblo pottery: a study of creative imagination in primitive art. New York: Columbia University Press.

Deetz, J.
   1965   The Dynamics of Stylistic Change in Arikara Ceramics.   University of Illinois Press: Illinois Studies in Anthropology no. 4

Hardin, M.F.
   1970   Design structure and social interaction: archaeological implications of an ethnographic analysis. American Antiquity 35:332–343.

Hill, J.N.
   1970   Broken K Pueblo: prehistoric social organization in American Southwest. Anthropological Papers of the University of Arizona no. 18. Tuscon: The University of Arizona Press.

Lathrap, D.W.
   1962   Yarinacocha: Excavations in the Peruvian Montana. Unpublished Ph.D. dissertation, Department of Anthropology, Harvard University.

Longacre, W.A.
   1970   Archaeology as anthropology: a case study. Anthropological Papers of the University of Arizona no. 17. Tuscon: The University of Arizona Press.

Mitchell, W.P.
   1976   Irrigation and community in the central Peruvian highlands. American Anthropologist 78:25–44.

Murdock, G.P.
   1949   Social Structure.   New York: The MacMillian Co.

Roe, P.G.
   1980   Art and residence among the Shipibo indians of Peru: a study in microacculturation.   American Anthropologist 82:42-71.

Rowe, J.H.
   1959   Archaeological dating and cultural process.   Southwestern Journal of Anthropology 15:317-324.

Shepard, A.O.
   1948   The symmetry of abstract design with special reference to ceramic decoration.   Contributions to American Anthropology and History no. 47, Washington: Carnegie Institution of Washington

   1956   Ceramics for the Archaeologist.   Carnegie Institution of Washington, Publication 609.   Washington.

Stanislawski, M.B.
   1977   Ethnoarchaeology of Hopi and Hopi-Tewa pottery-making: styles of learning. In, Experimental Archaeology, D. Ingersoll, J.E. Yellen, and W. MacDonald, eds.   Pp. 378-408.   New York: Columbia University Press.

   1978   If pots were mortal.   In, Explorations in Ethnoarchaeology, R.A. Gould, ed.   Pp. 201-277.   Albuquerque: University of New Mexico Press.

Stanislawski, M.B. and B.B. Stanislawski
   1978   Hopi and Hopi-Tewa ceramic tradition networks.   In, The Spatial Organization of Culture, I. Hodder, ed.   Pp. 61-76.   London: Gerald Duckworth and Co. Ltd.

Washburn, D.
   1977a A symmetry classification of Pueblo Ceramic designs.   In, Discovering Past Behavior: Experiments in the Archaeology of the American Southwest, P. Grebinger, ed.   Pp. 101-121.   New York: Gordon and Breach.

   1977b A symmetry analysis of upper Gila area ceramic design.   Papers of the Peabody Museum of Archaeology and Ethnology, Harvard University, Vol. 68.

Zaslow, B.
   1977   A guide to analyzing prehistoric ceramic decorations by symmetry and pattern mathematics.   In, Pattern Mathematics and Archaeology, G.A. Clark, ed.   Arizona State University Anthropological Research Papers no. 2.   Tempe.

Zaslow, B. and A.E. Dittert, Jr.
   1977   The pattern technology of the Hohokam.   In, Pattern Mathematics and Archaeology, G.A. Clark, ed.   Arizona State University anthropological research papers no. 2.   Tempe.

PART III

Technological Analysis of Pottery

Part III

The papers in Part III of <u>Pots and Potters</u> center on an advancing field in ceramic studies, that of technological analysis. Technological analysis refers to the characterization and description of pottery by means of precise, objective, and replicable standards. It focuses on the composition and characteristics of the clay body (paste) and decorative substances, and on recovering information bearing on the manufacture of the vessel (firing temperature, use of molds, etc.).

Technological studies have a number of significant advantages in the context of contemporary research interests in archaeology. Much of the ceramic material passing through archaeologists' hands is in the form of sherds, rather than whole vessels. Although a lot of information about the pot is incompletely known from fragments (e.g., form, volume, design structure), paste composition can be studied in even the tiniest sherds. Paste study allows a broader basis for comparison through time and through the rigors of differential preservation and, with the analytical methods currently available, permits more objective detailed quantitative comparison than do many other approaches. In addition, study of paste composition of archaeological sherds can form a data corpus for comparison with local ceramic resources—clay and tempers—and with the products of contemporary potters, should they live in the area, facilitating the extension of the ethnographic present back into the ethnohistoric and/or archaeological past.

Technological studies thus accommodate current methodological and theoretical trends in archaeology focusing on regional and ecological analyses, and study of techno-environmental variables. The advantages of technological analyses can easily be seen to satisfy the need for more comparable units of analysis between ethnographic and archaeological studies, and are useful adjuncts to ethnoarchaeological studies.

The only problem may be that of adequately refining anthropological concepts to take advantage of the technological precision now available to archaeologists.

Technological studies, in terms of microscopic or chemical analyses of pottery, are not new; indeed, their beginnings can be traced back to the late 1800s. At the 5th International Congress of Americanists meeting in 1883, Anatole Bamps discussed the value of microscopic studies of pottery, summarizing and criticizing some earlier work (1895). Among the important observations in this survey was reference to an earlier study demonstrating that red and black "layers" in the same sherd represented incomplete oxidation in firing, rather than "sandwiching" of different clays. Bamps also suggested that microscopic study could be important in discovering the manufacturing centers of pottery with wide geographic distributions, and pointed out that chemical analyses of pottery should be accompanied by mineralogical examination too. The first study to use petrographic thin sections of pottery was Nordenskiold's examination of Mesa Verde (Colorado) sherds in 1893, which included as well a consideration of possible sources of locally available clay and temper. Chemical analyses of pottery go back earlier, to analyses of the composition of pottery from Nineveh in the 1850s (which was the focus of Bamps' later criticism), and later chemical study of some Athenian pottery, published in 1895 (Richards 1895).

It was not until the development of X-ray diffraction analysis and electron microscopes in the 1920s that it was realized that clays were minerals, that is, crystalline rather than amorphous solids. This discovery led to greater understanding of the formation, occurrence, and properties of these materials, and their relevance to aboriginal potters and pottery.

Ceramic technological studies of archaeological pottery began to achieve importance in the late 1930s, when the two major researchers in the field began work. Anna O. Shepard concentrated principally on pottery of the Southwestern United States and Mesoamerica; her technological studies of the pottery of Pecos (1936), RioGrande glaze paint ware (1942), and Plumbate ware (1948) are monuments to the visionary accomplishments of this chemist who was so easily able to integrate technological data into the research problems of archaeologists. The other giant of ceramic technological analysis is, of course, F.R. Matson, whose contributions to the field of ceramic technology, particularly in the Old World, have been cited repeatedly throughout this volume. Additional mention must be made here of his Seleucia restudy (1971), however, which is one of the most thorough examinations of the variables and problems involved in assessing firing temperatures of ancient pottery.

Unfortunately, many of the early technological studies of pottery were undertaken with little mutual understanding between archaeologist and technical specialist, and the analysis itself was often published only as an appendix buried at the end of a report, to be subsequently ignored. It will always be necessary for both archaeologists and technical specialists to bear in mind the observations of Thompson drawn from his study of modern Yucatecan Maya pottery-making (1958:6-7):

> Although a correlation between the artifact type and various cultural generalizations is the ultimate goal of an archaeological reconstruction, the first inferences must be made on technological generalizations. The material bias of the basic archaeological

evidence dictates this technological beginning of the inferential construct. The technical and ecological factors which condition the properties, source, and availability of raw materials define a specific range of possibilities for the manufacture of any class of artifacts. . . . The significance of much technological information is often not readily apparent. Whenever an archaeologist receives technical or noncultural information from another discipline, he accepts the responsibility for identifying and exposing its interpretive significance. . . . The significance . . . is obscured unless the technological data are rephrased to emphasize some use which man makes of this . . . property. This shift of emphasis [creates] a technicultural combination—technical data in a cultural frame of reference. . . . This transition from a technological to a cultural orientation is a fundamental step in archaeological inference because it establishes a cultural context. . . .

In recent years technological analyses have become increasingly important, in large part because of changes in the theory and goals of archaeology. These changes have resulted in a need and desire to obtain more and different kinds of information from pottery, information that cannot be supplied by traditional qualitative or typological studies. Because they deal with quantitative measurements from instrumental analyses and multivariate statistics, these techniques might almost better be termed ceramic "technometry," reserving ceramic "technology" for the often-less-precisely-quantitative experimentation with clays and manufacturing methods that were discussed under experimental archaeology.

Broadly speaking, the kinds of data yielded by technometric and technological analyses fall into two areas of application: characterization studies and provenience studies. Characterization studies provide the foundation, allowing precise quantitative description of chemical (major, minor, and trace) and mineralogical composition of ceramic pastes and pigments. Such characterization of "types" or of decorative styles allows assessment of variability in composition, which may suggest the existence of single or multiple loci of manufacture, imitations, forgeries, and developments in the history of manufacturing technology. Provenience studies are usually done after characterization of not only the vessels in question but also of locally occurring ceramic resources. Intercomparison of the data sets permits some interpretations as to local manufacture vs. trade (i.e., provenience) of the objects.

The techniques themselves focus on analysis of mineralogical, chemical, and structural properties of a ceramic body, all of which are complementary, as Bamps observed. Among the techniques or instruments that are frequently employed in mineralogical analysis of clays and/or inclusions are petrography (for inclusions), X-ray diffraction and differential thermal analysis (clays and inclusions), and electron microscopy (clays and inclusions). Investigations of the chemical composition of ceramics include neutron activation analysis, X-ray fluorescence, atomic absorption, optical emission spectrometry, and electron microprobe analysis. Structural properties, including particle size, shape, and orientation, may be investigated through binocular or petrographic microscopy and scanning electron microscopy for finer resolution and higher magnification. Discussion of each of these methods is beyond the scope of this volume; the reader is referred to Tite (1972), Levey (1967), Carter (1978), Aitken

(1974), Shepard (1971), and references contained therein for more complete explanations.

The development and wider understanding of the application of these techniques have had a far-reaching impact in ceramic studies. Aside from the fact that many archaeologists now know far more about physics, chemistry, and statistics than was necessary in the past, the archaeological research problems and published literature are increasingly reflecting this new emphasis. No longer are technological reports simply buried at the end of reports; now there are books (e.g., Tite 1972; Aitken 1974) and journals (e.g., Archaeometry, Journal of Archaeological Science) dealing with technical analyses of archaeological materials. A greater variety of research problems—in ancient trade and production, history of technology, detection of forgeries—is being attacked with greater precision and gratifying success. Continuing methodological specialization among archaeologists is also reflective of the increasing importance of technometric analyses, as archaeologists with extensive training in chemistry and physics are able to work closely with physical scientists in productive analyses of archaeological materials.

Part III of Pots and Potters, then, reflects the importance of this area of ceramic research. The first two papers survey some of the past applications of technological analysis, and together provide an appropriate introduction for the more technical case studies which follow. Kingery's paper is an evolutionary overview of some of the interactions between technological developments and the demand for such technology in prehistoric societies. His examples, drawn largely from the Near East, include ceramic materials other than pottery, for example, pigments, plasters, and refractory materials, and he relates their development to contemporaneous changes in other technologies. The paper by Stross and Asaro reviews some instructive case studies in which technological analyses were applied to problems of provenience, history of technology, and detection of forgeries. The authors' discussions elaborate on the research problems and the steps involved in their solution, amply illustrating the benefits of close cooperation between chemical and archaeological studies.

The Steinberg and Kamilli paper makes a strong methodological point in the many-faceted area of provenience studies: that is, a combination of methods and techniques is more fruitful than a single technique in investigating a problem. Painted Halaf pottery from Mesopotamia shows a great deal of similarity from site to site over a broad area, leading to the suggestion that it was either distributed from a single center of manufacture or that itinerant potters made it. A combination of petrographic, scanning electron microscope, and microprobe analyses in investigation of the composition and texture of pastes and paints on the Halaf wares led to rejection of the first hypothesis, since pastes vary locally. However, paints share wide conformity to certain "rules," suggesting a distinctive shared technological tradition.

"Thin Orange" pottery, the subject of Kolb's paper, is associated with the large prehistoric city of Teotihuacan, in Central Mexico. Thin Orange was an important trade ware, found widely throughout Mesoamerica, but its location of manufacture was uncertain. Kolb synthesizes the results of numerous technological studies, primarily petrography and neutron activation analysis, which show that the pottery was not produced at Teotihuacan, though merchants from that site probably controlled its distribution. An origin of manufacture south of the Basin of Mexico is suggested, with only late imitations being made locally at Teotihuacan, and perhaps elsewhere.

A similar proveniencing objective is at the core of the paper by Kaplan, Harbottle, and Sayre, treating Tell el Yahudiyeh ware. Traditionally associated with the Hyksos, the ware was widely traded and has been found from Cyprus through the Levant and into Egypt and Nubia. Statistical similarity groupings established a typology of vessel forms which, together with their geographic distribution, suggest two areas of manufacture, one in the Levant and one in the Nile Valley. The products of each region showed differences in inclusions, manufacturing technique, and firing, and called into question the traditional identification of this ware with the Hyksos invasions and/or trade control in Egypt and elsewhere in the Near East.

REFERENCES

Aitken, M.J.
  1974   Physics and Archaeology. 2nd ed. Oxford: Clarendon Press.

Bamps, A.
  1895   La ceramique americaine au point de vue des elements constitutifs de sa pate et de sa fabrication. Ve Int. Congres des Americanistes. Copenhagen.

Carter, G.
  1978   Proceedings of the Annual Conference on Archaeological Chemistry. American Chemical Society, Archaeological Chemistry Division.

Levey, M. (ed.)
  1967   Archaeological Chemistry. Philadelphia.

Matson, F.R.
  1971   A study of temperatures used in firing ancient Mesopotamian pottery. In, Science and Archaeology, R. Brill, ed. Pp. 65-79. Cambridge: M.I.T. Press.

Richards, T.W.
  1895   The composition of Athenian pottery. Journal of the American Chemical Society 17:152-153.

Shepard, A.O.
  1936   Technology of Pecos Pottery. In, The Pottery of Pecos, Vol. II, A.V. Kidder and A.O. Shepard, eds. Papers of the Phillips Academy Southwestern Expedition 7:389-587. Andover.

  1942   Rio Grande Glaze Paint Ware, A Study Illustrating the Place of Ceramic Technological Analysis in Archaeological Research. Carnegie Institution of Washington, Pub. 526, Contribution 39. Washington, D.C.

  1948   Plumbate, A Mesoamerican Trade Ware. Carnegie Institution of Washington Pub. 573. Washington, D.C.

  1971   Ceramics for the Archaeologist. Carnegie Institution of Washington Pub. 609. Washington, D.C.

Thompson, R.H.
    1958   Modern Yucatecan Maya Pottery Making. Memoir No. 15, Society for American Archaeology. American Antiquity Vol. 23, part 2.

Tite, M.S.
    1972   Methods of Physical Examination in Archaeology. London: Seminar Press.

Chapter 11

Interactions of Ceramic Technology with Society

W. David Kingery

As Matson (1965:204) suggested some time ago, the study of ceramics, "in ecological terms, can be approached through a consideration of the needs of the people living in the region. . . .," and any study of ceramics which does not provide a better understanding of the people who make and use them is of pretty limited value. About this same time, I was interested in the relationship between modern society, ceramic science and technological developments. I concluded that "almost with the force of law, the level of technology always rises to meet the market for technology. When . . . a market for technology is established and recognized and technological innovations are rewarded, technological developments proceed at a rapid rate. . . ." (Kingery 1966).

Here, I should like to bring together these two streams of thought, take an explicitly scientific point of view, and propose a conjecture, an hypothesis if you like: "Within the internal limitations of the available materials, the level of ceramic technology rises to the level for which there is a well-perceived market within society." If this hypothesis is true, then various subsidiary conjectures might be developed and tested which could extend and perhaps quantify some particular aspects. The hypothesis is testable in that over a very long history one can evaluate the changing requirements for ceramic materials which have accompanied various social and cultural changes. In many ways, ceramics are an optimal medium for this purpose in that we know of no example in which the development of a new ceramic material or technique has been sufficiently decisive that it has led to substantial changes in society and culture, although the local availability of particular materials and techniques can certainly affect trade patterns. That is, the development of ceramic techniques and materials is always a consequence of societal change rather than a cause.   Although ceramics are often used to characterize an archaeological stratum or epoch, ceramics are never more than a minor characteristic of any culture.

We shall define ceramics as the art and technology which consists of shaping and manufacturing products made from earthy materials, and the application of heat to these materials to form useful products.   Defined in this manner, the first use of ceramics may have been by Palaeolithic hunters and gatherers, cave dwellers, responding to aesthetic and perhaps religious requirements which led to wall paintings and personal decoration.   The most common pigments were prepared by grinding manganese dioxide, ochre and other iron-containing materials.   Primitive New Guinea tribes today calcine sea shells, which have the same chemical composition as limestone, to form a fine-particle size white material for use as a pigment (J.J. Laurent, personal communication, 1971), while Aborginal Australians mine ochre and also collect and use a special mineral, huntite, as a white pigment (Clarke 1976).

In our laboratory, we are commencing to investigate the suggested hypothesis that Palaeolithic cave dwellers may have searched out and specially treated earthy materials to form improved pigments (and would welcome receiving information from readers on this subject).   In any event, necessary earthy pigments were used and did contribute to early development of civilization.

The demand for substantial amounts of manufactured ceramics first came with the cultural revolution which led to permanent settlements and the development of agriculture.   In the period 8000 to 7000 B.C., permanent settlements were developed in the Near East, there was a need for developing materials for architectural purposes, and suitable materials were found.   Archaeologists and the archaeological literature are often somewhat lax in distinguishing various sorts of building materials and plasters, but in the Near East clay was first used for architectural purposes, sometimes mixed with grass to form a composite material having the necessary tensile strength (Schmandt-Besserat 1977a, 1977b).   In addition to clay or mud plaster, gypsum plasters were also used that can be formed at low temperatures, but which are still moderately soluble and soft.   Lime plaster is much more durable, hard, and insoluble and has superior properties, but it requires temperatures of above 850°C to be sustained for several hours during preparation.   Gypsum plaster and lime plaster share the characteristic that after forming and use they have exactly the same chemical composition as the rocks from which they are formed.   In addition, they often contain one another as impurities, so that chemical analysis cannot distinguish between the plaster product and the chemically identical rock; simple field tests may also be misleading.

One of the modern tools of materials science is the use of high-magnification electron microscopes to characterize the structure of materials.   The traditional ceramic method has been to examine thin slices of the material optically, while the traditional metallurgical method has been to examine polished surfaces.   However, the structure of a material can also be evaluated by fracturing a surface, which is the method used for all of our illustrations (Figure 1) (Kingery 1975; Gourdin and Kingery 1975).   If we examine a sample of gypsum rock as shown in Figure 2, we find blocky grains of gypsum which are cemented or compressed together to form a hard structure.   When this material is heated it decomposes.   Then, when mixed with water to form a plaster, it sets and takes on a structure with a typical platey or acicular appearance as illustrated in Figure 3.   Even though the chemistry is identical, the microstructures clearly distinguish gypsum plaster from gypsum rock. A sample from Anau in south Turkistan (Figure 4) which was prepared about 6000 B.C. has been shown to be a gypsum plaster (Gourdin and Kingery 1975). This was a common building material from the very beginning of permanent settlement and remains so today.

A limestone rock is very similar in appearance to the gypsum rock illustrated in Figure 1. Lime plasters are made by decomposing the rock at high temperatures. When mixed with water and used as a plaster, a very different structure is formed, as shown in Figure 5, which is a modern (ca. 1895) plaster from Cambridge, Massachusetts. It has a very fine particle size consisting of little balls of calcium carbonate, and is very similar to the microstructure of a plaster used at Jericho about 6000 B.C. (Figure 6), during what is usually referred to as the pre–pottery Neolithic Period.

There has been some discussion in the archaeological literature about the ease of making a bit of plaster without too much difficulty. However, we know the density of the material and, when we examine the size of ancient structures built from plaster, it is a simple matter to calculate the volume. We find that several tons of limestone had to be calcined at a high temperature for each one (Gourdin and Kingery 1975), and cannot imagine such quantities being prepared a few pounds at a time. Clearly, at the early stages of permanent settlements, there developed a technological capability for heating tons of materials to temperatures well above red heat, to about 850°C, at a time when substantial or extensive metallurgical and pottery production was unknown. Indeed, the rapid appearance of fired pottery on the archaeological scene may well be explained on the basis that the capability for heating substantial amounts of material to high temperatures was already known as one of the early technological achievements in the development of permanent settlements.

That is, from the time of the earliest market for architectural materials, there rapidly developed a capability for high-temperature processing of tons of raw material in what may be thought of as one of the first manufacturing efforts. Our conjecture, then, seems a bit more plausible. Almost as soon as the cultural demand for permanent architectural materials was created and perceived, construction materials roughly equivalent to those now in use were developed and applied.

Perhaps the next major cultural development was the rise of large urban centers. There resulted a perceived need for specialized crafts, for luxury items, and a market for mass production. From Tepe Yahya in Iran we find one result, shown in Figure 7; mass production of ceramics was done by development of the fast wheel throwing process at just this time. This undecorated clay cup is clearly thrown on a fast wheel and represents the development of a new technological process that met new demands for increased production rates. Henceforth, the ubiquitous potter's wheel would be found in all urban centers.

At the same time, the market for metallurgical products increased to such an extent that smelting ores became a skilled craft necessary to produce the amounts of material required by a more complex urban civilization with more than a subsistence economy. One of the restrictions hampering this development in the Near East is the scarcity of suitable refractory clays, which are commonplace in northern Europe and China but uncommon in the calcareous environment of the Near East. The solution found for this was to mix sandstone with a little clay to prepare a special composition having the necessary refractory capabilities.

One example of this technical development is a tuyere nozzle from an Egyptian smelting site in the Sinai from about 1500 B.C. (Figure 8), when a substantial amount of metal production was required (Rothenberg 1970; see also Kingery and Gourdin 1976). Lumps of sandstone were mixed with clay and used as coating material to allow multiple use of the tuyere. (The tuyere itself was necessary to provide air to the reaction vessel to obtain temperatures necessary for the metallurgical process.) These quite different observations of ceramic developments in the field of mass production requirements and refractory requirements (both of which are still in use today) occurred very soon after the need was recognized—adding to the plausibility of our conjecture.

By A.D. 1000 or so there was a substantial trade from China to the West, where there was a market for Chinese porcelain, but the Chinese method of manufacture was unknown and remained so for many centuries. The China clay and China stone that were essential ingredients were not available in the Near East. This led to much experimentation and the early development of an imitation material which would come to be called "soft-paste porcelain." A sample from Iran of the 12th century is an example. In Figure 9 we see a sherd of material of light color with a light blue cobalt glaze, in which the microstructure is very uniform. The material contains a good deal of glass of uniform particle size which acts as a viscous glue to hold the material together in the same way that later compositions were made (perhaps the best known is that from Sevres in France). Here again, we find that once a market was recognized, within the limitations of available materials, technical solutions were quite actively and rapidly obtained.

In the 15th century, the widened communications networks resulting from printing and from geographical discoveries called for and led to many new requirements for ceramics in the Western world. The industrial and manufacturing revolution led to the need for substantial iron and steel production, which, in turn, required refractory materials capable of withstanding the higher temperature necessary for more rapid production. Refractories became a recognized speciality of ceramics. With steels available, the possibility of mass production required development of metal-working production lines which made essential the availability of abrasives, and fused silicon carbide and fused aluminum oxide became manufactured products of the ceramics industry. Similarly, revolutions in architecture, transportation, communications and computations systems, and even medicine have given rise to perceived needs and to new ceramics.

In both archaeological and historical contexts, the conjecture that the level of ceramic technology has rapidly risen to the level for which there is a perceived need seems highly plausible.

NOTE

[1] Abstracted in part from the 1978 Jacob Kurtz Memorial Lecture presented at the Technion, Haifa, Israel. The author also acknowledges the support of the M.I.T. Sloan Fund.

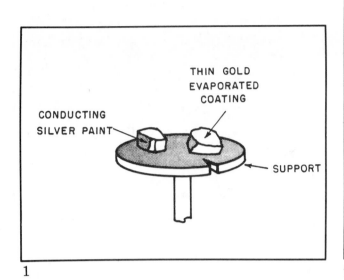

1

2

Figure 1. Samples embedded in silver paint and coated with a thin layer of evaporated gold. Notch in sample holder is for orientation.

Figure 2. Microstructure of a natural gypsum rock.

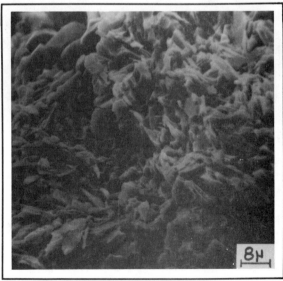

3

4

Figure 3. Microstructure of a "hard-burned" (3 hours at 450°C) and rehydrated gypsum plaster.

Figure 4. Microstructure of plaster from Anau, ca. 6000 B.C.

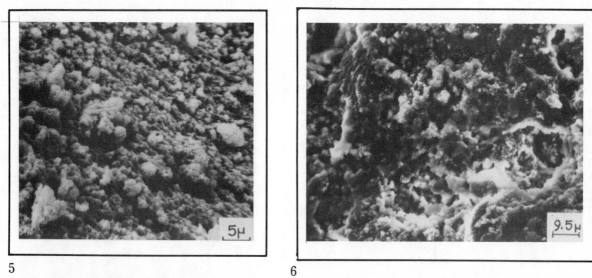

5   6

Figure 5.   Microstructure of a late 19th century plaster, showing the fine particle size of recarbonated lime.

Figure 6.   Microstructure of plaster from Jericho, ca. 6000 B.C.

7   8

Figure 7.   Cup thrown on potters wheel, from Tepe Yahya, ca. 3000-3500 B.C. (courtesy of C.C. Lamberg-Karlovsky, Peabody Museum, Harvard University).

Figure 8.   Cross section of tuyere nozzle from Sinai Site 350 illustrating clay-sandstone refractory composition (courtesy Beno Rothenberg).

Figure 9. (a) 12th century sample from Dvin, Iran, with (b) uniform microstructure which shows (c) bubbles and conchidal fracture of a glass-bonded ware.

REFERENCES

Clarke, J.
  1976 Two aboriginal rock art pigments from Western Australia: their properties, use, and durability. Studies in Conservation 21:134-142.

Gourdin, W.H. and W.D. Kingery
  1975 The beginnings of pyrotechnology: Neolithic and Egyptian lime plaster. Journal of Field Archaeology 2:133-150.

Kingery, W.D.
  1966 On the interaction between basic science and technological development in ceramics. Paper presented at the Tenth International Ceramic Congress, Stockholm, Sweden.

  1975 Observation of the microstructures of some Medieval ceramics with the scanning electron microscope. Paper presented at the Conference on the Application of the Physical Sciences to Medieval Ceramics, Lawrence Berkeley Laboratory, Berkeley, California.

Kingery, W.D. and W.H. Gourdin
  1976 Examination of furnace linings from Rothenberg Site #590 in Wadi Zaghra. Journal of Field Archaeology 3:351.

Matson, F.R.
  1965 Ceramic ecology: an approach to the study of the early cultures of the Near East. In, Ceramics and Man, F.R. Matson, ed. Pp. 202-217. Viking Fund Publication no. 41. Chicago: Aldine.

Rothenberg, B.
  1970 Palestine Exploration Quarterly (Jan-June):25.

Schmandt-Besserat, D.
  1977a The earliest uses of clay in Syria. Expedition 19:28.

  1977b The beginnings of the use of clay in Turkey. Anatolian Studies 27:133.

Chapter 12

Time's Wheel Runs Back or Stops:

Potter and Clay Endure

Fred Stross and Frank Asaro

The ability of clay to take on an endless variety of appearances is a challenging and attractive property for the ceramic artist, and a boon to the aesthete, whose mission it is to enjoy the product. It also poses a continuous challenge to one who desires to study and characterize a sherd, especially when it has been separated from its maker by space and time. The experienced eye often can tell us a great deal about the antecedents of the ware. However, in our tinkering with the structure of matter we have succeeded in making more penetrating eyes, eyes that go to the heart of things and that can perceive patterns of a different kind than those provided by the artist. Information on the pattern of the elemental make-up of the material with which we are dealing is highly diagnostic and is one of the most useful approaches to the problems in our studies.

The combination of precise analysis and typological-stylistic study, that is, the close association of the archaeologist with the chemist-physicist, has resulted in many new answers to old questions, and in many new questions no one thought to ask before. The methods developed or sharpened during the last few decades, which provide precise patterns of elemental composition, have enabled us to make a great leap forward, and here, as in other contexts, the cost can be staggering. But we will not dwell here on methodology, rather we shall look at a few examples of what has been done with these methods.

The Near Eastern pot has been boiling for as many millenia as history and tradition can account for; the eastern Mediterranean has been a crossroads for countless conquerors and migrations. The resulting complex trade patterns are well reflected in the pottery excavated in that region. Some pottery was widely traded, some is only found locally. Where did the widely distributed ware originate? Who were the originators, who importers, or imitators? Such questions have been vigorously debated by armies of scholars as they put together the pieces of this jigsaw puzzle by typological and stylistic comparison. A major contribution to this work was made by H.W. Catling of the Ashmolean Museum and by the forces of the Oxford Research Laboratory (Catling, Blin-Stoyle and Richards 1961) when they introduced elemental analysis by emission spectroscopy on a massive scale, and showed that this method could be used systematically and independently to determine provenience of pottery.

The development of gamma-ray solid-state detectors enabled neutron activation to yield a method for elemental analysis that can hardly be touched for sensitivity, accuracy, and general flexibility. This can, in propitious circumstances, provide a considerable degree of certainty in determining if a given sherd is locally made or imported, by comparing its composition with that of local pots of established pedigree, or that of local clay (Perlman and Asaro 1969; Perlman, Asaro, and Michel 1972).

CYPRIOTE BICHROME WARE

In the late twenties, a handsome, wheel-made type of pottery was found regularly by archaeologists in Cyprus, Palestine, and coastal Syria, and it became known as "Bichrome Ware." It was often embellished with birds or fish or goats or kine. It was dated to the middle of the 2nd millenium B.C. or earlier. At the time of the excavations there was a general belief that, at that period of the Late Bronze Age, use of the wheel in making pottery was not known, or at least not practiced, in Cyprus. The conclusion was that the ware originated on the eastern mainland and was imported into Cyprus. At least some major Cypriote styles, such as the White Painted Ware (of which the Bichrome Ware was later shown to be an outgrowth) and the Base Ring Ware seem indeed to be almost exclusively hand-made. These styles were earlier than, and contemporary with Bichrome, and hand-made examples persisted for a considerable time after the introduction of the wheel-made pottery. Whatever the genesis of the idea, signs that ceramic ware was turned on the wheel made it, in the eyes of many, automatically into an article of import, as far as Cyprus was concerned. However, some scholars did not share this opinion (e.g., Sjöqvist 1940:87-90).

In a chemical study at the Lawrence Berkeley Laboratory of some 1,500 Cypriote pottery sherds excavated in the Swedish Cyprus Expedition a marked similarity was found between Bichrome Ware and locally made pottery. This prompted an extensive chemical study (Artzy, Asaro, and Perlman 1973).

In such a project one tries, for each site relevant to a particular problem, to select a substantial number of sherds which reasonably might be expected to be of local manufacture, based on archaeological criteria. Ideally, the collection from each site will show chemical homogeneity and be different from all others tested. Fact obeys the ideal well enough at least to make this method workable. One can then compute the mean value for each chemical element found, and the standard deviation from the mean for the sherds in the group. The array of mean values and standard deviations for all the diagnostic elements becomes the chemical profile or fingerprint for the group. Examples of Bichrome Ware from primarily two sites were studied, Milia, in Cyprus, and Tel el Ajjul in what was then Palestine. The major portion of each group was chemically homogeneous to about 10 percent for

17 major, minor, and trace elements, and the means of those abundances differed on the average by less than 9 percent.

When compared with material of local derivation from several sites in Cyprus and Palestine, it was found that these two homogeneous groups matched local pottery from Cyprus closely, but were quite different from any of the Palestinian ware. Most of the remainder of the Milia and Tel el Ajjul assemblages showed appreciable differences for several elements, but fell into the general pattern characteristic of Cypriote origin. A number of these could actually be matched with local ware from other sites on Cyprus. Among the approximately 100 pieces analyzed, only six all from Ajjul were found to resemble (not match) Palestinian plain ware. It is noteworthy that these few pieces all are atypical in style and material of the bulk of Bichrome Ware. It may be rash to suggest that these might be local imitations of the popular Bichrome Ware, and the authors prefer to leave this question unresolved. But we may definitely conclude that the evidence is excellent that the Bichrome Ware originated in Cyprus and was exported from Cyprus, rather than the other way around. This then is an example where careful elemental analysis provided strong support for conclusions in a situation where typological evidence alone was ambiguous, if not outright misleading—a situation by no means unique.

TERRA SIGILLATA AND ATTIC FIGURED WARE

But chemistry can do more in the study of ancient pots than determine their composition. Theodor Schumann, for instance, a ceramic chemist, ventured into the colloid chemistry, thermal behavior, and oxidation-reduction reactions of clay and its components to solve his problem. Just before World War II he had become interested in the brilliant red color and the smooth lustrous surfaces of the Roman Terra Sigillata Ware, and the beautiful combination of matte red and glossy Black surface of Attic red- and black-figured vases (see Chapter 1, this volume), as had many archaeologists, artists, and ceramic chemists before him. Schumann reasoned that in view of the antiquity of the pieces they must have been made by relatively simple techniques, and he set about to duplicate them (1942).

Attacking the problem of the bright red gloss surfaces of the Terra Sigillata first, he considered the more obvious possibilities. They were: (1) polishing the surface (fired or unfired) of a sherd made from a clay similar to that used in making Terra Sigillata, (2) using a glaze, and (3) using an engobe. His experiments with polishing did not succeed in producing surfaces that looked anything like Terra Sigillata. Moreover, many Terra Sigillata pieces showed surfaces not accessible to polishing, which nevertheless showed the characteristic lustre. Glazes—siliceous fluxing agents typically contained alkali, borates, phosphates, lead or iron oxide—did not give the lustre of the Terra Sigillata or the black Attic surfaces, and they formed thicker layers than found on these types of ceramic. The same was true of engobes ("slips"), which are clay suspensions often used as a prime coat for glazes, or as modifiers for the surface of the clay body.

Careful analysis showed that the surfaces of both types of ware were essentially identical in composition with that of the body of the sherds; however, microscopic examination showed that the glossy surfaces incorporated particles of far smaller size than could be found in the body by inspecting breaks. Proceeding from this clue, Schumann made fine clay slips by allowing the clay to settle in water for long periods of time, and painting them on the dried form before firing, but without success.   He then prepared especially fine-particled slips by adding a peptizing (deflocculative) agent such as might have been accessible to the ceramicists in antiquity, i.e., potash, humus, blood, liquid manure, urine, or bile.   These slips could be applied to the clay body so as to give a layer only ten microns thick, and when fired, they produced a surface of the same lustrous red that was characteristic of the fine Roman Terra Sigillata ware.

This first success also proved to be an important stage in solving the mystery of the Attic red and black ware.   Early work had shown Schumann that the Attic ware resembled the Terra Sigillata in that there was no easily observable distinct layer over the body of the sherd, and that, within the limits of error of his analysis, the compositions of surface and body were identical.   This meant specifically that no manganese or cobalt could be detected in the black areas.   It is common practice today to produce black-colored ceramic surfaces by addition of oxides such as those mentioned.   The absence of any metals that would produce black color under ordinary firing conditions meant that the black on the Attic ware must be due to the black lower oxides of iron, Fe_3O_4 or FeO.

It was known that untreated clay rich in iron could be fired in an oxidizing atmosphere to produce the characteristic bright red color with a matt surface that we know from many examples in pottery, notably from bricks.   On firing in a reducing atmosphere, such as will exist when the supply of air to the kiln is curtailed, the sherd will turn black, and stay black if the ware is cooled under reducing conditions. However, it will turn red again if sufficient air is admitted while the temperature is still in the operating range (ca. 875°C).

With this information as a guide, and not without profiting from some lucky accidents, Schumann at last was able to reproduce also the distinctive black and red of the Attic ware.   He found that the same slip he used for producing the lustrous red of the Terra Sigillata ware could also serve to produce the fine black of the Attic vases.   He simply added a very small amount of alkali, which acted as a milk fluxing agent.   To produce the red and black surfaces of the Attic ware, Schumann finally arrived at the following procedure: the formed clay body is allowed to dry "leather-hard."   The areas meant to be black when finished are painted with the peptized, slightly alkaline slip.   Firing is begun with an oxidizing atmosphere--all surfaces of the ware turn bright red.   The reducing cycle is started; in antiquity this was done by adding green wood or wet brush to the fire--and the temperature of firing is raised.   The iron oxide is reduced to the black, lower oxides by the carbon monoxide generated, and the alkaline slip sinters just enough to block the pores of the painted surfaces.   The temperature then is slightly reduced, and the reoxidizing cycle is started by allowing air again to reach the ware freely.   The surfaces painted with the slip, however, are no longer permeable to the air, and remain black, and lustrous, while the other, unprotected surfaces are brought back to the original red color.   This procedure was entirely successful in reproducing the color and character of the Attic ware that had been the object of Schumann's study (see also Chapter 13, this volume).

Schumann's work was published in 1942, but did not come to the attention of the American audience until after the war.   In 1960 the suggestion was made (Noble

1960) to consider essential identity in the composition of surface and body as a criterion of authenticity for pottery of that type (at least for pieces purchased before publication of this article. . . .). The presence of common colorants such as manganese or cobalt in the black areas might be taken as evidence that the pieces were not of the true "Attic" type.

It is well known how Nobel "unmasked" the modern forged Etruscan Warrior pieces of the Metropolitan Museum—colossal examples of the red and black "Attic" technique—how Dietrich von Bothmer went to Rome, where he found the last surviving member of the creators of the Warriors, and how the latter signed a deposition describing the construction, and even contributed the missing thumb of the Big Warrior, some fired test pieces, and some unfired clay, which produced the same ceramic as the statuary under study. It is not unreasonable to suppose that the statute of limitations had run out when the "artist" confessed to his larcenous enterprises.

THERMOLUMINESCENCE

Another fine instrument for determining authenticity is that which measures the thermoluminescence (TL) of ancient sherds. This technique, like a fine violin, is capable of great performance in the hands of one who knows how, but can be highly disappointing when used by one who doesn't. It would be bringing owls to Athens to discuss the procedure here at length (see Aitken 1974), but a caveat or two, and an example or two may be in order.

The glow (below red heat) that one can observe on heating an ancient sherd is a function not only of the time passed since last firing (usually identical with that producing the ceramic), but also a number of other factors: the porosity, the water content of the ceramic, the radon (a radioactive disintegration product of radium) present, the nature of the soil or other substance in which the object had resided since its firing, and the intrinsic radiation susceptibility of the clay material resulting from its composition, including the size of the tiny quartz crystals it typically contains. If all these factors can be taken into account, it may be possible to make age determinations on a "typical" sample to ca. 10 percent of the age, or even better (Aitken and Allred 1972; Aitken 1976); however, more often than not, the material and the information will not be available and the error can be much greater. In any case, determinations should be made on at least half a dozen samples from each context for which a date is required.

The objectives in making TL determinations are varied, however, and the interest in the magnitude of the error is not always the same. It may be desirable to find the archaeological age to cross-check a radiocarbon date of associated material. Or the age of the artifact may fall outside the best capability of the radiocarbon method. Sometimes no radiocarbon-datable material from the same context is available. And of particular interest to the museum world and collectors-at-large, TL can provide one of our most accepted criteria for authenticity of ceramic antiquities.

Intriguing use of the method has been made with metal artifacts associated with ceramic material in some way. A striking example is the "Udo Bronze Head," a Benin culture casting (Fleming and Fagg 1977). A portion of the clay casting-core was still stuck to the cavity behind the nose. None of the surrounding soil that would have contributed to the irradiation was available, but soil from another head of similar provenience was; the assumption was made that the information was valid for the Udo style group of castings, of which the Head was a part. The age determined on the clay material by TL was 395 ± 35 years (A.D. 1580). Had the soil from nearby Benin been used to estimate the environmental dose rate, an age of 355 years would have resulted. This may give an idea of the magnitude of the influence of ambient material, and at the same time demonstrate the validity of the method. In either case, it gave a date only a few decades earlier than the estimate would have been on stylistic grounds. A recently developed procedure actually appears to make us nearly independent of the activity of the burial environment, as we shall see later on.

But TL can probe far deeper into the past—far beyond the time when pottery appeared on any archaeological horizon. Such a challenge was posed by burnt flint from the Palaeolithic site of Terra Amata, Nice. Special techniques had to be developed; thin-sections were made from the core of the stones with the help of special diamond wire saws, because the conventional "vising" or grinding to produce a powdered sample resulted in triboluminescence and other interference (Göksu and Fremlin 1972). It is particularly remarkable that here the environmental dose-rate is responsible for more than half of the TL. In other words, the radioactivity of the soil or sand in which the flint had been buried was an important factor in the determination, and any uncertainty in its effect was correspondingly reflected in the result. The results on two samples were considered reliable, and the time of firing was computed to be 230,000 ± 40,000 B.P., compared to millions of years estimated for unburnt or partially burnt specimens.

THE GREEK HORSE

Let us come back from the remote past to classic times, and to a truly classic case of double peripety. The Greek horse, cast in bronze and long a pride of the Metropolitan Museum of New York, one day found itself suspected of being forgery. We remember how it was banished to the Metropolitan Netherworld until the astute eye of Kate Lefferts discovered that the prime target of suspicion, the "casting fin," lacked substance, at least metallic substance. And again TL had the last word. The ceramic core, which had quite unreasonably caused raised eyebrows, now came to the rescue.

The core consisted of sand, clay, and other mineral inclusions. Because of many imponderable factors relating to the ceramic, one could not expect the highest precision of results. But if one needs only to distinguish between time periods of approximately two millenia and of a few decades, there is no need for outstanding precision.

Calculations showed that the process of casting would have raised the temperature within the core enough to erase the "geological" TL, and a full-scale TL testing program was initiated (Zimmerman, Yuhas, and Meyers 1974). This was a fine opportunity to use a modification of the TL technique suggested by the senior author (Zimmerman 1971) not long before: inclusions of high uranium content often found in potsherds (such as zircon grains) have a high internal alpha-particle dose rate, and therefore the TL produced by these grains is almost completely independent of the external beta- and gamma-dose rates, hence of the burial conditions. This was all to the good, since these were uncertain. In fact, the piece was recovered in 1908 from a shipwreck near Mahdia in Tunisia, according to the dealer who sold the bronze to the Metropolitan, a gentleman by the interesting name of Feuardent. Aside from the zircon grain procedure, two earlier techniques, known as the "fine-grain" and the "quartz-inclusion" methods, were also employed.

The doses measured in the experiments clearly show for each of the three mineral fractions that the core material had been subjected to a considerable amount of natural radiation from within the body. The difference in the large radioactive dose received by the zircon grains and the bulk material can be due only to internal alpha-particle doses accumulated over an extensive period. Even though the actual numbers were far from precise in this sequence of tests, the results showed unambiguously that the precious beast had been made anciently and not in modern times. The zircon method was later improved (Sutton and Zimmerman 1976); subsequent work by Zimmerman on the core material of the horse confirmed the earlier results, and it has narrowed the time range limits to the first five hundred years B.C. (Kate Lefferts, personal communication).

In the case of this amiable animal the old adage that one should not go by external appearance is not entirely pertinent. Here the patina, certainly an eye-catching component of external appearance, had looked suspect to the original doubter, but it was judged entirely sound and unforgeable by as keen as eye as that of Cyril Smith of M.I.T., whose expertise in ancient metals it would be hard to match. Now we may call out once more "'Bring forth the horse!' - the horse was brought; in truth, he was a noble steed" (Lord Byron, Mazeppa).

REFERENCES

Aitken, M.J.
   1974   Thermoluminescent dating. In, Physics and Archaeology, by M.J. Aitken. 2nd ed. Oxford: Clarendon Press.

   1976   Thermoluminescent age evaluation and assessment of error limits: revised system. Archaeometry 18:233-238.

Aitken, M.J. and J.C. Allred
   1972   The assessment of error limits in thermoluminsecent dating. Archaeometry 14:257-267.

Artzy, M., F. Asaro, and I. Perlman
   1973   The origin of the "Palestinian" Bichrome ware. Journal of the American Oriental Society 93:448-461.

Catling, H.W., A.E. Blin-Stoyle, and E.E. Richards
   1961   Spectrographic analysis of Mycenaean and Minoan pottery. Archaeometry 4:31-38.

Fleming, S.J. and B.E.B. Fagg
    1977   Thermoluminescent dating of the Udo Bronze Head. Archaeometry 19:86-87.

Göksu, H.Y. and J.H. Fremlin
    1972   Thermoluminescence   from   unirradiated   flints: regeneration   thermo-
           luminescence. Archaeometry 14:127-132.

Noble, J.
    1960   The technique of Attic vase-painting. American Journal of Archaeology
           63:307-313.

Perlman, I. and F. Asaro
    1969   Pottery analysis by neutron activation. Archaeometry 11:21-52.

Perlman, I., F. Asaro, and H.V. Michel
    1972   Nuclear applications in art and archaeology. Annual Review of Nuclear
           Science 22:384.

Schumann, T.
    1942   Berichte der Deutschen Keramischen Gesellschaft 23:408.

Sjöqvist, E.
    1940   Problems of the Late Cypriote Bronze Age. Stockholm.

Sutton, S.R. and D.W. Zimmerman
    1976   Thermoluminescent dating using zircon grains from archaeological ceramics.
           Archaeometry 18:125-134.

Wintle, A.G. and M.J. Aitken
    1977   Thermoluminescence dating of burnt flint: application to a Lower
           Palaeolithic site, Terra Amata. Archaeometry 19:111-130.

Zimmerman, D.W.
    1971   Uranium distributions in archaeologic ceramics: dating of radioactive
           inclusions. Science 174:818-819.

Zimmerman, D.W., M.P. Yuhas, and P. Meyers
    1974   Thermoluminescence authenticity measurements on core material from the
           Bronze Horse of the New York Metropolitan Museum of Art. Archaeometry
           16:5-15.

Chapter 13

Paint and Paste Studies of

Selected Halaf Sherds from Mesopotamia

Arthur Steinberg and Diana C. Kamilli

Halaf ware has long been a subject of interest, both because of its beauty and because of the questions it raises concerning its origins. Halaf ceramics have a characteristic surface texture and color, and are elaborately painted in geometric or surprisingly naturalistic designs. The paints may be monochrome, bichrome or trichrome, and colors include black, browns, red, orange, green, and white. This is the only polychrome ware of the early period (latter part of the 6th and well into the 5th millennium, B.C.) and it appeared without obvious antecedents (Oates and Oates 1976:109). Most of the sites where it is found are in northern Mesopotamia, but it is widely distributed, and has been found beyond the upper Khabur basin to the west, Begum to the east, near Lake Van to the north, and Choga Mami to the south.

It is strikingly different in style, color, and texture from the Samarran and 'Ubaid materials with which it commonly coexists; however, Oates and Oates (1976:109) mention that, in many cases, neutron activation studies of the pastes indicate that this Halaf ware was actually made at the sites where it was found. Therefore, either itinerant potters were active, or the pottery indicates a separate group of people living in the area. The latter is likely since the Halaf people's architecture is unique: where they moved into an area (for example at Yarim Tepe) they founded new villages nearby rather than build on existing ones. In short, they seem to have been a distinct ethnic group, but so far there is little evidence to indicate their origin.

Several scholars have worked on the interesting technological problems posed by Halaf pottery. Matson (1945:22) comments on the use of vitrified paint on certain Halaf wares, and suggests that they may have been made by itinerant groups of potters (1965:212). Davidson and McKerrell (1976) used neutron activation analysis on Halaf wares from northern Iraq and eastern Syria, to compare paste compositions with local clays and study trade. Tite and coworkers (Tite and Maniatis 1975a, 1975b; Tite 1969) used SEM methods to illustrate the reaction of different types of clays to different temperatures of firing. Extensive work on the Halaf paints has involved a broad battery of techniques, including scanning electron microscope (SEM) and X-ray diffraction (XRD) to name only a few (Noll 1976; Noll et al. 1975).

In this study the pastes and paints of 25 Halaf sherds, part of a larger study of Mesopotamian pottery and chosen to represent a range of paint types and site distribution (Figure 1), were studied by petrographic and electron microprobe analysis. These methods have not been used before to any extent on this ware, and were selected to give further information on mineral textural relationships and composition. The objective of the study was an investigation of the technology of Halaf paints, contrasting the relative uniformity of their execution site-to-site with the variability in local pastes. Because of the small number of sherds used for this paper (Figure 2), we will make no attempt to trace technological change through time, although Halaf wares are well stratified at several sites.

PASTE ANALYSES

The pastes of seven sherd samples from Tell Halaf, two from Arpachiyah, eight from Tepe Gawra, eight from Choga Mami, and two from Abu Maria were examined optically and by SEM (Table 1). Electron microprobe was used on occasion to determine the composition of feldspars and micas. Mineralogy of the pastes, together with information on the local geology, allows one to define an assemblage that is typical of sherds from a given site. Anomalous samples and possible trade items may be identified in this way. Although the main purpose of this paper is to discuss certain aspects of the paint technology, we have included a section on the pastes to show that many of the samples were locally made and that not all were traded from a few central sites. Study of paste textures allowed observation of the level of fusion of the paste constituents, and comparison from site to site of the methods used in firing. In some cases, the level of fusion of the paste correlates with that of the paint; in others, special fluxes were used in the paints to facilitate melting.

Tell Halaf

Halaf ware takes its name from the site of Tell Halaf (Oppenheim 1943); unfortunately, none of the ceramics discussed in his report were from stratified deposits and they are useful only for comparative purposes. Five of the Tell Halaf samples we chose for this study are monochrome and two bichrome. The mineral assemblages in the pastes (both coarse and fine fractions) are uniform, and include quartz, calcic plagioclase, pyroxene, and primary calcite. This combination is different from any of the others in this study and the uniformity suggests that all the sherds that happened to be chosen were made locally. This is reinforced by the presence of large areas of basalt and Neogene sandstones and limestones near the site. The coarse mineral fraction averages 13 percent, which is somewhat higher than in Halaf wares from the other sites.

TABLE 1

Coarse Fraction Assemblages of Sherd Pastes

SAMPLE	Letter on Figure 2	Estimated percent coarse fraction	Quartz	Calcic Plagioclase	Sodic Plagioclase	Alkali Feldspar	Untwinned Feldspar	Pyroxene	Amphibole	Chlorite	Biotite	Muscovite	Magnetite	Hematite Grains	Hematite Stain	Ilmenite	Chromite	Primary Carbonate	Secondary Carbonate	Microfossils	Chert	Other Rock Fragments	Chaff	Sherd Grog
TELL HALAF																								
Monochrome																								
JH-2	m	15	X	Tr	—	—	Tr	X	?	—	Tr	Tr	X	X	Tr	—	—	X	Tr	?	Tr	—	—	—
JH-4	j	15	X	Tr	—	—	Tr	X	—	—	Tr	Tr	Tr	Tr	—	—	—	X	—	Tr	—	Gab	—	Tr
JH-6	k	15	X	Tr	—	—	Tr	X	—	—	Tr	Tr	X	X	Tr	—	—	X	—	—	Tr	—	—	?
JH-8(32-43-15)	l	10	X	Tr	—	—	Tr	Tr	Tr	—	Tr	Tr	Tr	X	Tr	—	—	X	Tr	Tr	—	Volc	—	?
JH-9(32-43-1)	q	10	X	—	—	—	Tr	Tr	—	—	Tr	Tr	Tr	Tr	Tr	—	—	X	—	Tr	Tr	—	—	—
Bichrome																								
JH-3	x	10	X	Tr	—	—	Tr	—	Tr	Tr	Tr	Tr	Tr	X	X	—	—	Tr	Tr	—	Tr	—	—	-
JH-5	w	15	X	Tr	—	—	Tr	Tr	—	—	Tr	Tr	X	X	Tr	—	—	X	—	—	Tr	Volc	—	Tr
TELL ARPACHIYAH																								
Monochrome																								
A-a	—	2	X	—	?	?	Tr	—	—	—	Tr	Tr	Tr	Tr	Tr	—	—	?	Tr	-	Tr	SS	—	X
A-c	—	2	X	—	?	?	X	—	—	—	X	X	—	Tr	X	—	—	Tr	—	—	Tr	Sch,Volc	—	X
TEPE GAWRA																								
Monochrome																								
38-13-480 (31)	a	2	X	—	—	—	X	—	—	—	Tr	—	—	X	—	—	—	—	Tr	—	—	—	—	—
*38-13-471 (32)	c	4	X	—	Tr	Tr	X	—	—	—	X	X	=	X	X	—	—	—	—	—	Tr	Sch,Volc	—	X
38-13-878 (69)	e	4	X	—	Tr	—	X	—	—	—	X	X	=	Tr	X	—	—	—	—	—	Tr	Sch,Grn	—	?
*38-13-716 (53)	d	15	X	—	Tr	—	Tr	—	—	—	Tr	Tr	X	Tr	Tr	—	X	—	—	Tr	—	—	—	—
*38-13-875 (70)	n	5	X	—	Tr	Tr	X	—	—	—	X	X	Tr	Tr	Tr	—	—	?	X	—	Tr	Sch,Volc	—	X
37-16-509 (93)	r	2	X	—	Tr	—	X	—	—	—	X	X	Tr	Tr	X	—	—	Tr	—	—	Tr	—	—	—
Bichrome																								
*38-13-705 (54)	u	1	X	—	Tr	Tr	X	—	—	—	Tr	Tr	—	—	Tr	—	—	Tr	Tr	—	Tr	—	—	?
38-13-836 (68)	v	2	X	—	Tr	—	X	—	—	—	Tr	—	Tr	Tr	—	—	—	Tr	Tr	—	Tr	—	—	—
ABU MARIA																								
Monochrome																								
N 115 E	o	0	Tr	—	Tr	?	Tr	—	—	—	X	X	—	Tr	Tr	—	—	—	—	—	Tr	Sch	—	—
N 115 N	p	7	X	—	X	Tr	Tr	—	—	—	X	X	Tr	Tr	Tr	—	—	X	Tr	—	X	Sch,SS	—	—
CHOGA MAMI																								
Monochrome																								
CM 369 A	b	5	X	—	Tr	—	X	—	—	—	Tr	—	Tr	Tr	—	—	—	X	X	—	X	—	—	—
CM 369 B	f	2	X	—	Tr	—	X	—	—	—	—	—	X	X	—	—	—	X	X	—	X	Volc	—	—
CM 369 C	g	4	X	—	Tr	—	X	—	—	—	Tr	—	Tr	Tr	—	—	—	X	X	Tr	X	Sch,Sed	—	—
*CM 369 D	h	10	X	—	Tr	Tr	X	—	—	—	X	—	X	X	X	—	—	Tr	Tr	—	X	Sch,Sed	—	Tr?
*CM 369 H	i	2	X	—	Tr	—	Tr	—	—	—	Tr	Tr	X	Tr	—	—	—	?	X	—	X	Sch	—	?
CM 110	s	2	X	—	Tr	—	Tr	Tr	?	—	X	Tr	Tr	X	X	—	—	X	Tr	X	X	Sch,Volc	—	—
CM 352/23	t	4	X	—	Tr	—	X	—	—	—	Tr	X	Tr	X	Tr	—	—	X	X	X	Tr	—	—	—
Bichrome																								
*CM 184	y	4	X	—	Tr	Tr	X	—	—	—	X	Tr	Tr	X	Tr	—	—	X	—	—	X	Sed,Volc	—	?

Note: Samples are arranged by site and paint type. Tr = trace, Volc = volcanic, Gab = gabbro, Sed = sediment, SS = sandstone, Sch = schist, X = present.

*Samples with mineral assemblages different from most others from the site.

Five of the pastes are well fused, showing a predominantly isotropic paste matrix. Under polarized transmitted light, an alignment--almost a cellular structure--is evident in the paste. This is typical of the better-fused Halaf sherds from this site (and several others; see Noll 1976:270). The structure is shown in the SEM picture in Figure 3a (JH 8; Figure 21). We have seen this structure only rarely in other ware types, no matter how well fused, and it may contribute to the characteristic Halaf ware surface appearance noted so frequently. Tite and Maniatis (1975a) used SEM to examine various calcareous and noncalcareous clays fired to different temperatures. The elongated cellular structure formed best in fine-grained clays that contained aligned packed micaceous minerals, and few equigranular quartz grains to destroy the alignment. In their experiments, the number and extent of the glass areas increased with firing temperature, and the temperature at which certain features occurred varied with the refractory nature of the individual clay.

The different appearances of the clays in our Halaf sherds from all sites probably results from variation in temperature, presence or lack of fine matrix equigranular quartz, dominance of fine aligned clay minerals, and the refractory nature of the clay. The conditions necessary to form the cellular structure are more common in the Halaf pastes than in Samarran or 'Ubaid materials, which suggests exceptionally careful selection and clay treatment by the Halaf potters.

Arpachiyah

Arpachiyah has the best stratification of Halaf material yet found (Mallowan and Rose 1935). Most of the Halaf sherds come from outside the tell, except for the ceramics in the extraordinary "burnt house" in TT6. Unfortunately, we were able to work with only four Halaf and four 'Ubaid sherds from Arpachiyah, and only two of the Halaf sherds were used in this report because of loss of paint during the thin sectioning process.

On the basis of these few samples, the mineral assemblage appears to be typified by quartz, sherd grog, a variety of feldspars (all suggesting nearby granite or metagranitic rock), and micas (suggesting a metamorphic schist source). Coarse mineral fraction makes up only 2 percent in each sherd. The paste matrices are partly melted but contain more relict micas and clay minerals than do the Tell Halaf pastes. This is probably due in part to lower temperatures of firing, or possible lack of some flux; no cellular structure was noted in these two samples.

Tepe Gawra

Six monochrome and two bichrome Halaf style sherds were chosen from Tepe Gawra, excavated by Tobler (1950). The paste and paint mineralogy of these sherds is somewhat variable through time and by ware; in addition, there are clearly intrusive pieces. A characteristic paste mineral assemblage does emerge, however. Four of the eight Halaf sherds chosen for this study match this, and these four sherds were probably made locally. This assemblage includes quartz, untwinned feldspar, biotite, muscovite, and traces of sodic plagioclase and chert. Several also have traces of primary calcite, but this is rare. Of the four anomalous samples, one (38-13-716; Figure 2d) has this assemblage but also abundant primary calcite, magnetite, and

15 percent coarse fraction. These features are not incompatible with the site assemblage, just unusual, and may represent a local variant in the Tepe Gawra assemblage. The other three (38-13-471, 875, 705; Figures 2c, n, u) contain minerals suggesting that they may have been brought in from nearby Arpachiyah. Fusion levels of the pastes vary among the eight samples and several of the better-fused ones show cellular structure. There is no apparent correlation with whether they were imported (Figure 3c) or local (Figure 3b).

Choga Mami

Choga Mami is one of several mounds near the Mandali area (Oates 1969a, 1969b). The Halaf monochrome, bichrome, and trichrome wares were found in a late Halaf well and are similar in style to those found at Arpachiyah in level TT6. Comparison of the paste mineral assemblages of the Choga Mami Halaf wares with those of other wares from the site (and with the local geology) indicates that most of this Halaf ware was made locally, although the potters used very different firing and painting methods. This information is reinforced by the neutron activation data of Davidson and McKerrell (Oates and Oates 1976:109).

The mineral assemblage typical of the Choga Mami Halaf samples includes quartz, sodic plagioclase, micas, primary calcite, and spherulitic chert. This assemblage is different from any other in the study. The presence of primary calcite coarse fraction is somewhat unusual in sherds from Choga Mami; it does appear in certain earlier Samarran and coarse ware sherds, however, and is probably a variant in the local clays chosen by the different potters. Coarse fraction is less than 5 percent, which is typical of most wares from the site. The fusion level and texture of the pastes vary, but the cellular structure appears in several (Figure 3d: local sample CM 110; Figure 2s). As at Tepe Gawra, three anomalous samples (CM 369D, H, and CM 184; Figures 2h, i, y) may have been brought in from Arpachiyah.

Abu Maria

A mound near Abu Maria yielded two Halaf pieces used in this study, which were chosen for their black glassy paint. Unfortunately their pastes are somewhat indeterminate. The mineral assemblage is similar to that in sherds from Arpachiyah except for the lack of sherd grog, but it is unlike any other. Coarse mineral fraction is absent in one sample and 7 percent in the other.

PAINT ANALYSES

As many authors have noted, Halaf ware is extraordinary for the apparent degree of control the potters had over the paint colors. These are true polychrome colors and are not effects of uneven firing. The paints on all the Halaf sherds analyzed for this study are iron oxide- and silicate-rich, and, in the case of the polychrome samples, each appears to have been subjected to a single firing. The only exception to this is the white fugitive paint which, on one trichrome sample from Choga Mami (not included in this study), turned out to be kaolinite-rich and barely fused. In this case, the pot was apparently well-fired first, then the white decoration was added after firing (although it may have been refired at a very low temperature).

The iron oxide-rich paints have been arranged in Table 2 according to whether they are monochrome or bichrome, according to their general color category, and whether they are matte or shiny. Patterns immediately emerge and it is evident that the potters controlled these colors by a number of quite sophisticated composition and firing methods.

Slabs from each sherd were made into polished, uncovered thin sections. This allowed not only the usual optical study of the paste body, but also transmitted and reflected light analysis of the paint (or paints) as well. In this way, we could identify certain iron oxide phases (hematite is blood red in transmitted light; maghemite, brown to yellow; magnetite, black opaque; and hercynite, greenish), estimate the relative free iron oxide-to-silicate ratio, and determine the textural relationships between the minerals. The form of the crystals and their textural relations suggest the level of fusion of the paint. This is especially important in the discussion of the red vs. black matt paints, and the orange vs. black shiny ones. These data could not have been obtained by using X-ray diffraction, microprobe, or SEM alone.

After optical examination, we used the electron microprobe on the same thin sections to analyze individual metallic grains in the paints for iron, magnesium, manganese, and titanium content; also, we studied the unstructured, poorly-fused matrix mixtures, glass, and melt-produced silicates. From past observation, we have found that certain concentrations of elements in a paint affect its reaction to firing temperature and atmosphere. Therefore, in Table 2, "trace" amounts of iron means less than 6 percent; magnesium, 8 percent; manganese, 4 percent; calcium, 10 percent; aluminum, 15 percent; and potassium plus sodium, 5 percent. Silicon is usually present in amounts between 40 and 50 percent, since many of the paints are mixtures of iron oxide with clay mineral binder. The clay minerals also control the aluminum content.

The three major components that vary in these paints and that appear to control the final appearance most are iron oxide (in its various forms, and as a flux under reducing conditions), alumina (which may act as a refractory), and the alkali elements (which act as strong fluxes). In the case of these sherds, potassium is the major alkali, and sodium is rare. Most of the iron oxide appears to be hematite (translucent deep red in transmitted light) as is shown in Table 2. All the bright reflecting grains in Figures 4a and 4b, for example, are translucent red. The "dust" in the glass-rich paints is black opaque and is probably magnetite (powder was magnetic). Undoubtedly there are other forms mixed in, however. Magnesium and titanium are present only in traces. Manganese occurs in only three paints, all from Tepe Gawra (although two may have been imported from Arpachiyah). Calcium is in traces in some samples, but is quite abundant in others; we could find no real pattern, and it does not appear to correlate with fusion level or texture.

The paint-to-paste interfaces in our samples, viewed optically rather than by SEM, are sharp with little gradation (see Figure 4a and b, and Figure 5a and b), even in the better-fused, iron oxide-rich samples. This is very different from the interfaces between paste and paint in 'Ubaid samples. The texture and quality of the paint

TABLE 2

Composition and Texture of Paints on Halaf Style Sherds

PAINT TYPE	SITE	SAMPLE NUMBER	Letter on Figure 2	Matt	Shiny	Aligned Micaceous Minerals (burnished?)	Sintered	Melted	Glass	Metal Oxide-to-Silicate Ratio	Clay Minerals	Hematite; D = dust	Magnetite (?); D = dust	Melt Silicates	Iron	Magnesium	Titanium	Manganese	Calcium	Silicon	Aluminum	Potassium + Sodium
MONOCHROME																						
Red or Brown Matt	Tepe Gawra	38-13-471	e	X	-	—	X	—	-	10:90	X	X	-	—	X	X	—	X	Tr	X	X	X
		38-13-716	d	X	-	—	X	—	-	25:75	X	X	-	—	X	Tr	—	—	Tr	X	X	Tr
		38-13-878	e	X	-	—	X	—	-	10:90	X	X	-	—	X	Tr	—	—	Tr	X	X	X
	Choga Mami	CM 369 B	f	X	-	—	X	—	-	80:20	Tr	X	-	—	X	Tr	—	—	X	X	X	Tr
		CM 369 C	g	X	-	—	X	—	-	80:20	Tr	X	-	—	X	Tr	—	—	X	X	Tr	Tr
		CM 369 D	h	X	-	—	X	—	-	60:40	Tr	X	-	—	X	—	—	—	Tr	X	Tr	—
		CM 369 H	i	X	-	—	X	X?	-	60:40	Tr	X	-	Tr	X	Tr	Tr	—	Tr	X	Tr	Tr
Black Matt	Tepe Gawra	38-13-480	a	X	-	—	-	X?	-	40:60	?	X	-	Tr	X	Tr	—	Tr	X	X	Tr	Tr
	Choga Mami	CM 369 A	b	X	-	—	-	X?	-	80:20	?	X	-	Tr	X	Tr	—	—	—	X	Tr	—
Orange, Light Brown or Red Shiny	Halaf	JH-9(32-43-1)	q	-	X	X	X	—	-	10:90	X	D	-	—	X	Tr	Tr	—	X	X	X	X
	Arpachiyah	A-a	-	-	X	X	X	—	-	30:70	X	D	-	—	X	—	—	—	—	X	X	Tr
		A-c	-	-	X	X	X	—	-	20:80	X	D	-	—	X	—	—	—	—	X	X	Tr
	Tepe Gawra	37-16-509	r	-	X	X	X	—	-	10:90	X	D	-	—	X	Tr	—	—	—	X	X	Tr
	Choga Mami	CM 110	s	-	X	X	X	—	-	20:80	X	D	-	—	X	Tr	Tr	—	Tr	X	X	Tr
		CM 352/23	t	-	X	X	X	—	-	20:80	X	D	-	—	X	Tr	Tr	—	X	X	X	Tr
Black Shiny	Halaf	JH-4	j	-	X	?	-	X	X	5:95	—	—	D	—	X	Tr	Tr	—	X	X	X	Tr
		JH-6	k	-	X	?	-	X	X	60:40	—	—	D	—	X	Tr	Tr	—	Tr	X	X	X
		JH-8	l	-	X	?	-	X	X	50:40	—	—	D	—	X	Tr	—	—	Tr	X	X	X
		JH-2	m	-	X	?	-	X	X	60:40	—	—	D	—	X	Tr	Tr	—	Tr	X	X	X
	Tepe Gawra	38-13-875	n	-	X	X	X	X	X	10:90	X	—	—	—	X	Tr	Tr	—	Tr	X	X	X
	Abu Maria	N 115 E	o	-	X	?	-	X	X	10:90	—	—	—	—	X	Tr	—	—	Tr	X	X	X
		N 115 N	p	-	X	?	-	X	X	10:90	—	—	D	—	X	Tr	—	—	Tr	X	X	X
BICHROME																						
Red Matt	Tepe Gawra	38-13-705	u	X	-	—	X	—	-	40:60	?	X	-	—	X	Tr	Tr	—	Tr	X	X	—
Black Matt				X	-	—	X	X	-	40:60	?	X	X	—	X	X	—	Tr	Tr	X	Tr	X
Brown Matt	Tepe Gawra	38-13-836	v	X	-	—	-	X	-	30:70	—	X	X	Tr	X	Tr	Tr	—	X	X	Tr	Tr
Green Matt				X	-	—	-	X	-	10:90	—	Tr	-	X	X	Tr	—	—	X	X	Tr	—
Brown Shiny	Halaf	JH-5	w	-	X	?	-	X	X	15:85	—	D	-	—	X	Tr	Tr	—	Tr	X	X	X
Orange Shiny				-	X	X	X	—	-	15:85	X	D	-	—	X	Tr	—	—	Tr	X	X	Tr
Orange Shiny	Halaf	JH-3	x	-	X	X	X	—	-	15:85	X	D	-	—	X	Tr	—	—	Tr	X	X	Tr
Brown Matt				X	-	—	X	—	-	50:50	Tr	X	-	—	X	Tr	Tr	—	Tr	Tr	Tr	Tr
Red/Brown Shiny	Choga Mami	CM 184	y	-	X	X	X	—	-	10:90	X	D	-	—	X	—	—	—	Tr	X	X	—
Brown Matt				X	-	—	X	—	-	40:60	Tr	X	-	—	X	—	X	—	Tr	X	Tr	—

Note: Samples are arranged by paint monochrome and bichrome types. The metal oxide-to-silicate ratio refers to the relative amount of free metallic iron oxide in the paint as determined optically. All chemical analyses were obtained using electron microprobe methods. X = present, Tr = trace, D = the very fine grains of iron oxide referred to as dust in the text.

surfaces vary according to whether the paint is coarsely crystalline (producing a matt paint) as in Figures 4a and 4b; or fine grained or glass-rich (producing a shiny paint) as in Figures 5a and 5b. This is true for all samples we examined, unless they were highly weathered.

Table 3 presents all the paint data in a convenient summary form.

The paints on monochrome samples will be discussed first to demonstrate the patterns of manufacture. Bichrome combinations will be considered later.

Brown or Red Matt Paints

All the paints considered in this section are shades of brown and none are a true red. The four samples from Choga Mami are brown and matt for different reasons than the three from Tepe Gawra, and the two sets will be discussed separately.

The four sherds from Choga Mami contain abundant free metallic iron oxide in the form of hematite. Figure 4a (CM 369D; Figures 2h and 6a) shows, however, that this hematite is only partly fused and the original grain shapes are still evident. Both the bright areas and the darker gray in this picture are deep red in transmitted light. Much of the darker gray however is actually composed of strongly hematite-stained clay minerals, and there are considerably more of these than in the black paints discussed in the next section. This hematite is still partly in the earthy form, as opposed to the specular hematite in Figure 4b. SEM photographs of the pastes suggest that fusion is only partial, and it is possible that these samples were actually fired to a somewhat lower temperature than the black matt painted samples. It is also possible that the firing history of these samples was entirely oxidizing, which would discourage the dissociation of the hematite or its change to a more reduced form. Finally, potassium in these four paint samples occurs only in traces and clearly did not act as a flux.

The three brown matt paints on samples from Tepe Gawra contain much less free metallic hematite (less than 30 percent), and are predominantly stained clay minerals. They are only sintered, and resemble the clay mineral-rich orange shiny paints discussed below. The surface is matt, however, and under the microscope the clay minerals are randomly oriented and obviously have not been burnished. The alternate way, therefore, to produce a brown matt paint is to use a clay mineral-rich mixture and not polish it (Figure 6c); the brown color is produced by the fine hematite grains and stain.

In summary, the Halaf potters produced brownish matt paints by two distinctly different methods. One way was to use an iron-rich paint, consisting mostly of coarse hematite and less clay minerals, which was fired at a relatively low temperature and possibly only in oxidizing conditions (found at Choga Mami). Another way was to use a very clay mineral-rich paint with some hematite dust and stain in it but no alkali flux (found at Tepe Gawra). Both kinds are used in monochrome and bichrome applications.

Black Matt Paint

Only two true black matt paints were chosen, one from Tepe Gawra (38-13-480; Figure 2a), and one from Choga Mami (CM 369A; Figures 2b, 4b, and 6b). Both

TABLE 3

Summary of Paint Characteristics

Paint Type	Mineral Content, and Texture	Elements That Affect Fusion, Texture and Color	Fusion Level	Reason for Color	Reason for Surface Finish
RED MATT PAINT* Figures 2b and 6a (Choga Mami type)	Earthy hematite dominant; Hematite-stained clay minerals are present, but less than in red shiny paints, more than in black matt paints	Low K_2O Intermediate Al_2O_3 High Fe_2O_3	Sintered; poorly fused	Red, poorly crystalline, earthy hematite	Coarsely crystalline texture
BLACK MATT PAINT Figures 2a and 6c	Specular hematite (originally probably ochre, reduced to magnetite (?) during reducing high temperature part of firing cycle, then reoxidized during final stage); clay minerals present only in traces	Low K_2O Low Al_2O_3 High Fe_2O_3	Hematite disassociated and recrystallized; no original grain forms; reaction probably subsolidus; associated silicates melted	Black, crystalline, specular hematite	Coarsely crystalline texture
RED or ORANGE SHINY PAINT* Figures 2c and 6d	Hematite-stained clay minerals dominant; less than 30% red hematite dust	Low K_2O High Al_2O_3 Fe_2O_3 only as dust and stain	Sintered; poorly fused	Red hematite dust and stain on clay minerals	Alignment of fine grained clay minerals from burnishing; no coarse iron oxide grains
BLACK SHINY PAINT Figures 2d and 6e	Brown translucent glass; variable amounts of fine grained, black opaque iron oxide (type?)	High K_2O High Al_2O_3 Variable Fe_3O_4(?)	Melted	Black magnetite (?) dust and brown glass	Glass content; no coarse iron oxide grains
GREEN MATT PAINT Figure 2v	Melt silicates (fayalite, hedenbergite)	Low K_2O Low Al_2O_3 Intermediate FeO	Melted	Dominance of green silicates	Coarsely crystalline texture

*The red matt paints from Tepe Gawra are similar to the orange shiny paints, but unburnished (Figure 6b).

195

contain abundant coarse free metallic iron oxide, in this case hematite. This hematite, although translucent red in transmitted light, is in the metallic specular crystalline form, and this gives the black color to the paint. There is no magnetite, and as can be seen from Table 2, few manganese minerals. The paint layer on the sherd from Tepe Gawra has a trace of fayalite (Fe_2SiO_4) at the paint-to-paste interface.

In Table 2, we refer to the paint as melted as opposed to sintered, which may not be strictly true. The silicate fraction has melted to form the green silicates, and the iron oxide has certainly lost all original grain shape, reforming as evenly spaced individual crystals of metallic hematite. We are not sure, however, if this is a result of actual crystallization from a melt, or of subsolidus transformation. Actual melting of such a super-saturated hematite-rich mixture would require very high firing temperatures, and there is little alkali flux present. Iron, however, may act as a flux if transformed into the reduced Fe^{+2} form during a reducing part of the firing cycle. Magnetite (Fe_3O_4 or $FeO \cdot Fe_2O_3$) has a Fe^{+2} component and would suggest reducing conditions. Alumina can act as a refractory and retard reduction of iron and therefore the forming of Fe^{+2} as a flux; however, aluminum content is low in these samples, due to few clay minerals, and this may explain the higher level of fusion in the black rather than in the more alumina-rich brown matt paints.

Noll et al. (1975:604) have suggested that the more hematite in a paint (as opposed to magnetite or maghemite), the browner it gets. This is not true in these two samples; the black color is related entirely to the specular crystalline state of the hematite. The thickness of the layer (or the thickness of the mixture in terms of free metallic iron oxide) does not here appear to affect the color either; thin brush strokes are still black, although grayer.

Orange, Light Brown, or Red Shiny Paints

The paints on one sample from Tell Halaf, two from Arpachiyah, one from Tepe Gawra, and two from Choga Mami are light colored and shiny, and all have the same chemical and textural characteristics. All are sintered and contain less than 30 percent free metallic iron oxide. Clay minerals dominate. Alumina content is high and may have acted as a refractory. Potassium in all but one is low and did not act as a flux. The iron oxide is in the form of extremely fine-grained hematite (translucent red) dust and stain, and the percent of this dust causes the different color tones. Several authors have said that these light paint colors were produced by using a thinner paint mixture or brush stroke, but this is not the case here.

The gray paint layer in Figure 5a (JH 9; Figures 2q and 6d) shows the nearly total lack of coarse granular bright hematite. In polarized transmitted light, the clay minerals are undestroyed, anisotropic, and aligned. The lack of coarse equigranular grains provided no obstruction to alignment in burnishing, and because of this these fine-grained micaceous mixtures have shiny surfaces.

Black or Brown Shiny Paint

These melted dark shiny paints are on partly-fused bodies and are similar to the ones commented on by Matson (1945:22) and Noll et al. (1975:605). All are black except for two samples from Tell Halaf (JH 6; Figure 2k; and JH 2; Figures 2m, 6e and 5b), which are brown. All are similar in textural and chemical characteristics. They are melted, contain abundant glass (translucent brown in transmitted light), have bubble holes, and most contain extremely fine-grained, black opaque iron oxide dust. In some, this dust makes up more than 50 percent of the paint layer; in others, it is less than 15 percent. As noted earlier, we did not identify this dust, but it is slightly magnetic.

Chemically, these paints are the same as the orange burnished, clay mineral-rich paints except that they contain abundant potassium, which clearly acted as a strong flux and glass former. This flux appears to have overridden any refractory properties of the high amounts of alumina.

Several of these melted paints are on well-fused but not completely melted pastes that show cellular structure (e.g., JH 8, and Tepe Gawra 38-13-875), while several are on pastes that are less well-fused and have their fine-grained matrix intact. This is the classic case where a flux was added to a paint and not to the paste, allowing differential fusion. It must have been done on purpose, as it is employed on several bichrome samples. For example, dark glassy paint coexists with orange shiny paint on JH 5 (Figure 2w) from Tell Halaf. There is no actual evidence, but it is possible that the potters added potassium-bearing wood ash to the paint that they wanted to melt. It is doubtful that the clay minerals alone were the source of the potassium as the unmelted orange burnished samples are also clay mineral-rich, and it might be unusual for two clay mineral species to be available (and known) to potters at a single potting site.

These dark shiny paints were also clearly subjected to a reducing phase in the firing cycle, as shown by the black opaque form of the dust. It is probable that the impermeable glass coated the reduced iron oxide grains and insulted them from the oxygen of the final stage of the firing cycle. All of these factors explain the presence of melted black glass on a less well-fused, pink sherd body.

A monochrome sample from Tepe Gawra (38-13-875; Figure 2n) has a paint layer that is entirely glass with some traces of fine-grained iron oxide dust, and some subaligned remnants of clay minerals. This is a particularly interesting sample in that it is transitional, and shows that the unmelted equivalent of the black glassy paint is the aligned clay mineral-rich, low iron, orange shiny paint, but with potassium added. The other black glass samples have been completely melted and have lost the transitional features.

The black color of these magnetite dust- and glass-bearing paints is commonly truer black than in paints with coarse iron oxide grains, despite the very low amounts of black opaque phases. We noticed this also in potassium-rich glass paints on sherds from Tepe Giyan in Iran, and it seems to be a characteristic of the type.

Bichrome Paints

The paints on the bichrome samples follow, for the most part, all of these observations, and the following examples show the variations used by the potters.

The first example, a bichrome sample from Tepe Gawra (38-13-705; Figures 2u and 7a) has red matt and black matt paints. The red matt layer has abundant sintered hematite (showing original grain forms), and considerable amounts of clay minerals (and therefore aluminum). There is no potassium or manganese. Due to the lack of flux and manganese, this hematite remained in its earthy red porous form, and is similar to the paint in Figure 4a. The coexisting black matt paint contains abundant coarse, dissociated grains of specular hematite and magnetite(?), and only traces of clay minerals (and therefore aluminum). Potassium is abundant and probably helped flux the mixture. This paint is one of the few to contain manganese, which may have added to the black coloring. Except for the potassium and manganese, this paint layer is quite similar to the type in Figure 4b. Note again that the difference in color of the two pigments is not due either to differences in thickness of brush stroke, or to amounts of free metallic iron oxide in the mixture, but to the crystalline state of the hematite. The matt surfaces of both are due to their coarsely granular nature.

The second bichrome sample (Tepe Gawra 38-13-836; Figures 2v and 7b) includes a color we have not yet discussed, and is painted in green and brown. Both layers have the same general chemistry (low potassium, low aluminum), but the green layer is composed entirely of green melt silicates, both fayalite (Fe_2SiO_4) and hedenbergite ($CaFeSi_2O_6$). There are only traces of metallic iron oxide (hematite). The brown layer contains about 30 percent coarse hematite which has produced the browner color. Both color layers appear to be truly melted, and it may be that these represent "overfired" anomalous paints that otherwise would have been shiny orange (now green) and matt brown.

The third bichrome sample is from Tell Halaf (JH 5; Figures 2w and 7c) and is painted with shiny brown and shiny orange paints. Again these follow the above observations. Both contain about 15 percent fine hematite dust; however, the brown paint is glass-rich and contains much potassium, which acted as a flux and glass former. The orange shiny layer contains no glass, but 85 percent unmelted, aligned, anisotropic clay minerals. Microprobe investigation showed that there is little potassium. Both paints were burnished (although the glass in the brown layer creates its shine) and there are no coarse grains in either to make a matt surface. The potassium may have been selectively added to the brown layer in the form of wood ash.

The last two bichrome samples (JH 3 from Tell Halaf, Figure 2x; and CM 184 from Choga Mami, Figures 2y and 7d) have similar paint combinations and will be discussed together. The Tell Halaf sherd has orange shiny paint and the Choga Mami sample, a red-brown shiny layer. Each is sintered, contains less than 15 percent fine-grained hematite dust, and abundant clay minerals. Each has much aluminum (from the clay minerals) and little potassium to act as a flux. The clay minerals are aligned and have been burnished.

Both sherds have, in addition, a brown matt design. Each is rich in coarse-grained, sintered hematite. These layers contain little potassium to act as a flux, and fewer clay minerals than in the coexisting shiny paint. Here, as in the sintered brown paint of Figure 4a, the abundant earthy hematite gives the darker brown color. The burnishing that shined the coexisting fine-grained paints did not affect these brown, coarse-grained layers and they remained matt. We suspect that these two bichrome vessels were fired only under oxidizing conditions, and possibly at lower temperatures than some of the vessels with more fused paints.

SUMMARY

Some of the information in this report, summarized in Table 3, merely reinforces what others have already suggested; however, much is new and could only have been obtained by using the combination of methods we chose. We hope that this will give others ideas and encourage further work.

The paste mineral assemblages of our Halaf style sherds suggest that most of the pieces selected from Choga Mami, Tell Halaf, and Tepe Gawra were made at those sites, although several anomalous samples were noted. The poor sampling from Arpachiyah and Abu Maria does not allow us to draw conclusions, but the data suggest that these pieces have assemblages distinct from the others.

SEM pictures of the pastes show that many are partly melted and have developed an elongated cellular structure that may be related to original alignment of fine-grained clay minerals and micas in the matrix. This texture is common in our Halaf wares, and rare in other ceramic types. The level of paste fusion does not always correlate with that of the paints.

The iron oxide-based paints on these sherds come in various colors and may be matt or shiny. Potters appear to have used the same methods to produce these effects no matter at what site the pot was made. This suggests that either itinerant potters were involved or that actual colonies of Halaf people with a shared painting technology lived in each place.

There were two ways that the Halaf potters produced the brown or red matt paints. Those from Choga Mami (similar in composition to the matt black paints) contain abundant coarse hematite, which is only partly fused and still earthy. Clay minerals are somewhat more abundant than in the black matt paints. The brown matt paints from Tepe Gawra are different in that they contain abundant hematite-stained, unaligned clay minerals with only minor fine-grained hematite dust. These paints are similar to the shiny orange, sintered clay mineral-rich paints, but have not been burnished.

Matt black paint contains abundant specular (well-crystallized) hematite, black in handsample, with minor associated silicates. The iron oxide has been recrystallized and the associated silicates have been melted. Manganese oxide is present in only one sample from Tepe Gawra, and was not a major source of the black color in other samples.

Orange, light brown, and red shiny paints are composed of abundant aligned clay minerals, and extremely fine-grained hematite dust. There is little potassium to have acted as a flux and the mixture is only sintered. These fine-grained paints have been burnished to produce the shine.

The shiny black or dark brown paints contain abundant brown glass and varying amounts of a fine-grained, black opaque iron oxide dust. There is evidence that this paint type started out being similar to the clay mineral-rich, orange shiny paints, but had potassium added as a flux, perhaps in the form of wood ash. The addition of potassium to the fine-grained paints allowed them actually to melt and form a glass phase, while the paste bodies remained only sintered. Upon final reoxidizing firing, this glass phase remained impervious, retaining its reduced black color.

The different colors on the bichrome samples follow these patterns, and it is evident that the effects could have been achieved in a single firing, as long as it involved both reducing and oxidizing phases.

Our studies of these paints have shown that the Halaf potters had an extraordinary control of materials and firing conditions. They varied the color and texture of the paints by varying: the amount of iron oxide used (i.e., the ratio of iron oxide to clay mineral slip); the form of the iron oxide (coarse granular vs. fine powdery hematite); and the method of application of the paint (merely brushed on, or carefully burnished in addition). They also controlled the use of fluxes. The addition of potassium enabled glass to form in some paints during reduction firing; this allowed them to retain their black color even when the final kiln atmosphere was an oxidizing one. Lack of potassium but abundant aluminum (in the clay minerals) in other paints tended to retard the effects of reduction firing and sintering. The combination of several paint types on a single vessel which underwent a complex firing cycle shows just how well controlled these materials were.

We have noted several times that the body paste of these Halaf vessels is well fused but not excessively so. Overfired pots are rare, contrary to the 'Ubaid wares from southern Mesopotamia, and wasters are not generally noted in the archaeological reports. On the other hand, the paints on these bodies cover the range from barely sintered to recrystallized to downright glassy, with several different types coexisting on the same body. Moreover, the paints and bodies are apparently cured in the same firing achieving a well-matched ensemble of polychrome painting on strong bodies. This is further evidence that the potters had an unusually keen knowledge of their materials and control of their kilns since they produced oxidation and reduction firing at high temperatures without adversely affecting the structure of the bodies of their vessels.

This kind of material and kiln control is also responsible for the magnificent productions of 6th and 5th century B.C. Athenian potters (see Chapter 12, this volume), whose technological antecedents appear here in 5th millenium Mesopotamia.

This is merely a preliminary study of some Halaf wares with the intent of illustrating the range of paints used and how various effects were attained. It remains now to attempt to localize this remarkable pottery production, and discover how these techniques were disseminated throughout northern Mesopotamia, and how they may have influenced other local pottery industries; we hope that others will take up this worthy task.

ACKNOWLEDGMENTS

The results reported in this paper are part of a larger project on 'Ubaid and related ceramics in southern, central, and northern Mesopotamia. The petrographic and electron microprobe work was funded by National Science Foundation Grant #SOC75-17430. Chemical analyses were run on the MAC automated electron microprobe in the Department of Earth and Planetary Sciences at MIT. We wish especially to thank Joan Oates at Cambridge University for loaning many of the samples; also Tom Davidson who supplied some of the samples from Tell Halaf. Certain sherds from Tell Halaf and Tepe Gawra were acquired from the University of Pennsylvania Museum. Leo Morris, Jr., helped with the preparation of text and illustrations at MIT. Finally, we wish to thank Fred Matson for discussions in the spring of 1978 concerning several technological issues related to aspects of this study.

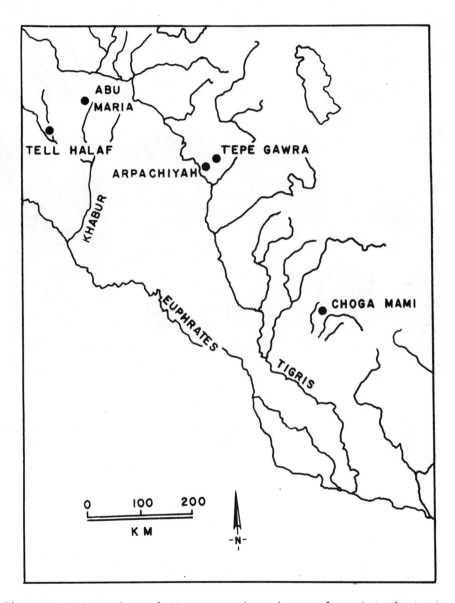

Figure 1. Location of Mesopotamian sites referred to in text.

Figure 2. Halaf sherds used in this study, arranged according to paint type: (a, b), monochrome black matt; (c – i), monochrome reddish brown matt; (j – p), black or brown shiny; (q – t), monochrome orange, light brown, or red shiny; (u – y), bichrome sherds. The two samples from Arpachiyah were not available for illustration. Letters can be correlated with site and sample numbers on Table 1. Scales are not the same for each sherd. Bichrome colors are represented by solid black lines and stippling.

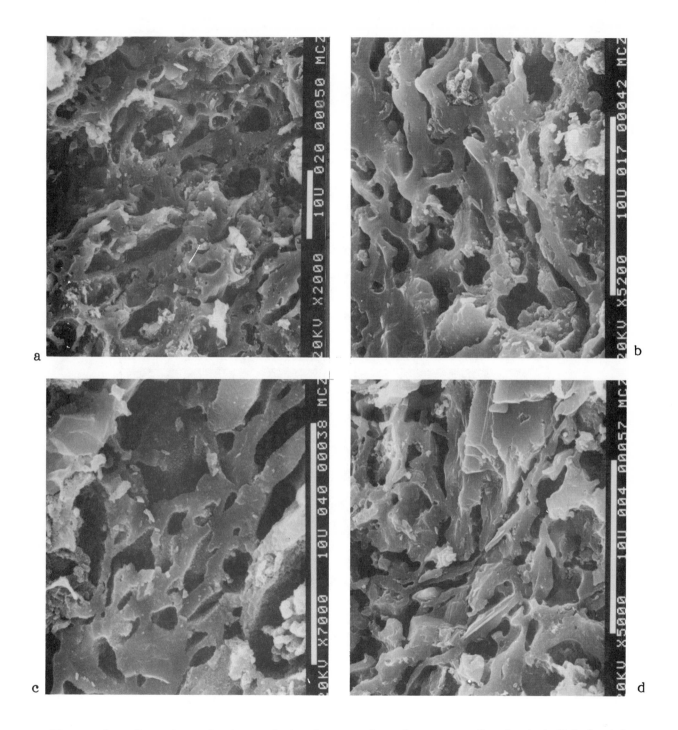

Figure 3. Scanning electron photomicrographs of pastes of selected Halaf style sherds. Note elongate cellular structure. Power and scale as shown. (a) Sherd JH-8 (32-42-15) from Tell Halaf (Figure 2l). (b) Sherd 38-13-878 from Tepe Gawra (Figure 2e). (c) Sherd 38-13-875 (Figure 2n), found at Tepe Gawra, but may have been brought in from Arpachiyah. (d) Sherd CM 110 (Figure 2s) from Choga Mami; cellular structure present but not well developed. Reproduce at 85%.

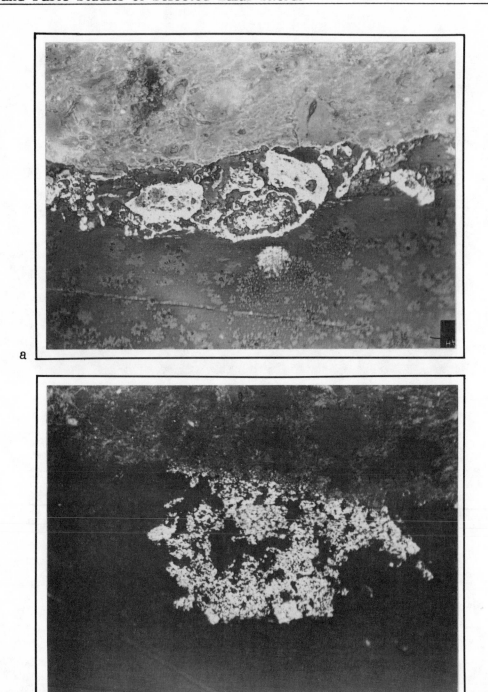

Figure 4. Reflected light photomicrographs of matt paints on Halaf style sherds. Magnification 500x. (a) Sintered, red matt paint on monochrome sherd from Choga Mami (CM 369D; Figure 2h and 6a), containing abundant bright hematite and less abundant hematite-stained silicates. Note the relict coarse grain shapes. (b) Recrystallized, black matt paint on monochrome sherd from Choga Mami (CM 369A; Figure 2b and 6b) containing abundant bright light-reflecting specular hematite grains and minor silicates.

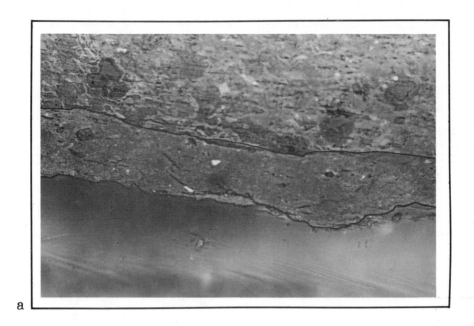

a

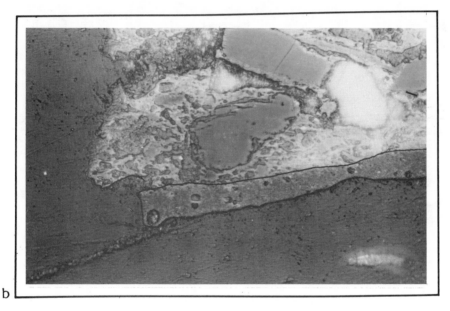

b

Figure 5. Reflected light photomicrographs of shiny paints on Halaf style sherds. Magnification 500x. (a) Partially fused, light brown shiny paint on monochrome sherd from Tell Halaf (JH-9; 32-43-1; Figure 2q and 6d), containing fine-grained, hematite-stained clay minerals. These cannot be distinguished in reflected light but make up most of the solid gray paint layer. In polarized transmitted light, the clay minerals are anisotropic and semi-aligned (probably a result of burnishing). (b) Melted, brown shiny paint on monochrome sherd from Tell Halaf (JH-2; Figure 2m and 6e), containing abundant glass and black iron oxide dust. Note the similarity of appearance in reflected light to the paint layer in Figure 4c. In unpolarized transmitted light, the glass is clear brown except for the disseminated fine-grained magnetite (?) dust.

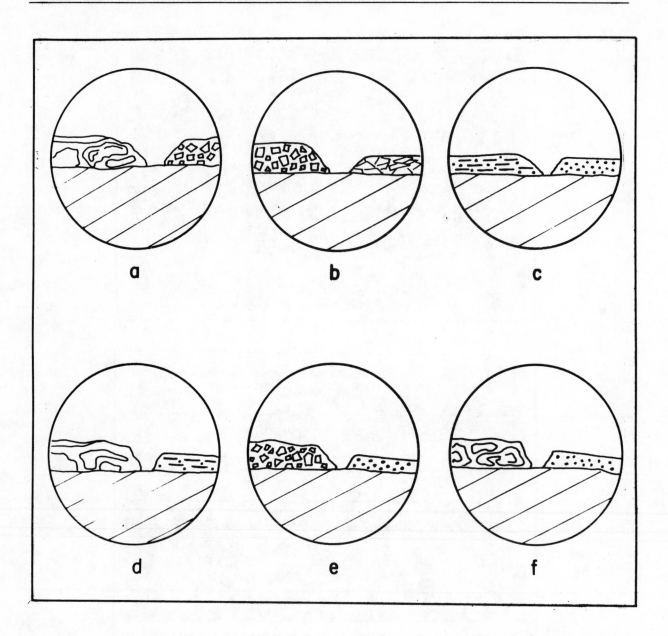

Figure 6. Idealized drawings of monochrome paint textures, as if seen through a petrographic microscope using a combination of transmitted and reflected light. (a) Red matt paint (Choga Mami type); hematite is only sintered leaving relict grain shapes (Figure 4a; CM 369D). (b) Black matt paint; the hematite is in specular form and appears to have recrystallized (Figure 4b; CM 369A). (c) Red matt paint (Tepe Gawra type); unaligned micaceous minerals with disseminated hematite dust, all sintered. (d) Orange or red shiny paint; aligned micaceous minerals with hematite dust, all sintered (Figure 5a; JH-9). (e) Brown or black shiny paint; mostly clear brown glass and disseminated magnetite (?) dust (Figure 5b; JH-2).

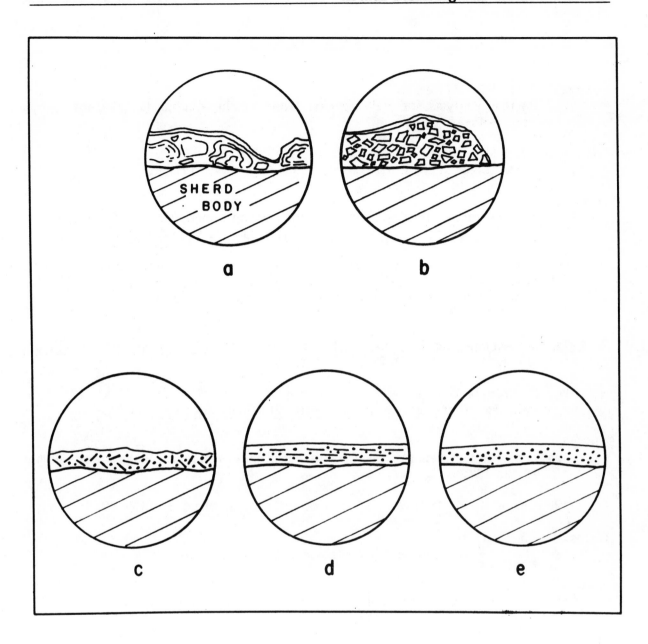

Figure 7. Idealized drawings of bichrome paint combinations. (a) Red matt and black matt paints (Tepe Gawra sample 38-13-705; Figure 2u). (b) Black matt and green matt paints (Tepe Gawra sample 38-13-836; Figure 2v). (c) Orange shiny and brown shiny paints (Tell Halaf sample JH-5; Figure 2w). (d) Red matt and orange shiny paints (Tell Halaf sample JH-3, Figure 2x; Choga Mami sample CM 184, Figure 2y). (e) Black matt and black shiny paints. (f) Red matt and black shiny paints.

REFERENCES

Davidson, T. and H. McKerrell
  1976   Pottery analysis and Halaf period trade in the Khabur headwaters region. _Iraq_ 38:45-56.

Mallowan, M. and J. Rose
  1935   Excavations at Tell Arpachiyah, 1933. _Iraq_ 2:1-178.

Matson, F.R.
  1945   Technological development of pottery in northern Syria during the Chalcolithic age. _Journal of the American Ceramic Society_ 28:20-25.

  1965   Ceramic ecology: an approach to the study of the early cultures of the Near East. In, _Ceramics and Man_, F.R. Matson, ed. Pp. 202-217. Viking Fund Publication no. 41. Chicago: Aldine.

Noll, W.
  1976   Mineralogie und Technik der fruhen Keramken Grossmesopotamiens. _N. Jb. Miner. Abh._ 127:261-288. Stuttgart.

Noll, W., R. Holm, and L. Born
  1975   Painting of ancient ceramics. _Angew. Chem. Internat._ 14:602-613.

Oates, J.
  1969a A preliminary report: the first season's excavations at Choga Mami. _Sumer_ 25:133-137.

  1969b Choga Mami, 1967-68: a preliminary report. _Iraq_ 31:115-152.

Oates, D. and J. Oates
  1976   _The Rise of Civilization_. Elsevier.

Oppenheim, M.
  1943   _Tell Halaf, v. I. Die Prahistorische Funde._ Bearbeitet von Hubert Schmidt. Berlin: Walter de Gruyter and Co.

Tite, M.
  1969   Determination of the firing temperature of ancient ceramics by measurement of thermal expansion: a reassessment. _Archaeometry_ 11:132-143.

Tite, M. and Y. Maniatis
  1975a Scanning electron microscopy of fired calcareous clays. _Transactions and Journal of the British Ceramic Society_ 74:19-22.

  1975b Examination of ancient pottery using the scanning electron microscope. _Nature_ 257:122-123.

Tobler, A.
  1950   _Excavations at Tepe Gawra, v. II, Levels IX-XX._ Philadelphia: University of Pennsylvania Press.

Chapter 14

Technological and Cultural Aspects of Teotihuacan Period "Thin Orange" Ware

Charles C. Kolb

Thin Orange pottery is a luxury ware associated with the large Mesoamerican city of Teotihuacan. Teotihuacan, located in a valley to the northeast of the Valley of Mexico, site of modern Mexico City, was the center of political, religious, and economic activity in the Meseta Central (Central Plateau; Figure 1) of Mexico during the Classic Period (approximately A.D. 50-750). The city comprised some 20.5 square kilometers during its apogee, with a population of 85-125,000 inhabitants (possibly as many as 200,000; Millon 1970:1077). Sanders and Price (1968:29-31) considered Teotihuacan to be a pan-Mesoamerican culture since its influence was felt during the Classic as far away as the Yucatan Peninsula and the southern Maya area. It is probable that the Teotihuacan sphere of contact in Mesoamerica included an area of 1.79 million square kilometers (ca. 700,000 square miles), with perhaps as many as a million inhabitants.

Thin Orange was apparently in great demand at the urban center and larger rural sites in the Teotihuacan Valley. It was undoubtedly associated with religious activities, especially with funeral rites and as burial offerings, and perhaps with all rite de passage events among at least the elite or upper classes at Teotihuacan. In addition to its ritual functions it may have acquired heirloom status and been passed from generation to generation as Wedgwood pottery, Waterford crystal, Hummel bone china figurines, etc., are in present-day western culture.

First reported by Penafiel (1890), Thin Orange was described by Seler (1915), who called it dunnwandinger hellgelber ("thin-walled bright yellow" ware). It also acquired other names, including "yellowish-red" pottery (Linne 1942, 1947), "eggshell orange" ware (Longyear 1940:269), "Thin Orange" ware (Vaillant 1938; Shepard 1946), and ceramica anaranjada delgada (Armillas 1944). Its spatial distribution extends from Teotihuacan and Calpulalpan in the northern sector of the Mexican Meseta Central southward as far as the sites of Kaminaljuyu in Highland Guatemala, and Copan in Honduras (Figure 2). "Abundant occurrences" have been reported throughout central, western, and southern Mexico in the states of Colima, Hidalgo, Puebla, Tlaxcala, Guerrero, Morelos, Jalisco, and Oaxaca. In the Maya area, the pottery has been noted in both the Highlands of Guatemala and Honduras and the Lowlands of Yucatan.

Although references to Thin Orange appeared as early as 1890, detailed typological-chronological and technological studies have been conducted only since the early 1930s. Most authorities do not believe Thin Orange was made by the resident artisans at the urban center of Teotihuacan, but instead that it constituted an import from one or more pottery-making centers south of the Basin of Mexico. The importation argument rests upon the fact that geologically/petrographically, the clay and aplastics of Thin Orange found at Teotihuacan did not match the clay and aplastic constituents of wares which were known to have been manufactured locally at that city, including Monochrome Black, Monochrome Brown, and Tan Monochrome Copoid wares, to name only a few. The present report summarizes and updates the technological studies and cultural postulates concerning supposed centers of manufacture of Thin Orange ware.

SUMMARY OF TECHNOLOGICAL STUDIES

Mineralogical Studies

A study of 46 thin sections, 7 of which were from Teotihuacan, resulted in creation of three groupings of Thin Orange ware on the basis of analyses of aplastic content (Sotomayor and Castillo Tejero 1963). These aplastic groupings were as follows: (1) Group A (n = 43) contained particles of quartziferous schists, chlorite schists, iron oxides (hematite), quartite, and quartz. Three subgroups were identified on the basis of relative abundance of calcite, from abundant (n = 6), to scanty (n = 28), to none (n = 9). (2) Group B (n = 2) included andesine, orthoclase, hypersthene, hornblende, biotite mica, magnetite, titanite, and quartz. (3) Group C (n = 1) contained banded quartz, quartz, biotite mica, andesine, with abundant fragments of diorite quartz and orthoclase. The seven Teotihuacan specimens were all of Group A, four with abundant calcite, two with scanty calcite, and one with no calcite. Group A tempers were concluded to be the "ideal type" and had originated in a metamorphic zone. Consulting the Carta Geologica de la Republica Mexicana (1960), Sotomayor and Castillo Tejero discerned ten areas in central Mexico as possible centers of Thin Orange manufacture (1963:18-19, Fig. 2). All of these were in northern and southern Puebla, or northern Guerrero and northern Oaxaca.

Later surface surveys and excavations by the Pennsylvania State University Teotihuacan Valley Project (William T. Sanders, director), provided a collection of 4,370 sherds of Thin Orange ware. This total Thin Orange sample was examined by the author in order to discern typological, chronological, and technological data (Kolb 1973), and 1300 of the 2890 sherds from excavation contexts were utilized in an analysis of aplastics. Since the original report, the remaining 1590 excavated and 1480 surface sample sherds have also been intensively examined regarding tempering material. The analysis was conducted using a binocular microscope (60x magnification) and tangental nonfluorescent lighting source. A fresh break in the paste was made with pliers to facilitate the examination of worn sherd edges, and the same researcher (Kolb) made all of the evaluations. It was determined that basic distinctions can be made between the types by using a 20x hand lens in normal daylight. This technique has been used in the field, and the same sherds were rechecked in the laboratory to determine accuracy (98.5 percent). The analysis of 4,370 sherds of Classic Period Teotihuacan Thin Orange pottery showed that the light colored clay was thickly strewn with opaque, translucent, lustrous, and crystalline aplastics; few clear grains were found. The major constituents included: quartzite, calcined calcite, talc, quartz, muscovite mica, and hematite. Minor inclusions were: feldspars, hornblende, chlorites, and scoria. No vegetal fibers or seeds of any kind were observed.

The sherds examined were originally divided into two distinctive groups, Type Alpha and Type Beta, and these groupings were later reconfirmed by petrographic analyses (Kolb 1965, 1969, 1973). Table 1 summarizes the findings which have been detailed elsewhere (Kolb 1973, 1977).

One notable inclusion found in both types was scoria or basalt. Scoria is essentially "pyroclastic ejecta, usually of basic composition, characterized by marked vesicularity, dark color, heaviness, and partly crystallized" (American Geological Institute 1960:439). "Basalt" is here defined as a fine-grained dark colored igneous rock composed mostly of microscopic calcium-sodium (plagioclase) feldspar, pyroxene, and olivine (Pough 1955:15-16; American Geological Institute 1960:41). Scoria and basalt particles may have been natural, fluvially weathered residuals in the raw clays, or accidentally added during the crushing of the clay or grinding of temper when the abrading surfaces of the implements (manos and metates of basalt, and mortars and pestles of tezontli, a scoria) wore away.

Type Alpha, which occurred in Teotihuacan Valley sites from Late Tzacualli through Oxtotipac Phases (A.D. 50-850), contained substantial quantities of quartzite, calcite, talc, and quartz, with lesser quantities of muscovite mica and hematite. It corresponded with previous mineralogical studies of Thin Orange conducted by Beskow (Linne 1934:213-214) and Shepard (1946:198-201), as well as with Sotomayor and Castillo Tejero's Group A (1963:10). Type Beta, which was limited to Metepec and Oxtotipac Phase sites (A.D. 700-850), had substantial quantities of muscovite mica, quartzite, and calcite, with lesser quantities of quartz, talc, and hematite. The Beta had no reported parallel in the technological literature, but corresponded to a type of Thin Orange ware referred to descriptively as "Coarse Thin Orange" (Kolb 1965, 1973), which may readily be discerned with a hand lens. Shepard reported micaceous fragments present in all pastes, but failed to note if there were quantities as great as one-third of the total aplastic content (1946:200). She, too, found sherds without calcite content, but reported calcite to be as abundant as quartzite in some sherds, which was also noted in both Alpha and Beta types.

Field observations were made in 1968 and 1972 at six sites in Hidalgo, Tlaxcala, and Puebla. These sites had a total of 1205 Thin Orange sherds, all of the Alpha type. I have not seen the "near-Thin Orange" pottery from Huajuapan described by Paddock (1966), but this may possibly consist of copies or imitations of Thin Orange or a minor local variant.

A preliminary examination of non-Thin Orange Classic Period sherds from urban and rural Teotihuacan sites indicated a radical difference in aplastic inclusions when

TABLE 1

Inclusions in <u>Alpha</u> and <u>Beta</u> Thin Orange

Minerals/Other Inclusions	Approximate Percentages
Type <u>Alpha</u> (n = 4,258)	
Quartzite (angular and subangular)	35-25
Calcite (angular)	25-20
Talc	15-5
Quartz (angular and rounded)	10-5
Muscovite mica	10-5
Hematite (lumps and crystals)	5-0
Feldspar (angular)	1-0
Hornblende (angular)	1-0
Various chlorites/schists	1-0
Scoria or basalt	1-0
Unidentified minerals	Traces
Type <u>Beta</u> (n = 112)	
Muscovite mica	65-30
Quartzite (angular and subangular)	30-20
Quartz (angular and rounded)	10-5
Calcite (angular and subangular)	10-0
Talc	10-0
Hematite (lumps and crystals)	5-0
Feldspar (angular)	1-0
Hornblende (angular)	1-0
Various chlorites/schists	1-0
Scoria or basalt	1-0
Unidentified minerals	Traces

compared to the Thin Orange pottery. The temper of these sherds was predominantly volcanic ash or volcanic sand with considerable quantities of quartz and epidote, the latter a common mineral in metamorphic rock. The quartz was generally angular and averaged 0.5 mm. in size, i.e., "medium" on the Wentworth scale. Quartz fragments were found in the slips and throughout the paste cross-sections of other Teotihuacan wares. Epidote, always present in the slip and paste cross-sections of Teotihuacan wares, appeared as dark green or blackish green to dark brown, transparent to translucent, and in sizes of 0.2 to 0.5 mm. (i.e., both "fine" and "medium" size grades). Mica, quartzite (rounded and subangular), and minute silicon dioxide fragments (angular)--probably obsidian--were also found, as were occasional plant impressions. Other minerals occasionally present in the Teotihuacan sherds include: quartzite, olivine, vesicular rhyolite (?), ferruginous clay, gypsum/talc, basalt (?), felsite, and various mafics.

Neutron Activation Analyses

Neutron activation analyses of 41 Thin Orange sherds, including 20 from Teotihuacan, indicated a high incidence of cerium and chromium in this ceramic compared to other Mesoamerican archaeological pottery (Abascal, Harbottle, and Sayre 1972, 1973; Abascal 1974). Additional neutron activation studies included more comprehensive analysis of 69 samples of Thin Orange (including the original 41) (Harbottle, Sayre, and Abascal 1976), plus samples from El Salvador (n = 4), Guatemala (n = 5), and Honduras (n = 1). Five clay samples from modern pottery manufacturing centers in the state of Puebla (Acatlan, n = 3, and San Juan Ixcaquixtla, n = 2) were also analyzed. This comparison of Thin Orange specimens with 160 Mesoamerican pottery and clay samples resulted in determination of at least 5 Thin Orange groups. Fifty-two specimens fell into a homogeneous grouping termed "Core Thin Orange," which correlated directly with Sotomayor and Castillo Tejero's Group A Thin Orange (1963) and Kolb's Alpha Thin Orange (1969, 1973, 1976).

In summary, the distinctive Thin Orange Mesoamerican pottery has been found by several studies to comprise a coherent mineral and chemical analytical group, referred to variously as Type Alpha, Group A, and "Core Thin Orange." Small numbers of Thin Orange or Thin Orange-like sherds differ in a number of characteristics, principally mineralogical, leading to definition of Type Beta, or texture ("Coarse Thin Orange") (Kolb 1965). Classic sherds of other wares from urban and rural Teotihuacan sites, undoubtedly manufactured locally, contained a different group of aplastics, including volcanic ash, volcanic sand, quartz, and epidote. This would suggest that Thin Orange ware of the Classic Period was not manufactured at Teotihuacan, but instead was imported. Various considerations for determining the locale of production and means of distribution will be developed below.

CULTURAL POSTULATES

Little is actually known about the acquisition of raw materials (aplastics and raw clays) or manufacturing techniques involved in pottery-making at Teotihuacan, although a "pottery-making area" has been located in the vicinity of the Moon Pyramid. Others have been located in the modern settlement of San Sebastian, which is still a viable pottery-producing community (Millon 1973:40; Krotzer 1976; Rattray

1976). In order to try to compensate for this lack of knowledge, the following postulates and subpostulates will be examined:

1. The raw clay may have been locally obtained or imported into Teotihuacan, where it was made into various ceramic forms.

2. The aplastics (<u>Alpha</u> and/or <u>Beta</u>) may have been locally obtained or imported into Teotihuacan.

3. The ceramic artisans may have been:

    a. Local Teotihuacanos residing in or near the urban center.

    b. Non-Tetihuacano (foreign) emigrant potters from "foreign" areas who came to Teotihuacan during the Early Classic.

    c. Teotihuacanos who had migrated to "foreign" areas and had returned to Teotihuacan.

    d. Teotihuacanos who migrated to "foreign" areas and did not return to Teotihuacan.

    e. Non-Teotihuacano (foreign) potters who resided in the "foreign" areas and manufactured the ceramic in their own locales.

Conclusions from the technological and typological investigations and neutron activation analyses, as well as data presented in this paper, permit the elimination of several of the postulates.

Postulates One and Two

Regarding the first and second postulates, i.e., that the raw clays and/or the aplastics (tempering materials) were either local or imported, it should be noted that probably <u>any</u> finely-washed, strong, high-grade plastic clay (either domestic or foreign) could have been employed in making Thin Orange ware. However, neutron activation analyses of Basin of Mexico clays and ceramics have effectively eliminated the first postulate (Abascal, Harbottle, and Sayre 1973; Harbottle, Sayre, and Abascal 1976), because these studies indicated that Thin Orange ware contained a high incidence of cerium and chromium not found in the indigenous Basin of Mexico wares. Therefore, clays apparently from outside the Basin of Mexico and its Teotihuacan subvalley were employed in the manufacture of the ware. These investigators tried to determine the origin of the ware, but on the basis of analyses of sodium, barium, calcium, nickel, and titanium, plus computer-based clustering studies of other Mesoamerican pottery, they were forced to conclude that "there is nothing in our work that definitely suggests a geographic source for it" (1976:18). Nonetheless, they were able definitely to eliminate Acatlan, Puebla, suggested by Armillas (1944), and San Juan Ixcaquixtla, Puebla, suggested by Cook de Leonard (1956, 1957). In addition, the region near the mouth of the Rio Coatzacoalcos in Vera Cruz, postulated by Abascal (1974), was eliminated as the source. The researchers' findings also eliminated Oaxaca as a point of origin of "Classic Teotihuacan" wares and "Core Thin Orange" ware as well. Therefore, the importation of clay for Thin Orange manufacture may be a reality, although its source is presently unknown.

Other lines of evidence supported the importation of Thin Orange materials or finished vessels from outside Teotihuacan. The distinct variations in aplastic contents of the Alpha and Beta types strengthened the argument, despite the quantities of sherds in urban and rural sites in the Teotihuacan Valley. Design motifs which appeared on Thin Orange vessels, and their method and technique of execution, also supported the supposition that non-Teotihuacanos ("foreigners") made Thin Orange ware. These motifs, such as the incised "cumulus" cloud, interlaced lines, and multiple scallop), were infrequently duplicated on known indigenous Teotihuacan wares. When similar motifs did appear on the Teotihuacan Monochrome Brown, Black, or Tan Copoid wares (Kolb 1965), it was always after they had been used on Thin Orange, suggesting that the local Teotihuacan monochrome ware producers copied these "new" designs on their own craft products. This generally occurred from Early Tlamimilolpa through Early Xolalpan Phases (A.D. 250-550) (Kolb 1973). Also, the hemispherical bowl form with ring or annular base had no known antecedent at Teotihuacan, and appeared to have been introduced, as only a few hemispherical bowl forms in local monochrome wares had been reported at Teotihuacan (Kolb 1965). Thus, there appears to have been at least some contact between the two pottery-producing artisan groups.

Ethnographic data on modern Teotihuacan potters is lacking, as is sufficient petrographic study of other pottery from the areas suggested as centers of Thin Orange manufacture (northern and southern Puebla, northern Oaxaca, and northern Guerrero). Also, the problem of chronological depth cannot presently be totally resolved. Undoubtedly there was change over time in terms of the attitudes and behavior of the ceramic artisans, hence ceramic forms and modes of decoration would change. Nevertheless, the following might be a feasible explanation of the occurrence of Thin Orange at Teotihuacan.

During the Tzacualli-Miccaotli Phases (50 B.C. - A.D. 250) of Teotihuacan culture, non-Teotihuacan ("foreign") potters residing at the developing urban center produced Thin Orange ware using indigenous raw clays, imported aplastics, and methods of manufacture from their "home" areas. This would account for the introduction of new vessel forms (such as the hemispherical bowl), decorative techniques ("self-slipping"), and design motifs (incised "cumulus" cloud, etc.). These potters may have constituted an elite or special class (or perhaps caste?) of artisans separate from local Teotihuacan pottery-makers, and both groups produced their respective wares simultaneously. Heyden (1975:139) suggested that "residents of the southern part of the Valley of Mexico moved northward in the direction of Teotihuacan after the eruption of Xitle volcano (ca. 200 B.C.) in the Cuicuilco area." It is possible that these migrants began the production of Thin Orange ware at Teotihuacan, but this conjecture cannot be substantiated.

If Alpha/Group A/"Core Thin Orange" were reserved for ceremonial, ritual, and/or religious occasions, as has been suggested, these emigrant potters could have had a special status position above the local ceramicists. The locals copied the "new" design motif infrequently on outflaring wall, flat-bottom bowls, since the designs were reserved for certain wares and/or artisans, and the motifs could have had a prehistoric "copyright." Eventually local potters may have been integratred into the elite Thin Orange ware-producing group, but probably remained as elite craft specialists.

Postulate Three

This postulate, comprising five subpostulates, proposed that the ceramic artisans were: (a) local Teotihuacanos, (b) "foreign" emigrants to Teotihuacan during the Early Classic, (c) "returned" former Teotihuacanos who had previously migrated to "foreign" pottery-producing centers outside the Basin of Mexico and northern Puebla, (d) Teotihuacanos who had migrated to "foreign" pottery-producing centers and remained there, and/or (e) non-Teotihuacanos residing in "foreign" areas who manufactured pottery in their own locales. An additional supposition would be that the manufacture of certain types of pottery was restricted to special classes (or castes) of ceramic producers.

In the case of Alpha/Group A/"Core Thin Orange," since technological studies and neutron activation analyses revealed that the ware was not locally made (at least in San Sebastian), subpostulates 3a through 3c are rendered invalid. It is possible that some former Teotihuacan potters residing in the "foreign" area produced Thin Orange utilizing local clays and aplastics. New vessel forms and decorative techniques could have been "copyrighted" by this class of potters, which would account for the infrequency of making the hemispherical bowl form at Teotihuacan in local clays or wares, and using the "new" design motifs. Alpha Thin Orange could have been made in the "foreign" area using local clays but with "imported" aplastics from yet a third area. There is no evidence to suggest the viability of the "imported" aplastics conjecture. Subpostulates 3d and 3e are valid suppositions.

Therefore, Alpha Thin Orange seems to have been entirely a "foreign" ceramic produced in "foreign" areas by resident artisans who had little contact with Teotihuacan pottery-makers. Potential loci of manufacture exist in southern Puebla and adjacent Vera Cruz, as well as in northern Guerrero and northern Oaxaca. These "foreign" potters employed their own indigenous clays, indigenous aplastics, and local manufacturing and decorative techniques, which would account for the introduction of the new vessel forms and decorative motifs into Classic Teotihuacan culture. Artisans at Teotihuacan probably had no hand at making Alpha Thin Orange, but Teotihuacanos may have constituted the pochteca merchant importers and the redistributors of the ware and were certainly the primary, perhaps nearly exclusive, consumers. Local Teotihuacan potters could possibly have eventually adopted the design motifs of this popular import, perhaps to increase their own "sales." This latter conjecture is also a logical assumption based on data presented here and elsewhere.

"Classic Teotihuacan" Thin Orange, while not abundant, represents a totally different set of circumstances. This ware was made from clays identical to those from San Sebastian Teotihuacan and contained microcrystalline inclusions but little if any calcite aplastic—i.e., probably Sotomayor and Castillo Tejero's Group A-3 (1963:10). This might represent the attempt by local Teotihuacan potters to replicate Thin Orange ware using local clays and some aplastic of the "desired" calcite type. It would appear that Rattray's suggestion (1976) that a form of Thin Orange was being made at Teotihuacan by the Metepec Phase (A.D. 700-750) would be validated on the basis of temper materials and clay chemistry. This production may have continued into the Oxtotipac Phase (A.D. 750-850) (Kolb 1973). "Classic Teotihuacan" Thin Orange appeared to be Group A-3, and subpostulates 3a through 3c are valid for this variety of Thin Orange. The other chemical groupings of the ware determined by Harbottle and his colleagues (1976:16-18) probably represent other areas, such as the Gulf Cost and Oaxaca, where potters imitated Thin Orange using local materials.

Type Beta Thin Orange, containing muscovite mica, had no apparent parallel in the literature, but was reasonably similar to Sotomayor and Castillo Tejero's Groups B and C, both of which contained some biotite mica (1963:10). This type dated to the Metepec and Oxtotipac Phases (A.D. 700-850) but was not abundantly represented at rural Teotihuacan Valley sites. Beta ware was confined to large storage jars (amphorae) and carinated basin forms which normally lacked decoration (Kolb 1965, 1973). It may have been made in the Huajuapan de Leon area of Oaxaca near the Puebla border or in a similar geomorphic region (Kolb 1976). Subpostulates 3d and 3e appear valid.

The subpostulate that classes (or castes) many have existed among the pottery producers is one yet unresolved. The manufacturers of Alpha and Beta Thin Orange could have been of different artisan classes if one assumes on the basis of form and decoration that Beta type was produced apparently for domestic utility rather than for ceremonial/religious purposes. There is no supportive ethnographic analogy for this area.

IMPORTATION ROUTES

Alpha/Group A/"Core Thin Orange" was imported into both the Teotihuacan Valley and the Basin of Mexico from geomorphic areas to the south or southeast via one or more mercantile routes and by one or more mechanisms. There are two primary routes into the Teotihuacan Valley from the Basin of Puebla-Tlaxcala and areas to the south and east. One of these routes enters via the Texcoco Region of the Basin of Mexico and continues to Teotihuacan from the southwest, while the other arcs northward through northwestern Tlaxcala and the Plains of Apan into Teotihuacan from the northeast. I shall subsequently consider each of these routes in more detail.

By "mechanisms," I refer not only to the importation of the ceramic but also to its redistribution once it reached provincial centers and/or the urban center. Some of the more viable possibilities are briefly mentioned below but will not be elaborated since the proof of one versus another would be virtually impossible. If the mercantile mechanism were in private hands, it was probably organized on the basis of a clan (calpulli), lineage, or household compound. Alternatively, if the commercial mechanism were a function of the state, it was undoubtedly controlled by a bureaucracy and was staffed by state employees or contracted personnel. Therefore, one may propose a "private sector" model with independent or licensed importers, or an "imperial" model in which the state functioned as the importer. Another permutation would be whether the importer distributed/sold the ceramic to the consumer, or whether middlemen redistributors were also involved.

Teotihuacan, with a population perhaps only one-fourth that of the Postclassic Aztecs, was militarily unable to control vast areas of Mesoamerica, but its economic influences were relatively widespread (Sanders 1977:408). The Teotihuacan sphere probably consisted of those nearby territories that could be controlled by military means and included the Basin of Mexico, southern Hidalgo, northwestern Tlaxcala, and eastern Morelos (Hirth 1978:320-321). Since military political control of "foreign" areas was impossible, Teotihuacan influence was felt through mercantile institutions. By analogy with later Aztec trade activity, new settlements or barrios adjacent to existing communities would be established on the key routes to oversee commercial activities, and the settlers would marry into local or regional ethnic group lineages or clans, thus establishing kinship relations in "foreign" areas. The Teotihuacanos had craft production organized and the trade routes controlled.

Different trading or interaction spheres, each with its own "unionized" tumpline carrier organizations, may have been based on a kinship unit such as a clan (calpulli) or lineage. Sanders (1978) suggested that the merchants could have been organized on the same principle as obsidian workers at Tenochtitlan during the Late Postclassic (Aztec) Period. Sindicatos (unions) could have transferred their merchandise at distribution centers between the economic spheres. Figure 3 illustrates probable interaction spheres involved in the importation of Thin Orange ware into the Basin of Mexico, and especially to the urban center of Teotihuacan. The distances (in kilometers) illustrated are approximations, but demonstrate that tumpline carriers used by pochteca merchant-traders could have easily accomplished the importation and subsequent distribution of Alpha type and possibly Beta, Thin Orange ware. The thickness of the arrows suggests the intensity of the trade between the various Classic sites.

The present data concerning Alpha Thin Orange ware indicate one or more centers of manufacture outside the Basin of Mexico, most probably in southern Puebla, adjacent Veracruz, northern Guerrero, or northern Oaxaca. Beta type Thin Orange may have been made in northern Oaxaca, possibly in the Huajuapan de Leon vicinity, where muscovite mica, quartzite, and calcite were present. Numerous sites could have been part of the exchange network as transfer points and distributional centers in the movement of Thin Orange from its center of manufacture out to consumers.

Southwest Texcoco Route

Parsons' Tx-EC-26 site with "relatively abundant" Thin Orange was a possible transfer point between regions. This site was a one-component Early Classic (A.D. 150-550) civic-ceremonial center of some four hectares extent at the lower edge of the Upper Piedmont in the southern Texcoco area (Parsons 1971:59). This settlement, a hamlet with fewer than one hundred people, was the only site in either Early or Late Classic that Parsons mentioned as having Thin Orange ware present in any quantity. The small size of the site would tend to preclude its function as a distributional center for Thin Orange. However, it could have served as a "transfer point" where pochtecan tumpline carriers from the Basin of Puebla-Tlaxcala area transferred their cargo to Basin of Mexico tumpline carriers, who distributed the ware throughout the Basin region. It is suggested that the Tx-EC-26 site simply served as a short-term transfer point between the major physiographic zones. Another probable distribution point was the Tx-EC-32 site, 6 kilometers west of Tx-EC-26 and 15 kilometers south of modern Texcoco. This site was the largest in the Texcoco Plain at this time (Parsons 1971:60-61).

Other transfer points or distribution centers probably existed in the Calpulalpan region of the northern Basin of Mexico (see below), and at San Juan Ixcaquixtla in southern Puebla, once hypothesized as a center of Thin Orange manufacture. A key site for the probable importation of the ware from the south into the Teotihuacan Valley was Classic Cholula, but unfortunately we know little about the nature of the Classic and of Thin Orange at this site (cf. Marquina 1970; Dumond 1972; Dumond and Mueller 1972). Cholula was the dominant urban polity in the southern Basin of Mexico/Puebla area, although it was probably under Teotihuacan political jurisdiction. Thin Orange pottery of at least the Alpha type is known from Cholula. It is possible that during the Late Classic, as Teotihuacan's political power reached its zenith and began to wane, Cholula, then at its peak, became more independent, and perhaps rival trading spheres emerged between the Basin of Mexico and Puebla-Tlaxcala.

Northwest Tlaxcala Route

The Calpulalpan region (including Las Colinas, San Jose, and San Nicholas sites, as well as others) is also a key to understanding Thin Orange ceramic importation into the northeastern sections of the Teotihuacan polity. Less work has been done in this area than in the southern Valley of Mexico, and it is difficult to draw firm conclusions. A trade route linking Teotihuacan and Calpulalpan with Puebla and Tlaxcala was in use during Terminal Formative Patlachique and Tezoyuca Phases (ca. 200 B.C.), and continued in use with varying intensity into Colonial times (Charlton 1977). Nine sites, dating to the Late Teotihuacan period, were situated between the Teotihuacan Valley and the Plains of Apan. Two of these sites had from 20 to 50 percent Thin Orange pottery in their ceramic assemblages, while the other seven had over 50 percent. Unfortunately the Thin Orange from these sites has not yet been technologically analyzed.

Distributions of Alpha Thin Orange from Teotihuacan to the nearby regions of Texcoco, Chalco, Ixtapalapa, etc., may be assumed along the eastern side of the Basin of Mexico southward around the lake complex. Dispersement from Teotihuacan to the regions of Zumpango and Azcapotzalco is also noted in Figure 3. The Thin Orange importation in the Xochicalco area may have been via Azcapotzalco or Chalco, or perhaps directly from the center(s) of manufacture.

A useful direction for future investigation would be to examine quantities of Thin Orange and other local wares found at all postulated southern centers of manufacture. Ceramic technological and neutron activation analyses of selected sherds from selected sites will be most beneficial in determining, or at least delimiting, the possible manufacturing centers. Intensive ethnographic studies of indigenous Mexican potters are needed, with emphasis on their techniques of production and particularly their methods of obtaining raw materials and finished product distribution. Such studies would make great strides in illuminating Classic Period pottery manufacturing and trading patterns.

SUMMARY

Ceramic typological-chronological investigations, ceramic technological (especially petrological-mineralogical) studies, and neutron activation analyses have yielded important new data on Classic Period Teotihuacan Thin Orange ware. Various researchers have identified groups or types on the basis of the examination of the finished ceramic, aplastic materials, and raw clays from supposed "centers" of manufacture.

Type Alpha/Group A/"Core Thin Orange" was produced in an area south or southeast of the Basin of Mexico and imported into the Teotihuacan Valley. "Classic Thin Orange" was a Late Classic period imitation of this ware and was made at Teotihuacan. Type Beta, designed for utilitarian purposes, was also produced in an area south or southeast of the Basin of Mexico, perhaps in northern Oaxaca. Types Alpha and Beta were made by non-Teotihuacanos in their own local areas. "Classic Thin Orange" was manufactured from San Sebastian clays, probably by Teotihuacanos.

A model of importation/distribution is suggested which involves several Classic Period sites, and a sindicato of pochteca; controlled tumpline carriers is postulated as the transport mechanism. The trade network and interaction sphere was undoubtedly under Teotihuacan control.

ACKNOWLEDGMENTS

This paper is a revision of an earlier one read at the annual meeting of the American Anthropological Association, November 29, 1973, in New Orleans, Louisiana. The initial field research was conducted under the auspices of the Instituto Nacional de Antropologia e Historia, Mexico, D.F., and the Pennsylvania State University. I wish to thank Florencia Mueller, the late Anna O. Shepard, Evelyn Rattray, Frederick R. Matson, Gordon Ekholm, William T. Sanders, Garman Harbottle, Dean Arnold, and Eva Tucker for their invaluable advice.

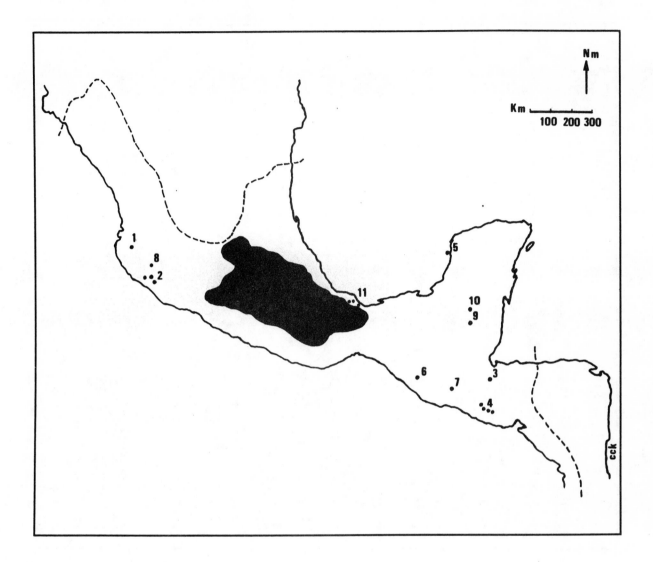

Figure 1. Basin of Mexico and Basin of Puebla-Tlaxcala physiography. Contour lines delineate the maximal Basin areas. Short dashed lines (- - -) illustrate the Teotihuacan Valley and the Texcoco Plain; long and short dashed line (-- - --) illustrates the division between the Basins. 1. Azcapotzalco; 2. Calpulalpan Region; 3. Chalco; 4. Cholula; 5. Cuicuilco; 6. Ixtapalapa; 7. Teotihuacan; 8. Tepeapulco; 9. Texcoco; 10. Tlaxcala Region.

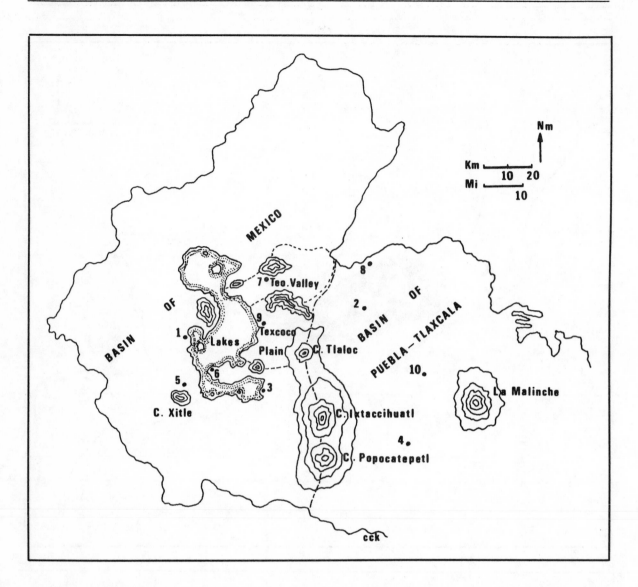

Figure 2. The distribution of Thin Orange Ware in Mesoamerica. The stippled area represents regions with significant quantitites of the pottery. The numbered sites or regions have lesser amounts of the ceramic: 1. Ahualuco, Jalisco; 2. Colima Region, Colima; 3. Copan, Honduras; 4. San Salvador region, El Salvador; 5. Isla de Jaina, Campeche; 6. Izapan, Chiapas; 7. Kaminaljuyu, Guatemala; 8. Sayula, Jalisco; 9. Tikal, Guatemala; 10. Uaxactun, Guatemala; 11. Rio Coatzalcoalcos region, Veracruz.

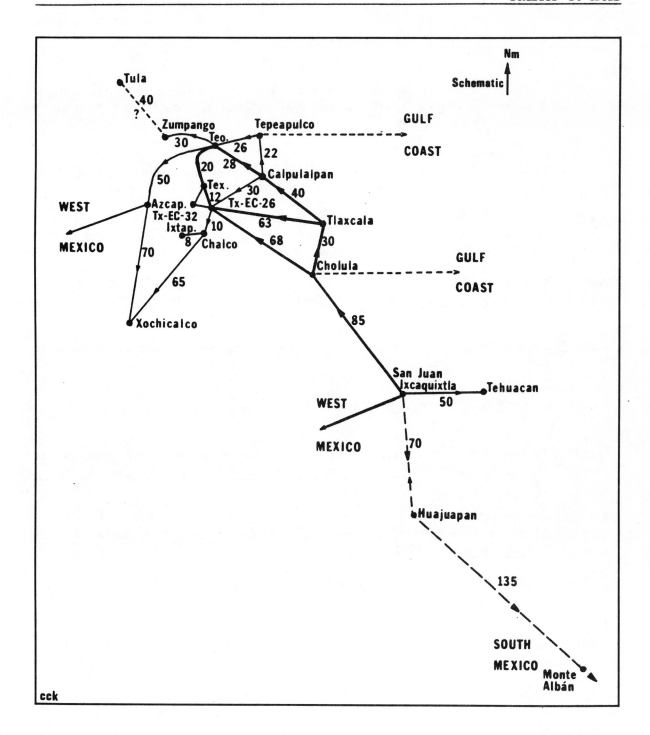

Figure 3. <u>Alpha</u> and <u>Beta</u> Thin Orange ware distribution routes in Central Mexico, showing the shortest distances (in km.) between sites and/or regions. Dashed lines indicate the probable route to southern Mexico, Yucatan, Guatemala, and Honduras. Shorter dashed lines depict possible routes to the Gulf Coast. Solid lines designate routes into the basin of Puebla-Tlaxcala and Basin of Mexico

REFERENCES

Abascal, R.
1974   Analisis por activacion de neutrones: una aportacion para la arqueologia moderna. Mexico, D.F.: Escuela Nacional de Antropologia e Historia y UNAM. Tesis.

Abascal, R., G. Harbottle, and E.V. Sayre
1972   Neutron activation study of Thin Orange. Paper presented at the Society for American Archaeology annual meeting, Bal Harbour, Florida.

1973   Correlation between terra cotta figurines and pottery from the Valley of Mexico and source clays by activation analysis. Paper presented at the American Chemical Society annual meeting, Dallas.

American Geological Institute
1960   Dictionary of Geological Terms, 2nd ed. Garden City: Doubleday.

Armillas, P.
1944   El problema de la ceramica anaranjada delgada. Escuela Nacional de Antropologia, Publicacion 1.

Carta Geologica
1960   Carta geologica de la Republica Mexicana. Mexico.

Charlton, T.H.
1977   Teotihuacan: trade routes of multi-tiered economy. Memorias de la Sociedad Mexicana de Antropologia, Guanajuato, Gto, Julio 31 - Agosto 6, 1977.

Cook de Leonard, C.
1956   Algunos antecedentes de la ceramica Tolteca. Revista Mexicana de Estudios Antropologicos 14:37-43.

1957   El origen de la ceramica anaranjada delgada. Escuela Nacional de Antropologia, Mexico, D.F. Tesis.

Dumond, D.
1972   Demographic aspects of the Classic Period in Puebla-Tlaxcala. Southwestern Journal of Anthropology 28:101-130.

Dumond, D. and F. Mueller
1972   Classic to post classic in highland Central Mexico. Science 175:1208-1215.

Harbottle, G., E.V. Sayre, and R. Abascal
1976   Neutron activation analysis of Thin Orange pottery. Paper presented at the Second Cambridge Symposium on Recent Research in Mesoamerican Archaeology, Cambridge, England, August 28-31, 1976.

Heyden, D.
1975   An interpretation of the cave underneath the Pyramid of the Sun in Teotihuacan, Mexico. American Antiquity 40:131-147.

Hirth, K.G.
1978   Teotihuacan regional population administration in eastern Morelos.   World Archaeology 9:320-333.

Kolb, C.C.
1965   A tentative ceramics classification for the Teotihuacan Valley (Patlachique through Aztec V Phases). Ms., Department of Sociology and Anthropology, Pennsylvania State University, University Park.

1969   Anaranjada delgada at Teotihuacan. Paper presented at the 1969 meeting of the Society for American Archaeology, Milwaukee.

1973   Thin Orange Ware at Teotihuacan.   Department of Anthropology, Pennsylvania State University, Occasional Papers in Anthropology 8:309-378.

1976   New data on Teotihuacan "Thin Orange" ware. Ms., Department of Anthropology, Pennsylvania State University, Behrend College (Erie).

1977   Technological investigations of Mesoamerican "Thin Orange" ceramics. Current Anthropology 18:534:536.

Krotzer, P.
1976   The potters of Teotihuacan. Paper presented at the Society for American Archaeology annual meeting, St. Louis, Missouri.

Linne, S.
1934   Archaeological researches at Teotihuacan, Mexico. Ethnographical Museum of Sweden, n.s., Publication 7.

1942   The yellowish-red pottery: a problem of Mexican trade relations. Ethnos 7:156-165.

1947   Thin Orange pottery of Mexico-Guatemala. Ethnos 12:127-136.

Longyear, J.M. III
1940   The ethnological significance of Copan pottery. In, The Maya and Their Neighbors, C.L. Hay, et al., eds. Pp. 268-271. New York.

Marquina, I. (coordinator)
1970   Proyecto Cholula. Instituto Nacional de Antropologia e Historia, Investigaciones, No. 19. Mexico.

Millon, R.
1970   Teotihuacan: completion of map of giant ancient city in the Valley of Mexico. Science 170:1077-1082.

1973   Urbanization at Teotihuacan, Mexico, Vol. 1: The Teotihuacan Map. Austin: University of Texas Press.

Paddock, J.
1966   Oaxaca in Ancient Mesoamerica. In, Ancient Oaxaca, J. Paddock, ed. Pp. 83-242. Stanford: Stanford University Press.

Parsons, J.
  1971 Prehispanic settlement patterns in the Texcoco region, Mexico. University
        of Michigan, Museum of Anthropology, Memoirs No. 3. Ann Arbor.

Penafiel, A.
  1890 Monumentos del artes mexicano antiguo, Tomo 1. Berlin: A. Asher.

Pough, F.H.
  1955 A Field Guide to Rocks and Minerals, 2nd ed. Boston: Houghton-Mifflin.

Rattray, E.C.
  1976 Thin Orange: a Teotihuacan trade ware. Paper presented at the Society
        for American Archaeology annual meeting, St. Louis, Missouri.

Sanders, W.T.
  1977 Ethnographic analogy and the Teotihuacan Horizon Style. In, Teotihuacan
        and Kaminaljuyu: A Study in Prehistoric Culture Contact, W.T. Sanders
        and J.W. Michels, eds. Pp. 397-410. Pennsylvania State University Press,
        University Park.

Sanders, W.T.
  1978 Personal communication.

Sanders, W.T. and B. J. Price
  1968 Mesoamerica: the Evolution of a Civilization. New York: Random House.

Seler, E.
  1915 Die Teotihuacan kultur des hochlands von Mexico. Gesammelte
        Abhandlungen zur Amerikanischen Sprachund Alterthumskunde, Band
        5:405-585.

Shepard, A.O.
  1946 Technological features of Thin Orange ware. Excavations at Kaminaljuyu,
        A.V. Kidder et al., eds. Carnegie Institution of Washington, Publ.
        561:198-201.

Sotomayor A. and N. Castillo Tejero
  1963 Estudio petrografico de la ceramica "anaranjado delgado." Instituto Nacional
        de Antropologia e Historia, Prehistoria No. 12.

Vaillant, G.C.
  1938 A correlation of archaeological and historical sequences in the Valley of
        Mexico. American Anthropologist 40:536:543.

Chapter 15

Tell El Yahudiyeh Ware:

A Re-evaluation

Maureen F. Kaplan, Garman Harbottle, and Edward V. Sayre

This article concerns Tell el Yahudiyeh ware (hereafter TY), an incised pottery, usually in juglet form, which occurs in Cyprus, Egypt, Nubia, and the Levant during the period ca. 1750-1550 B.C. This is the time of the Second Intermediate Period in Egypt, when the centralized government of the Middle Kingdom broke down, at least part of the land was occupied by foreign rulers (Hyksos), and, it is generally assumed, trade outside of Egypt ground to a halt. TY was first associated with the Hyksos (and therefore a Levantine manufacturing area) by Sir William Flinders Petrie (1906), an association which has grown so strong over time that Engberg (1939) and Van Seters (1966) included TY in their discussions of the Hyksos without hesitation.

This association has not gone unquestioned. Cyprus, Egypt, and Nubia have also been suggested as manufacturing areas (Dussaud 1928; Macalister 1912; Reisner 1923; Junker 1921). More recent work, however, has concentrated not on the basic question of its origin but on defining its geographic range (Amiran 1957), dividing it into types (Åström 1957; Van Seters 1966; Merrillees 1974), or using it to date the Middle Cypriote III-Late Cypriote periods in Cyprus (Åström 1957; Oren 1969; Merrillees 1971). Several of these studies reach contradictory conclusions in part because the authors concentrate on TY ware from a particular region (Cyprus, Egypt, or the Levant).

It was decided that a complete study of the ware was warranted and that it required an integrated, multidisciplinary approach. First, a typology of the ware was constructed on the basis of vessels from all areas, not just from one cultural region. These types were then plotted according to findspot and the geographic distribution of each type was inspected for indication of possible manufacturing areas. In a parallel effort, samples of the ware were analyzed by neutron activation to determine the area(s) of manufacture. A chronological analysis of the findspots would indicate which manufacturing area is the earlier if more than one exists. A high correlation between the results of the chemical and typological/geographical analyses would give us increased confidence in the conclusions we draw, while a lack of correlation would indicate a need for more study to identify the causes of the disagreement. It should be noted that the typological and chemical analyses were performed, for the most part, on different vessels; complete (or nearly complete) vessels were required for the typological work while samples for chemical analysis were most available from fragments and partial vessels. Each of these areas of investigation will be discussed below.

TYPOLOGY

The typology was established by form and other attributes such as base type, number of strands forming the handle, decoration, and so forth. The information on body form was coded as the three proportions shown in Figure 1 and subjected to a cluster analysis based on average linkage of the mean Euclidean distance between points (Sneath and Sokal 1973). Figure 2 is the resultant dendrogram for the 155 encoded vessels. Five distinct form categories are shown, as well as a "mixed" and "squat" cluster.

Each form category was then inspected to see whether it could be further subdivided on the basis of discrete attributes. (A discrete attribute, as opposed to a continuous variable, is one which takes a distinct series of values; i.e., a handle may be formed from one or more strands of clay. In contrast, there is a theoretically infinite number of values between the minimum and maximum possible proportions of a vessel. These two kinds of variables cannot be handled in the same cluster analysis.[2]) Because of the high frequency of some attributes (e.g., single handle) a cluster analysis using a coefficient of association was not suitable (Kaplan 1980). The form categories were therefore subdivided by eye. Tables 1 and 2 show the patterns evident for two attributes: handle type and orientation of the decoration. The remaining attributes show similar patterning. This subdivision resulted in ten major types of TY.

Three "mixed" vessels are illustrated in Figure 3. They are obviously different types, yet all three body proportions are identical for each vessel. This situation illustrates one of the difficulties with a cluster analysis based only on body form without information on other discrete attributes such as decoration, rim, handle, or base types. It also brings to mind G. Cowgill's caveat, "if the data are reasonably reliable and reasonably relevant one may expect reasonable but only reasonably correct results from statistical analysis" (Cowgill 1968). These vessels and the "squat" ones were not considered while the other clusters of body forms were being subdivided: they were later assigned to various types on the basis of the discrete information. The major types of TY are illustrated in Figure 4 and are described below.

The Cylindrical group is noticeably separated from the other form groups in the dendogram (Figure 2), yet can be further subdivided on the basis of other attributes. Cylindrical 1 juglets are small, with rounded bases and gentle angles

TABLE 1

Crosstabulation of Type by Handle

Type	Number of Strands in Handle		
	One	Two	Three
Cylindrical 1	11	–	–
Cylindrical 2	–	4	–
Piriform 1	–	13	1
Piriform 2a	20	–	–
Piriform 2b	–	5	–
Piriform 3	5	10	–
Ovoid	2	11	6
Biconical 1	43	1	1
Biconical 2	2	1	1
Globular	22	–	–

TABLE 2

Crosstabulation of Type by Decoration

Type	Decoration	
	Horizontal	Vertical
Cylindrical 1	9	2
Cylindrical 2	3	1
Piriform 1	12	2
Piriform 2a	2	18
Piriform 2b	—	5
Piriform 3	14	1
Ovoid	17	2
Biconical 1	45	—
Biconical 2	4	—
Globular	—	22

of transition from the shoulder to the body and from the body to the base. The rim is rolled-over and the handle is always single. The decoration is a wide band covering all of the available body area. Cylindrical 2 juglets are larger with flat or slightly rounded bases. The transition from the shoulder to the body and from the body to the base is sharply defined. The handle is always double and the decoration consists of one or two narrow bands of incision which cover only a fraction of the available body area.

The Globular type is very homogeneous. The rim is primarily rolled-over and the handle is always single. The most common form of decoration is three or four vertical gores or herringbone incision.

Biconical 1 juglets have two wide bands of horizontal decorations (usually chevrons), leaving only a narrow unincised band around the middle of the vessel. The rim is always rolled-over, the handle always single, and the base is always in the form of a button. Biconical 2 juglets are distinguished by the number of bands, their thickness, and narrower bases and rims.

The Piriform family is marked by slender-bodied juglets with high shoulders. Piriform 1 has two to four horizontal bands of geometric decoration covering most of the available body area. The bodies are often burnished all over, unlike the majority of other types. The rim is usually inverted, the handle is almost always multiply-stranded, and the base varies from a ring to an indented button. Piriform 2a bears a decoration which invariably consists of three or four vertical gores of herringbone punctures. The handle is always single and the base may be a ring or button. Piriform 2b is extremely similar to Piriform 2a; its distinguishing features are double handles, thinner rims, and a slight plumpness in the body. The base is a pronounced button, often ending in a point. Piriform 3 juglets are marked by one or two narrow bands of horizontal decoration which cover only a fraction of the available body area. The handle is usually multiply-stranded, though single handles do occur. The base is usually in the form of a button.

Ovoid juglets form a heterogeneous group. The predominantly light color of the vessels sets them apart from the majority of the dark-bodied vessels. The body is marked by the absence of a distinct shoulder, in contrast to the Piriform group. The handle is usually two or three strands of clay, and the base ranges from pointed to flat to button. The rim is never rolled-over, but varies from straight to slightly everted.   A more detailed discussion, including minor groups not included in this paper, may be found in Kaplan (1980).

GEOGRAPHICAL DISTRIBUTION

If the ware is to be associated with the Hyksos, it should be most common in the Levant, with some occurrences in the Nile Valley after their invasion of the latter area. It is also possible that a single type of TY may show a manufacturing area in the Levant and a later one in the Egyptian Delta (i.e., the potters moved after the conquest), but this would be more apparent in the chemical analysis. If two types from the same form category occur in separate geographical areas with minimal overlap, then separate manufacturing areas may be postulated. The validity of these hypotheses can then be tested by neutron activation analysis of the ware to determine the area of manufacture.

The difference in geographic distributions for Cylindrical 1 and Cylindrical 2 is striking (Figure 5). It is not illogical to propose a separate manufacturing area for each type. Piriform 1 (Figure 6) has the widest distribution of any type, ranging from Kerma (Sudan) to Ras Shamra (Syria) and Cyprus. Not evident from Figure 6 is the relative frequency with which it is found in Egypt, though it tends to occur as isolated examples in the Levant (except at the site of Byblos which is noted for its close ties with Egypt). This frequency suggests it was manufactured in the Nile Valley. Ovoid juglets appear restricted to the Levant, although two interesting vessels occur in Level F at Tell el Dab'a in the Delta (personal communication, M. Bietak). Tell el Dab'a is a fascinating site which shows a change in settlement plan and ceramic repertoire after a burning level (Bietak 1968a, 1968b, 1970, and 1975). It may well be a site which shows the arrival of the Hyksos into Egypt by conquest. If it is, then it is all the more important to note that these ovoid juglets are not the earliest pieces of TY found at that site. We will return to this point on the section correlating the typological and chemical analyses.

Piriform 2a has a distribution pattern similar to that of Piriform 1, but it lacks the sites in the Northern Levant. Piriform 2b and 3 have distribution patterns restricted to the Levant (Figure 7). Again, the patterns imply different manufacturing areas, the Nile Valley for Piriform 2a and the Levant for Piriform 2b and 3. Biconical 1 and Globular have similar geographic distributions, predominantly occurring in the Nile Valley. Biconical 2 occurs only in the Levant (Figure 8).

The geographical analyses, then, suggest that there are two "families" of TY with two manufacturing areas. The geographical spread of the types which are most frequent in the Nile Valley suggest that they were manufactured there. The relative infrequency of the types which are restricted to the Levant, and their resemblance to the more common Egyptian types, suggest that these are imitations of the Egyptian material. This is in direct contrast to what is generally believed and it is for this reason that the neutron activation analysis plays a necessary and integral part of this study.

NEUTRON ACTIVATION ANALYSIS

Neutron activation analysis has been applied to archaeological problems for over a quarter century (Sayre and Dodson 1957). It may therefore be considered a maturing discipline in which the procedures for sample preparation and irradiation have become standardized, at least within each laboratory. (The present work followed methods described in Abascal-M. et al. 1974). A more important aspect, however, is that these years of research have built up a substantial data base with which to work. Before the TY project began, Brookhaven already had reference chemical groups and statistical methods for distinguishing between the following areas: Egypt (Tobia and Sayre 1974); Cyprus (Bieber 1977; Bieber et al. 1976a, 1976b); and Southern Levant (Brooks et al. 1974; Brooks 1975; Bieber et al. 1976b)—i.e., nearly all the areas where TY could have been made. The TY project included supplementing known groups with additional samples in order to form a better statistical description of each group. Fred Matson supplied samples of Nile alluvium for this purpose, while one of the authors gathered samples of local ancient ceramics from Egypt, Sudan, and the northern Levant. (Fred Matson has been of great assistance in generating the Brookhaven data bank by supplying numerous clay and ceramic samples from many areas in the Near East.)

It is not the purpose of this paper to explain in detail the methods which were used to establish the chemical groups since they have been published elsewhere (Brooks et al. 1974; Bieber et al. 1976a, 1976b; Harbottle 1976). Statistical analysis of the new local material resulted in the identification of four additional chemical groups: (1) material from the site of Ras Shamra in Syria, (2) material from Aswan in Egypt, (3) material from the area of Nubia between the Second and Third Cataracts of the Nile, and (4) sherds made from a mixture of Nile alluvium and the underlying Pleistocene clay. A further description of the distinguishing chemical characteristics of each of these groups may be found elsewhere (Kaplan et al. 1982).

Once the reference chemical groups had been established, the 155 TY samples were compared to them. Methods of identifying the group to which they belonged included: (1) cluster analysis, (2) comparing each sample to each group individually (via the computer program ADCORR), and (3) comparing each sample to a number of groups at the same time. The latter technique, discriminant analysis, is one which can only be used with well-established reference groups; this again illustrates the importance of a data base which makes this type of analysis possible. These techniques are described in the references given above as well as in Doran and Hodson (1975).

The neutron activation analysis indicated TY was manufactured both in the Levant and the Nile Valley. (For the purpose of this study, this gross geographical attribution is more important than a finer distinction, such as whether a sherd was made from Nile alluvium or Nile alluvium-plus-Pleistocene clay.) There are more samples of Egyptian material (92) than Levantine (52), but in the absence of any archaeological data, we would not be able to say whether this was due to Egyptian material actually being more abundant in the archaeological record or if samples from it were more readily obtained. More information, however, can be obtained by combining the typological and chemical analyses.

CORRELATION OF TYPOLOGICAL, CHEMICAL, AND CHRONOLOGICAL ANALYSES

In the first two sections of this paper, we established a typology for TY and suggested areas of manufacture for these types according to their geographical distribution. This is what is meant by the heading "Archaeologically Predicted Areas of Manufacture" on Table 3. This table lists the number of samples analyzed by neutron activation for each type, where the archaeological data suggests the material was manufactured and where the chemical analysis says they were manufactured. Eleven TY samples could not be assigned to a chemical reference group, that is, they did not lie within the 95 percent confidence bounds of any of the reference groups.[3] The prediction rate is based upon the number of samples which could be classified. For example, 23 Piriform 2a samples could be assigned to manufacturing areas; 22 of them (96 percent) were made in Egypt.

There is a very high correlation between the archaeological and chemical analyses. The typological and geographical analyses suggest that Cylindrical 1 and Globular type vessels were manufactured in the Nile Valley. Every sample taken from a vessel of this type has a chemical composition which matches one of the Nile Valley sources. The archaeological analyses suggest that Cylindrical 2, Piriform

2b and 3, Biconical 2, and Ovoid were manufactured in the Levant.   Again, every sample from a vessel of these types matched a Levantine clay source.   Of the remaining types, Piriform 1 and 2a and Biconical 1, there are, at most, two samples which do not match the predicted area of manufacture.   There are two possible explanations for this.   Samples for neutron activation analysis were often taken from sherds; had more of the vessel survived, it might have been classified as a different type.   Second, we may have copies which even a trained archaeologist's eye cannot detect.   Except for these rare occurrences, the near perfect correlation allows us to postulate, with some confidence, the existence of two "families" of TY, one Egyptian and one Levantine.

It should be noted that there are only Levantine copies of Egyptian types. The reverse—Egyptian copies of Levantine types—is what would be expected if the ware were truly associated with the Hyksos.   The Egyptian material shows a wide geographic spread during a period in which her trade was thought to be in decline. The Levantine types, on the other hand, are restricted to the Levant.

The exception to this is the two ovoid juglets found at Tell ed Dab'a.   These were sampled, and they are manufactured from a Levantine clay.   Tell el Yahudiyeh ware occurs in an earlier level at that site and a sample of that material shows that it was Egyptian in manufacture.   The data from Tell el Dab'a are extremely important because it is the only site with such stratigraphic evidence.   Material from Egypt is often dated to the Second Intermediate Period because of the presence of TY ware.   When the remaining material is examined, however, a date in the late 12th or 13th Dynasty is often possible, i.e., before the arrival of the Hyksos.   In addition, several Egyptian types may continue as late as the early 18th Dynasty, i.e., after the expulsion of the Hyksos.   The pattern seen in the Levant is that those types appear after the Egyptian material.   (For a site-by-site analysis, see Kaplan 1980.)

So it appears that Tell el Yahudiyeh ware cannot be considered a homogeneous type of pottery affiliated with the Hyksos.   It can be divided into a "family" of Levantine types and a "family" of Egyptian types.   The former are more restricted in geographic distribution and include copies of Egyptian types.

Now that these "families" have been established, can we go back and discern other, more general differences between them?   Each vessel and sherd was examined by a hand lens for temper.   Both "families" can contain sand, chaff, or other materials but only the Egyptian ceramics contain mica, which is more visible on the surface rather than in cross-section.   None of the Levantine samples contain mica.   There are also differences in the manufacture of these vessels.   Piriform juglets manufactured in the Levant often have a heavy base but very thin walls near the point of maximum diameter.   This thinness leads to an unexpected lightness when contrasted with an Egyptian vessel of the same size, and many vessels break at this point.   The manufacturing areas also show differences in the ability of the potters to control the atmosphere in the kiln.   The ware is usually dark but the cores are often reddish, which suggests that the dark exterior was formed by changing the kiln atmosphere to a reducing one after a period of oxidation.   This kiln technique is not common to the Levant in this period, during which most of the pottery is red (Amiran 1970).   Only half of the Levantine vessels can be described as gray or black whereas 77 percent of the Egyptian vessels are those colors.   It may be suggested that the Egyptians had better control of their kilns.

CONCLUSIONS

Archaeology is ultimately more interested in the potters than the pots, and the TY project has some interesting implications for understanding the cultural interactions of this period. The Second Intermediate Period was one during which centralized government in Egypt collapsed and, it is generally assumed, so did her trade network. Foreigners—the Hyksos—were able to enter the country and rule at least part of it.

The results of this study, however, indicate the TY was primarily an Egyptian pottery which appeared before the Hyksos entered and may have continued in use after they left. It cannot, therefore, be tightly associated with the Hyksos, nor can it be used to judge the extent of their influence. Its wide distribution shows that Egypt continued to trade goods outside her boundaries throughout this period. Finally, not only goods travelled between what were generally considered to have been hostile neighbors, but the trade appears to have included ideas and technology as well.

NOTES

[1] Research performed at Brookhaven National Laboratory under contract with U.S. Department of Energy and supported by its Division of Basic Energy Sciences.

[2] Editor's note: Although this kind of "mixed-level" data cannot normally be handled in the same cluster analysis procedure, because of the limitations of the similarity coefficients, the Gower coefficient has recently been successfully applied to mixed-level ceramic data (see P.M. Rice and M.E. Saffer, Cluster analysis of mixed-level data: pottery provenience as an example. Journal of Archaeological Science 9:395-409 [1982]).

[3] This is not an unexpectedly large number of samples to remain unclassified; the use of the 95 percent confidence level implies that five samples of every hundred would not be assigned to a group to which it actually belonged.

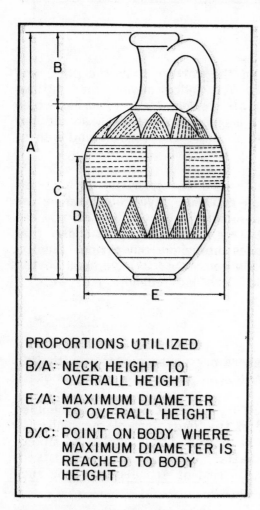

PROPORTIONS UTILIZED

B/A: NECK HEIGHT TO
OVERALL HEIGHT

E/A: MAXIMUM DIAMETER
TO OVERALL HEIGHT

D/C: POINT ON BODY WHERE
MAXIMUM DIAMETER IS
REACHED TO BODY
HEIGHT

Figure 1.   Measurements used to characterize the body proportions of Tell el Yahudiyeh ware. Reproduced by permission of Archaeometry and the Research Laboratory for Archaeology and the History of Art, Oxford University.

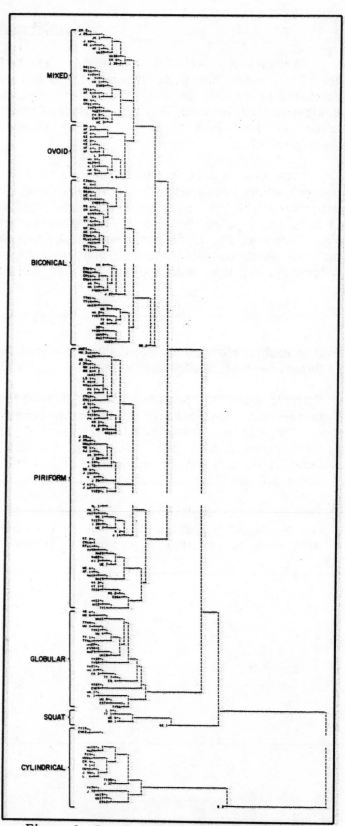

Figure 2. Dendogram of cluster analysis of Tell el Yahudiyeh ware by body proportions.

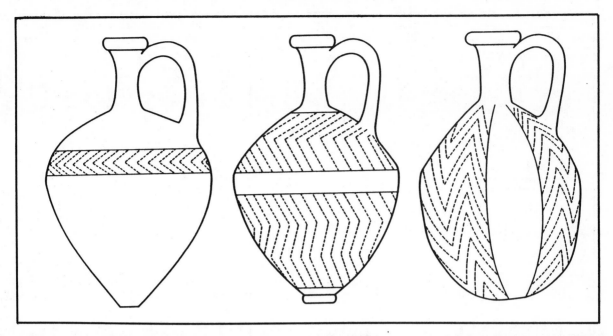

Figure 3. Three different types of Tell el Yahudiyeh ware with equal proportions. Reproduced by permission of Archaeometry and the Research Laboratory for Archaeology and the History of Art, Oxford University.

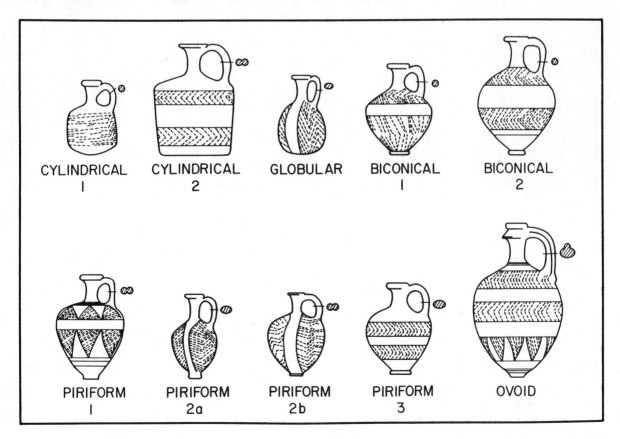

Figure 4. The major types of Tell el Yahudiyeh ware. Reproduced by permission of Archaeometry and the Research Laboratory for Archaeology and the History of Art, Oxford University.

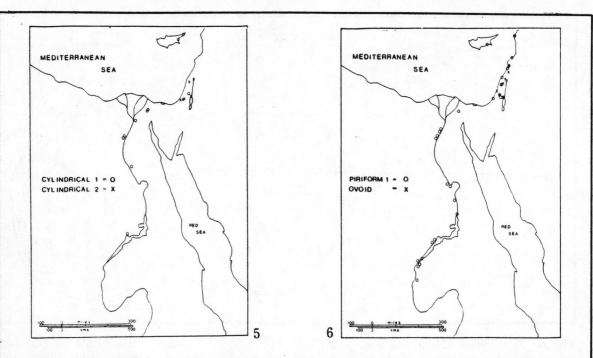

Figure 5. Geographic distributions of find sites of the Cylindrical 1 and 2 specimens.

Figure 6. Geographic distribution of find sites of the Piriform 1 and Ovoid specimens.

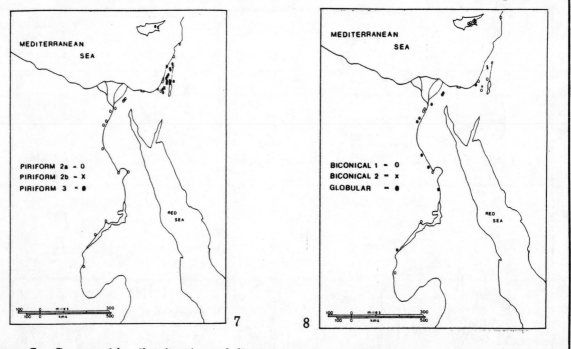

Figure 7. Geographic distribution of find sites of the Piriform 2a, 2b and 3 specimens.

Figure 8. Geographic distributions of the find sites of the Biconical 1 and 2 and the Globular specimens.

REFERENCES

Abascal-M, R., G. Harbottle, and E.V. Sayre
  1974 Correlation between terracotta figurines and pottery from the Valley of Mexico and source clays by activation analysis. In, Archaeological Chemistry, C.W. Beck, ed. Advances in Chemistry 138:48-80. Washington: American Chemical Society.

Amiran, R.
  1957 Tell el Yahudiyeh ware in Syria. Israel Exploration Journal 7:93-97.

  1970 Ancient Pottery of the Holy Land. New Brunswick, N.J.

Åström, P.
  1957 The Middle Cypriote Bronze Age, reprinted as Swedish Cyprus Expedition IV.1.B. Lund (1972).

Bieber, A.M. Jr.
  1977 Neutron Activation Analysis of Archaeological Ceramics from Cyprus. Unpublished Ph.D. dissertation, University of Connecticut, Storrs.

Bieber, A.M. Jr., D.W. Brooks, G. Harbottle, and E.V. Sayre
  1976a Application of multivariate techniques to analytical data on Aegean ceramics. Archaeometry 18:69-74.

  1976b Compositional groupings of some ancient Aegean and Eastern Mediterranean pottery. In, Applicazione dei metodi nucleari nel campo delle opere d'arte. Pp. 111-132. Rome.

Bietak, M.
  1968a Bericht uber die erste Grabungskampagne auf Tell el-Dab'a in Ostdelta Agyptens im Sommer 1966. Bustan 9:20-24.

  1968b Vorlaufiger Bericht uber die erste und zweite Kampagne der osterreichischen Ausgrabungen auf Tell el-Dab'a im Ostdelta Agyptens (1966, 1967). Mitteilungen der Deutschen Archaeologischen Instituts, Abt. Kairo 23:79-114.

  1970 Vorlaufiger Bericht uber die dritte Kampagne der osterreichisachen Ausgrabungen auf Tell el-Dab'a in Ostdelta Agyptens (1968). Mitteilungen der Deutschen Archaeologischen Instituts, Abt. Kairo 26:15-42.

  1975 Die Hauptstadt der Hyksos und die Ramsesstadt. Antike Welt 6:28-43.

Brooks, D.W.
  1975 Persian Period Relationships of Tell el Hesi as Indicated by Neutron Activation of its Imported Ceramics. Unpublished Ph.D. dissertation, Hartford Seminary Foundation.

Brooks, D.W., A.M. Bieber, Jr., G. Harbottle, and E.V. Sayre
  1974 Biblical studies through activation analysis of ancient pottery. In, Archaeological Chemistry, C.W. Beck, ed. Advances in Chemistry 138:81-99. Washington: American Chemical Society.

Cowgill, G.
1968   Archaeological applications of factor, cluster, and proximity analyses. American Antiquity 33:367-375.

Doran, J.E. and F.R. Hodson
1975   Mathematics and Computers in Archaeology.   Cambridge, MA: Harvard University Press.

Dussaud, R.
1928   Observations sur la ceramique du IIe millenaire avant notre ere.   Syria 9:131-150.

Engberg, R.M.
1939   The Hyksos Reconsidered.   Chicago.

Flanagan, F.J.
1973   1972 values for international geochemical reference samples.   Geochimica et Cosmochimica Acta 37:1189-1200.

Harbottle, G.
1976   Activation analysis in archaeology.   Radiochemistry 3:33-72.

Junker, H.
1921   Der nubische Ursprung der sogenannten "Tell el Jahudiye Vasen".   Osterr. Akad. d. Wiss., Phil.-Hist. Klasse, SB 198.3).   Vienna.

Kaplan, M.F.
1980   The Origin and Distribution of Tell el Yahudiyeh Ware.   Studies in Mediterranean Archaeology, vol. 62.   Goteborg.

Kaplan, M.F., G. Harbottle, and E.V. Sayre
1982   Multidisciplinary analysis of Tell el Yahudiyeh ware.   Archaeometery 24:127-142.

Macalister, R.A.S.
1912   The Excavation of Gezer, 1902-1905 and 1907-1909.   London.

Merrillees, R.S.
1971   The early history of Late Cypriote I.   Levant 3:56-69.

1974   Some notes on Tell el Yahudiya ware.   Levant 6:193-194.

Petrie, Sir W.M.F.
1906   Hyksos and Israelite Cities.   London.

Oren, E.
1969   Cypriote imports in the Palestinian Late Bronze I context.   Opuscula Athensia 9:127-149.

Reisner, G.A.
1923   Excavations at Kerma I-V.   Cambridge, MA.

Sayre, E.V. and R.W. Dodson
   1957   Neutron activation study of Mediterrranean potsherds. American Journal of Archaeology 61:35-41.

Sneath, P.H. and R.R. Sokal
   1973   Principles of Numerical Taxonomy. San Francisco: Freeman.

Tobia, S.K. and E.V. Sayre
   1974   An analytical comparison of various Egyptian soils, clays, shales, and some ancient pottery by neutron activation.   In, Recent Advances in Science and Technology of Materials III, A. Bishay, ed.   Pp. 99-128.   New York: Plenum Press.

Van Seters, J.
   1966   The Hyksos: A New Investigation.   New Haven.

PART IV

Conclusions

Chapter 16

Overview and Prospect

Prudence M. Rice

The papers in <u>Pots and Potters</u> have explored "ceramic archaeology" from a variety of viewpoints and with data representing a variety of periods and regions of human history. The divisions of the volume reflect three of the major methodological objectives and foci of ceramic studies today: achievement of an understanding of ancient potters within their society and their use of available resources; study of present-day potters and experimentation with pottery-making to gather observations that can be extended to the potters of prehistory; and, use of recent advances in physiocochemical analytical techniques to sharpen the precision of ceramic technological analysis and characterization of ancient pottery. Obviously these objectives are not mutually exclusive, and there is considerable overlap in data and methods in pursuing any of them. Equally obvious, as pointed out elsewhere in this volume, these methods and objectives did not suddenly appear out of nowhere in 1965. They have a long history in archaeological studies, but have perhaps been more systematically pursued over the last 20 years, as archaeology itself has become more systematic, eclectic, and specialized.

DEVELOPMENT OF CERAMIC STUDIES

It is useful to consider the development of ceramic studies within the overall historical framework of archaeology and anthropology. My limited experience enables me to make observations only with regard to the New World; I make no pretense of judging the extent to which these observations may or may not hold true for Old World ceramic studies.

The history of ceramic studies in the New World is very much tied into the overall development of archaeology as a discipline, which in turn has a strong grounding in anthropology. While pottery has always been studied to illuminate "the cultural context in which the objects were made and used," the definition of how that "context" itself should be interpreted has changed a great deal. The early years of American archaeology (1840-1914) comprise a stage that Willey and Sabloff (1980) have described as "classificatory-descriptive." The primary interest of archaeologists was that of describing sites and artifacts, paralleling similar concerns among ethnographers of the time. Collections of sherds or complete vessels from excavations in Southwestern puebloes, Southeastern shell middens, and Peruvian graves were segregated into categories, largely on the basis of style and/or decoration. These descriptive categories, and the stylistic changes they incorporated, then formed the basis for assessing temporal relationships of materials found within a site.

From 1914 to 1960, archaeology in the Americas was in a developmental stage that Willey and Sabloff call "classificatory-historical." The chief concern was the building of regional chronological syntheses, and the primary means of accomplishing this aim was still through artifact classification. The criterion of success for a typology, be it ceramic or lithic, was that it illuminate historical relationships between cultures. Pottery types, stylistic motifs, forms, etc., were often employed in a sequential ordering technique known as "seriation." Now performed by modern high-speed computerized data processing equipment, seriation as a method of chronology building has roots going back to Petrie's (1899) arrangement of pottery vessels from Egyptian tombs and, even earlier, to "Worsaae's law," which postulated that objects occurring together in a burial were placed there at the same time (at burial) and were in use together. A further development in pottery studies during this period provided the foundation for much of the current work in pottery analysis. This is the beginning of technological (especially petrographic and chemical) studies of pottery and clay resources, a field that really began its surge in the late 1930s (see introduction to Part III).

By the late 1950s a number of developments were taking place in the field of American archaeology as a whole, which had significant effects on the course of ceramic studies. The earlier antievolutionary, "historical particularistic" focus, emphasizing data collection and description and deemphasizing theory and generalizing, was being gradually supplanted by an evolutionary perspective and an interest in environmental and technological contexts of cultural development. In archaeology, the changes were in some ways profound, leading to the much abused term, the "new archaeology." The development of radiocarbon dating and other chronometric techniques took away much of the need to maintain chronology-building at the forefront of archaeological endeavor, and as regional chronologies began to be developed, archaeologists realized that other goals and methods were increasingly broadening their discipline.

Pottery, the foundation data for whatever archaeological objectives were current, gained added importance in the post-1960 stage of "processual" archaeology. It was in this context that the methodological trends exemplified by many of the papers in this volume gained their impetus. "Ceramic ecology," emphasizing resources and technoenvironmental concerns, was spurred by general cultural ecology and cultural materialism, and ultimately owes a debt to Steward and White. Technological and physicochemical analyses, including trace chemical, high resolution SEM microscopy, X-ray diffraction, and so forth, were dependent upon instrumental advances in other fields to increase our knowledge of material culture: physics and chemistry in understanding the structure and composition of clay bodies, and computer science for increasing ease of manipulation of large bodies of technical data. Ethnoarchaeology, the archaeological study of contemporary peoples, was significant in terms of development and testing of hypotheses about spatial interrelationships of behavior and material culture in the present, and in delineating similar relationships in the past.

This brief review suggests a need to examine the "role and scope" of pottery in archaeological inquiry. As suggested above, the archaeological "context" to which pottery has been related has changed from one of cultural or artistic description, to culture chronology, and now to inter- and intracultural relationships in time and space. As the field of ceramic archaeology has developed and broadened, so has the context in which the conclusions are interpreted. The "cultural context" mentioned in the quotation which opened this volume involves not only the social context of time and space, but economic patterns such as trade, production, and resource use, ritual or ceremonial behavior, value and belief systems, and so forth.

There has clearly been an advance in methodological sophistication in ceramic studies. This is most conspicuously true of the instrumentation available for application to ceramic analyses, which includes X-ray diffractometers, electron microscopes, and nuclear reactors. It is also true of the ceramic research designs through which these instruments are employed. Precise statements of research problems and hypotheses, and awareness of the need for careful checking of results for accuracy and replicability, are signs of this increasing sophistication.

Concomitant theoretical sophistication is not as striking, however, and this observation has several ancillary considerations. On the plus side, ceramic researchers are increasingly able and willing to deal with the multivariate nature of pottery. Variability in pottery, and the capability of measuring and interpreting the significance of such variability, depends in part on the understanding of the context of manufacture and use of that pottery. As American anthropologists and archaeologists have moved away from traditional normative approaches to cultural and behavioral contexts, and from seeking only chronologically sensitive variables in pottery, a fuller range of ceramic variables can be studied, analyzed, and interpreted. The breadth of our conclusions is determined by the breadth of our research problems, after all.

On the negative side, however, there is no real body of ceramic theory (are we waiting until "all the data are in"?) being consistently developed, advocated, or even denounced by ceramic archaeologists, suggesting that no defined "paradigm" or set of paradigms exists yet for ceramic research. Clearly the problems being addressed by ceramicists exist on a variety of levels. Taking the papers in this volume as examples toward achieving such a paradigm or paradigms, many are case studies involving specific issues in specific areas or periods. However, by and large they address themes and problems that are general rather than particularistic, and it is hoped that researchers in other areas with analogous problems will gain methodological insights from their work. If these or similar analyses cannot be or are not being used in a cross-time and cross-cultural manner, perhaps it reflects that in fact too many ceramic researchers conceive their problems too particularistically and narrowly, without reference to common theory.

In considering ceramic method and theory, or the lack thereof, two other issues bear additional consideration in the future. For one, it is regrettable that discussions of sample selection do not regularly appear in the context of physicochemical analytical methodology (cf. Wilson 1978; Reeves and Brooks 1978). To be sure, probabilistic sampling is not necessarily the best or the only means of selecting sherds for analyses. Judgmental sampling has traditionally been used and, considering the lacunae between archaeological target populations and sampled populations, be they of artifacts, sites, or cultures, it may be the best procedure to continue to follow. However, the legitimacy of creating vast inferential schemes on the basis of nonprobabilistic sampling deserves some critical attention.

The second issue is that of operationalizing anthropological and archaeological concepts to take advantage of the precision of the analytical devices currently at our disposal. Ceramic research is still largely at the stage where many variables of interest are capable of only nominal or ordinal levels of measurement (e.g., form, type, color, kind of inclusions, hardness), although others are continuous (thickness, diameter, volume, wall angle). But in the general absence of an agreed upon paradigm for research, there has been little effort at achieving a synthesis in which measurements of ceramic properties integrate with anthropological concepts. Or, perhaps it is clearer and more accurate to state this problem in reverse: concepts or behavior involving trade, production, ethnicity, craft specialization, acculturation, migration, centralization, segmentation, reciprocity, and so forth, in which archaeologists and anthropologists are clearly interested, have not been translated into operational models in which measurements of specific variables of pottery can be utilized. Until some agreement or discussion of ceramic models and ceramic theory is generated, in which these issues are taken into consideration, the incredible technical precision which we have available is virtually wasted.

FUTURE DIRECTIONS

I will conclude by offering some suggestions as to key issues and methods around which ceramic studies can be expected to revolve in the future.

Classification

One issue clearly ought to be ceramic classification. Archaeologists rarely work with sherds as individual sherds; rather, they group the sherds into categories or "types," which are more or less strictly formulated on a variety of attributes for delineating spatio-temporal relationships. Classifications of pottery began as descriptive categories created on the basis of decorative style in the early years of archaeology. Later, more rigorous classifications were developed for the explicit purpose of recovering chronology, and the variables chosen were those expected or known to be time-sensitive. Curiously, even in the so-called "explanatory period" of post-1960s, processual archaeology, the goals of ceramic classifications have remained focused on chronology-building, together with some interest in spatial relationships. Thus, despite the nominal interest of modern archaeology in "cultural dynamics," typologies are still static and descriptive, focused on elucidating spatio-temporal relationships. Plus ca change, plus c'est le même chose.

This is not to denigrate entirely the role of ceramic classifications. Classifications are basic to all sciences; they organize and systematize vast quantities of data, facilitate communication, and, by the criteria chosen to differentiate typological units, establish the significant features of variability or lack of variability in the objects of interest. Archaeologists have argued long and loud about whether types, ceramic, lithic, or whatever, are "created" or "discovered," whether classifications should be polythetic or monothetic, and whether the classificatory activity is best one of "lumping" or "splitting." But although some alternative or supplementary ceramic concepts exist (e.g., mode, ware, style, horizon, tradition, group), the type continues to be the major working unit of discussion and comparison.

Ceramic ecological, ceramic technological, and ethnoarchaeological studies are becoming more and more important in process-oriented ceramic archaeology. However, they are having very little feedback or impact at the process-oriented "dirt archaeology" level of excavation and descriptive synthesis, which still demands and depends largely on spatio-temporal index types. All too frequently, sites are excavated and the ceramic type descriptions are written, and that seems to be viewed as the termination of a successful ceramic analysis. Typologies in some cases are becoming even more formalized: consider the expansion of type-variety systematics into Mesoamerica and the Southeastern United States. On the one hand, this is all to the good insofar as regulation of terminology allows better communication between archaeologists comparing regional and local sequences. But classification schemes that are useful for one purpose—assessing time and space relationships—are not necessarily "best" for all other purposes. The real use-meaning of a pottery type has not changed in half a century, nor has there been much implementation of the idea that different "kinds of types" will be necessary both to accommodate the processual-explanatory goals of archaeology today, and to take effective advantage of the kinds of analytical techniques available more or less routinely today that were not available 25 or 50 years ago (Rice 1982).

There is an obvious paradox involved here, as there is in all sciences: we need to know the meaning and role of ceramic data in answering our questions, but we need to know how to ask our questions so that they can be addressed by ceramic data. Because classifications organize and structure data, they necessarily also organize and structure research problems. However, classifications are only tools; they are means to an end, not ends themselves. Thus it is necessary to ask continually if the two are existing in optimal and beneficial relationship, or if classifications, which are always conservative and slow to change, are impeding rather than enhancing ceramic research.

Dissatisfactions with ceramic classifications, and recognition of limitations of the type concept, are not new. Much of the debate of the 1960s "new" American archaeology focused on this topic, but for ceramic technologists specifically perhaps the most effective and thoughtful discussion of the problem is Shepard's (1971:xii-xv, 306-322). Study of ceramic "modes" is often recommended as a procedure to accompany standard typological analysis, but is all too rarely carried out, since the objectives of ceramic classification (creation of types) are more clearly integrated into standard archaeological field research. Perhaps modal analyses will help bridge the gap. In any case, it is to be hoped that increasing awareness among all archaeologists of the capabilities of ceramic data to address a variety of "processual" problems, and the potential disjunctions between traditional types and new avenues of investigation, will lead to careful reconsideration of ceramic classification units.

Concepts

Another topic of concentration for future ceramic researchers will necessarily involve a more systematic look at the interface of what we might call "ceramic variables" (the properties observed and measured in a ceramic object or raw material) and "sociocultural variables" or anthropological/archaeological concepts dealing with human behavior and social organization.

Most broadly speaking, the "ceramic" variables of archaeological pottery fall into four general categories: variables of the clay body (clay and inclusions); variables of form and dimension; variables of decoration and/or surface treatment; and variables reflecting the manufacturing procedures. Some variables will obviously fall into more than one category (e.g., a red color is a result of iron content of the clay, firing of the clay, and perhaps decoration as well). Also, some variables cannot be measured on sherds but only on whole or partially reconstructable vessels (e.g., volume of a container, or aspects of design structure). Many of these variables are used as the basis for classifying sherds into types, but consideration of the variables independently—as modes, rather than within types—will continue to be of use in ceramic analyses (see also van der Leeuw, this volume).

The anthropological/archaeological concepts to which these variables have been and will continue to be addressed might be divided into two classes: concepts of context and concepts of process. Concepts of context involve some of the sociocultural parameters within which pottery has traditionally been concerned. Space-time considerations are the most obvious of these, but also included is the relationship of pottery in general and specific variables in particular to other technologies. The relationship of pottery-firing technology and the origins of metallurgy in the Near East is an obvious example of such use, as is ceramic decoration and basketry in the Southwest. Less frequently or successfully attempted are identifications of pottery with specific communities, ethnic groups, or status levels. Can (and if so, how?) archaeologists define "ethnicity" ceramically? Can ethnohistorically known groups—e.g., the Itza of Postclassic Peten, Guatemala—be isolated archaeologically by patterns of frequency of occurrence of particular ceramic variables? Such contextual concepts, or associations of ceramic variables with a sociocultural context, are basically descriptive and static. They represent the more traditional of the uses of ceramic data and will continue to be important in future ceramic studies.

The second class of anthropological/archaeological concepts are those that might be loosely termed processual or dynamic. That is, these terms relate to pottery as it circulates within a society, its function and use, and changes in that use or function through time and space, particularly as pottery may be related to other processual objectives that do not necessarily use ceramics as their data base. For example, contemporary archaeological interest in trade and, increasingly, in production involves a variety of both static and dynamic concerns—organization of production, resource procurement, interactions locally and regionally in exchange. How can the concepts of such economic studies (e.g., reciprocity, craft specialization) be measured ceramically? The introduction of new elements into a ceramic assemblage used to be explained simply as "influence" from outside. Today "influence" is no longer an acceptable explanation, but how do acculturation, religious syncretism, conquest, centralization of authority, and so forth leave their impress on pottery?

There is no necessary one-to-one relationship between a given cultural change and a given ceramic variable or set of variables. Nevertheless, as processual archaeology has been the accepted <u>modus operandi</u> for many years now, it is due time to give some consideration to allowing ceramic studies to transcend their traditional descriptive focus and become more closely attuned to the method and theory demands within which they are conducted.

Change

This brings up another general area in need of consideration by future ceramic archaeologists: the meaning of change in ceramics and the relationship of ceramic change to general culture change. Change is all too often conceived of by ceramicists simply as change in type frequencies or replacement of one mode by another mode. The fact that different ceramic variables may change at different rates or under different circumstances is typically given scant attention. However, the relationship of ceramic change to general cultural change may be an even more serious difficulty.

A nagging problem in archaeological ceramic studies has been the fact that archaeologists employ sherds (more specifically, they employ type categories) to define and characterize time periods (phases) at a site or region, and then to intercompare time periods from early to late in that site or region. Culture historical sequences are built on the basis of presence/absence of types or frequencies of types, and the types themselves are defined on the presence/absence, frequency, or co-occurrence of particular attributes. However, virtually all ethnographers who have dealt with potters point to the conservatism of potters, to their general low status in the community (exceptions exist, of course), and to the conservatism of the entire pottery-making operation. If such is the case in the present and, in the absence of evidence to the contrary, assuming it is also true of the past, how can archaeologists continue to depend uncritically on ceramic data as their primary means of describing and detecting culture change? Changes in types and type frequencies are used as markers for the beginning of new phases or new "influences" within a culture. The ensuing "phases" are then viewed normatively, in terms of the pottery types and modes that are characteristic or diagnostic of that period, whereas what should be looked at, if archaeologists are truly interested in change, are the boundary periods where types characteristic of one period are ending and those of the next phase are beginning. We should be studying the transition itself, rather than the results, or the before-and-after states (phases) of the transition.

Archaeologists work under the assumption that changes in the cultural system as a whole will eventually make themselves felt in the ceramic subsystem. Yet it is known ethnographically and ethnohistorically that in many situations, under severe stress from conquest and acculturation, ceramic production has changed very little (Rice, in press). Are the changed sociocultural circumstances (phases) that archaeologists describe from their typological studies of material goods then really reflective of changes that occurred decades earlier because of a lag caused by conservatism among potters?

The concepts of systems theory applied to ceramic studies and combined with the observations of ethnographic work among potters may well provide the most useful means of addressing these problems. Rejection of a normative view of ceramically defined phases, and greater concern with internal variability of pottery units, be they types or modes, is another plus. Also, consideration of individual variables or categories of variables is more likely to be useful than are types in this regard. Since different variables are likely to change at different rates, greater attention to the kinds of ethnographic situations under which particular "ceramic variables" (form, decoration, manufacturing technology) do or do not change, and greater effort by archaeologists toward delineating which variables (or modes) are changing and which are relatively stable, might give clues as to the general kinds of cultural changes that may have been taking place. In consideration of current processual interests, archaeologists are clearly desirous of obtaining such information, but are in many cases constrained by the blinders of typologies from achieving their goal. Work apart from ceramic types, utilizing systems theory and the general procedures of ceramic ecology, may eventually result in the development of a body of ceramic theory that is reflective of current interests in sociocultural change and compatible with the highly precise analytical techniques currently available (see Arnold, in press).

Methods

This leads to a final problem with which future ceramic studies will be involved: methodology, or how to study pottery. It has been quite clear within the last few years that archaeologists are taking a harder and more critical look at techniques of pottery analysis. There is already a large body of discussion and debate concerning the methodologies of physicochemical analyses and multivariate statistics, and their reliability with respect to applications to ceramic data (e.g., Bishop et al. 1982). Part of this reconsideration is an expectable "backlash" against what was often a naive and starry-eyed enthusiasm for anything that smacked of science—and the more arcane the better. Most practitioners of the high-powered analyses, such as neutron activation analysis and scanning electron microscopy, never touted their methods as exclusive sources of "truth" in the first place. But rational assessment of their limitations, combined with their prohibitive cost, is increasingly forcing archaeologists to abandon the razzle-dazzle and return to simpler, cheaper techniques of measurement (Rice and Saffer 1982).

This, then, is returning us to the problem of "operationalizing" anthropological concepts. The desire to move beyond the mere descriptive characterization of pottery by physicochemical methods is manifesting itself in numerous ways. The study of "trade," and the differentiation of "local" from "nonlocal" pottery by petrography or neutron activation analysis is being elaborated in several directions (see papers in Peacock [1978], and Howard and Morris [1981]). One is the study of manufacturing techniques, which employs replicative experimentation and xero-radiography among other techniques (see papers in Olin and Franklin [1982]); another is the study of socioeconomic organization of production, which is incorporating study of technological and decorative variability (Plog 1980; Feinman et al. 1981; Rice 1981). A relatively "new" focus of study—new not as a general topic but in the methods currently used—is formal/functional analysis. Employing the techniques and principles of ceramic engineering, archaeologists are analyzing vessel shapes, sizes, and physical properties (strength, resistance to breakage, porosity) for the purpose of inferring their functions in the ancient societies in which they were made and used (Braun 1981; Hally 1983).

Quite obviously, these questions of function, production, manufacture, and trade are significant to the broader questions of sociocultural development and changes that are being asked by all archaeologists. However, although ceramic analytical techniques are being scrutinized, similar intensive consideration of the utility of ceramic variables or properties—differences in operationalizing anthropological concepts, reliability of measuring variables, and so forth—simply does not exist in the archaeological literature. The broad range of analytical techniques of the materials sciences show continued promise for ceramic ecological and ceramic technological studies. But somewhere along the line, the theoretical concepts of archaeology must be sharpened by ceramic archaeologists to take advantage of their precision.

CONCLUSIONS

The present volume was created in the spirit of enlarging the body of ceramic data by which generalizations can be made about human behavior and society. The methods exemplified by the studies in this volume are new in some senses and old in others. Ceramic ecology, ceramic technology, and ethnoarchaeology as ways of understanding and describing pottery are extensions of older approaches to archaeological data, but they are innovative as attempts to systematize ceramic data within broader processual objectives. A body of ceramic theory has not yet been created in which the relationships between these methods and archaeological goals are clearly articulated, however.

The key issues in ceramic archaeology, present and future, involve questions of how to study pottery and why to study pottery, in the sense of determining the objectives toward which the methods and concepts of ceramic analysis should be applied. Ceramic archaeology must address not only the pottery vessels but the people who made and used them, drawing on the present as well as the past. The focus must be on pots and on potters.

REFERENCES

Arnold, D.E.
  in press   Ceramic Theory: A Systems Approach to Cultural Process. Cambridge: Cambridge University Press.

Bishop, R.L., G. Harbottle, and E.V. Sayre
  1982   Chemical and mathematical procedures employed in the Maya Fine Paste Ceramics Project. In, Analyses of Fine Paste Ceramics, J.A. Sabloff, ed. Pp. 272-282. Excavations at Seibal, Department of Peten, Guatemala. Memoirs of the Peabody Museum of Archaeology and Ethnology, vol. 15, no. 2. Cambridge: Harvard University.

Braun, D.P.
  1981   Experimental interpretation of ceramic vessel use on the basis of rim and neck formal attributes. In, The Navajo Project, D.C. Fiero et al., eds. Pp. 171-231. Museum of Northern Arizona MNA Research Paper 11. Flagstaff.

Feinman, G.M., S. Upham, and K.G. Lightfoot
  1981 The production step measure: an ordinal index of labor input in ceramic manufacture. American Antiquity 46:871-884.

Hally, D.
  1983 Use alteration of pottery vessel surfaces: an important source of evidence for the identification of vessel function. North American Archaeologist 4:3-26.

Howard, H. and E. Morris (eds.)
  1981 Production and Distribution: A Ceramic Viewpoint. BAR International Series 120. Oxford.

Olin, J.S. and A.D. Franklin (eds.)
  1982 Archaeological Ceramics. Washington: Smithsonian Institution Press.

Peacock, D.P.S. (ed.)
  1978 Pottery and Early Commerce. London: Academic Press.

Plog, S.
  1980 Stylistic Variation in Prehistoric Ceramics. Cambridge: Cambridge University Press.

Petrie, Sir W.M.F
  1899 Sequences in prehistoric remains. Journal of the Royal Anthropological Institute 29:295-301.

Reeves, R.D. and R.R. Books
  1978 Trace Element Analysis of Geological Materials. New York: John Wiley.

Rice, P.M.
  1981 Evolution of specialized pottery production: a trial model. Current Anthropology 22:219-240.

  1982 Pottery production, pottery classification, and the role of physicochemical analyses. In, Archaeological Ceramics, J. Olin and A.D. Franklin, eds. Pp. 47-56. Washington: Smithsonian Institution Press.

  in press Change and conservatism in pottery-producing systems. In, Ceramic Approaches in Anthropology and Archaeology, S.E. van der Leeuw and A. Pritchard, eds. IPP, CINGULA series no. VII. Amsterdam.

Rice, P.M. and M.E. Saffer
  1982 Cluster analysis of mixed-level data: pottery provenience as an example. Journal of Archaeological Science. 9:395-402.

Shepard, A.O.
  1971 Ceramics for the Archaeologist. Carnegie Institution of Washington, Publication 609. Washington.

Willey, G.R. and J.A. Sabloff
    1980 A History of American Archaeology. 2nd ed. San Francisco: W.H. Freeman.

Wilson, A.L.
    1978 Elemental analysis of pottery in the study of its provenance: a review. Journal of Archaeological Science 5:219-236.